Early Adopter JXTA

Sing Li

Wrox Press Ltd.

Early Adopter JXTA

First Published December 2001

Published by Wrox Press Ltd,
Arden House, 1102 Warwick Road, Acocks Green,
Birmingham, B27 6BH, UK
Printed in the United States
ISBN 1-861006-35-7

Trademark Acknowledgements

Credits

Author
Sing Li

Foreword
Juan Carlos Soto

Series Manager
Jan Kolasinski

Technical Architect
James Hart

Technical Editors
Ismail Bhana
Benjamin Hickman

Project Manager
Beckie Stones

Technical Reviewers
Sandhya Ashok
William R. Bauer
Kevin Burton
Evan Shaw
Juan Carlos Soto

Production Co-ordinator
Natalie O'Donnell

Proof Reader
Chris Smith

Cover
Chris Morris

About the Author

Sing Li

First bitten by the computer bug in 1978, Sing has grown up with the microprocessor and the Internet revolution. His first PC was a $99 do-it-yourself COSMIC ELF computer with 256 bytes of memory and a 1 bit LED display. For two decades, Sing has been an active author, consultant, instructor, entrepreneur, and speaker. His wide-ranging experience spans distributed architectures, web services, multi-tiered server systems, computer telephony, universal messaging, and embedded systems.

Sing has been credited with writing the very first article on the Internet Global Phone, delivering voice over IP long before it becomes a common reality. Sing has participated in several Wrox projects in the past, has been working with (and writing about) Java, Jini, and JXTA since their very first available releases, and is an active evangelist for the unlimited potential of P2P technology.

Over the extremely short development cycle of this book, an incredible international dynamic 'peer group' is responsible for delivering (and sharing) the content between the covers of this small volume. In the true JXTA spirit, the synergy of this self-organized network is nothing short of phenomenal. I would like to take this opportunity to acknowledge these contributions.

To my lovely wife Kim Diep, for standing by me in the worst of times, and for the endless supply of nurturing TLC.

To James Hart, editor, evangelist, and author all rolled into one. Without your encouragement, the project would have never got off the ground. Without your follow-through and guidance, it would never have finished.

To Ismail Bhana and Ben Hickman, for their excellent editing which transformed an engineer's midnight murmurs into intelligible words and phrases. And to Beckie Stones and the rest of the Wrox team for putting things together in record time.

To Juan Carlos Soto, whose name is synonymous with jxta.org. Your indomitable energy permeates throughout the JXTA effort, and rubbed off onto me. Thank you for all the ideas, support, and encouragement – above and beyond the call of duty. With you on board, there is little doubt that the JXTA ship will sail far and wide.

To William R. Bauer, whose extraordinary reviewing had garnished my meager coverage with superb technical depth and supplanted my shallow thinking with seasoned design wisdom. Thank you also for your contribution to the JXTA community, and turning far-out concepts into actual reality for all of us.

To our excellent international team of reviewers, Sandhya Ashok, Kevin Burton, and Evan Shaw. Your thoughts and ideas were indispensable in realizing the concepts, and facilitating understanding between these pages.

Last, but definitely not least, a huge round of applause and buckets of kudos goes to Bernard Traversat, Dave Doolin, and all the jxta.org participants who are collaboratively pushing the bleeding-edge limits of modern day system design forward incrementally, one CollabNet build at a time!

early adopter

JXTA

Table of
Contents

Table of Contents

iv

JXTA

Foreword

Foreword

A little over a year ago I was at a career crossroads deciding what to do next for my primary job. I had been working several jobs part-time and enjoying the exciting energy level of high tech startups. However, I could not ignore the dot-com implosion around me in Silicon Valley. I decided to work at Sun Microsystems full-time, ideally in a position that would provide the opportunity to innovate, with the intellectual stimulation of a startup. I could immediately see that a new investigation inside Sun – Project Juxtapose – would provide such an opportunity.

A year later Project JXTA, as it is known externally today, has indeed proven to be very stimulating and is unique in many respects. It is run as a startup with limited resources, is tackling a new, unproven technology area, and is driving towards ambitious goals which can only be achieved with the participation of software developers outside of its control. There is never a day without many opportunities to learn new things on all sides – technology, business, community development, and operations.

Project JXTA represents a fresh way of thinking about the future of network computing and software development. It was initiated by Sun Microsystems, a leading innovator in network computing and sometime renegade. From its beginning, Sun has seamlessly embedded networking into all its products with their singular vision that "The Network is the Computer." Almost 20 years later, that concept is being embraced by the leaders in the information industry.

Project JXTA can be seen both as evolutionary and revolutionary. It is a logical direction for a technology leader like Sun to explore to evolve its current products. Today you can use JXTA on your computer at work to securely retrieve personal information from your computer at home. You can use JXTA to build collaboration applications that enable you to share documents and securely chat with colleagues all over the world. Of course, there are many other ways to do these things today. JXTA, in theory, makes doing them easier.

The revolution comes in several areas. First, JXTA allows you to do the things mentioned above without requiring any central administration and independent of your physical network connection and location. This effectively empowers members of a peer group to control their own interactions, and removes barriers to accessing information and resources. It works despite inherently unreliable and ever changing intermediaries on the Internet. Next, JXTA has a vision where any connected device can interact as a peer with any other. Today JXTA has been demonstrated on devices ranging from cell phones to super servers. Tomorrow we'll see meaningful, spontaneous peer interactions among the tiniest devices and a revolution where mere mortals are empowered to access and arrange their resources as they see fit. Your wristwatch will be able to securely retrieve calendar information from your colleague's PDA. Light switches in a building will not be directly connected to the lights, but rather both will be elements on a control network that discover and interact with each other and can be dynamically reassigned. Databases will not be central repositories, but will be virtual information stores distributed among collections of disparate resources.

JXTA's ambitious technical objective is logical and simple: Allow any connected device to interact in a peer to peer style with any other device regardless of their individual network connection or programming language. It is not about eliminating servers (after all, Sun initiated this project). Rather it is about establishing the missing agreement and base technology by which peer-to-peer innovation can run free and cooperatively with centralized services.

Project JXTA was set up to operate in the open and embrace the ideas of others. It uses a liberal open source model and actively encourages participation by everyone. All the technology, documentation, and demonstrations are freely available on the jxta.org web site. Unlike most open source projects, JXTA does not have existing functionality to emulate. It is breaking new ground in that it is being "invented" and refined as it goes by the community.

This approach seems to be working, as a vibrant, global community of developers has emerged. In its first 6 months, jxta.org had over 6 200 members and supported over 250 000 downloads of the technology and documentation. The seed technology provided by Sun has been significantly enhanced and over 40 projects are hosted on the open source site. Excellent books such as this one continue to expand its reach and ensure that knowledge of JXTA is available to all.

I encourage you to invest a little time in the following pages learning about the JXTA technology and its vision. Whether you conclude it is an obvious evolution or a radical revolution in network computing and software development, I am sure you too will find your encounter with JXTA very stimulating.

Juan Carlos Soto
Community Manager, jxta.org
Group Marketing Manager, Project JXTA, Sun Microsystems, Inc.

December 2001

early adopter

JXTA

Introduction

Introduction

JXTA, the brainchild of Sun Microsystems' chief scientist, Bill Joy, represents the first real opportunity for developers to get to grips with the theory and practice of developing applications using a peer-to-peer communication model. Unlike traditional client-server systems, peer-to-peer offers the possibility of extremely scalable, fault-tolerant networked applications. However, it also requires us to think about development in completely different ways, embracing non-deterministic, unpredictable communications, and communication across unknown physical transports to an unknown destination.

JXTA is an exciting project, and this book aims to give the enthusiastic experimenter some initial grounding in the concepts and ideas that underpin it, and then to move on to show how it can be used to develop real applications that get real work done.

Who is this Book For?

This is a Wrox 'Early Adopter' series book, so we're going to assume that you are already a capable developer who simply wants to know everything they can about working with JXTA. This book goes into as much depth as it can on this new technology as it stands today, but please bear in mind that this book was written against pre-release technology that is very subject to change.

The technologies and protocols that the reference implementation of JXTA is based upon (Java, TCP/IP, XML) are not covered in themselves, and it is assumed that you already have some knowledge of them prior to reading this. If you aren't familiar with Java, but have a good knowledge of object-oriented programming, you will still be able to understand the concepts expressed in this book, and hopefully apply them using the ports that exist of JXTA's core to other languages.

What does the Book Cover?

Early Adopter JXTA explores this technology by taking the following path:

Chapter 1: P2P and Architecture Juxtaposition explores the nature of peer-to-peer systems, and the role JXTA is designed to play in the development of such systems.

Chapter 2: JXTA Basics begins with the installation and testing of the JXTA core, then goes on to explain the key concepts that go to make up the JXTA framework. A solid understanding of the terminology introduced and explained in this chapter is vital for deep exploration of JXTA application development.

Chapter 3: Taming the JXTA Shell looks at the default JXTA application, the shell, and explains how the shell is used to interact with the JXTA environment. In addition, we look at how to write shell extensions ourselves. If you want to get your hands dirty quickly, this should be your first stop after installing the JXTA core.

Chapter 4: JXTA Applications and Services introduces a view of how applications can be built onto the JXTA framework, and talks about the conceptual models we need to apply to designing applications for a peer-to-peer context. This chapter introduces the EZEL library, an easy way to partition the logic of a peer-to-peer application into 'clients' and 'services' that are deployed onto the network.

Chapter 5: Programming the JXTA Platform goes under the hood of JXTA to look at the platform APIs that make JXTA applications work.

Chapter 6: WroxShare: A JXTA Application Case Study presents a complete file-sharing application developed using the JXTA CMS (Content Management System) library, and shows how such an application can be taken from concept to deployment using the JXTA platform.

Chapter 7: The Future of JXTA examines where JXTA stands now, and what possibilities lie in its future.

What do I Need to Use this Book?

To follow this book you will need a copy of the JXTA Java reference implementation, and a Java 2 platform standard edition SDK, version 1.3.1 or later. You can obtain a J2SE 1.3.1 SDK for Windows, Solaris, and Linux from Sun Microsystems (http://java.sun.com/j2se). A version of the SDK for Mac OS X is included with the operating system.

Full instructions on downloading and installing JXTA are in Chapter 2.

Conventions

To help you get the most from the text and keep track of what's happening, we use a number of conventions throughout the book.

Code examples are generally highlighted like this:

```
public static void main(String args[])
{
    SimpleService myapp = new SimpleService();
    myapp.init();
    System.exit(0);
}
```

If the example is repeated again, for example, when updating it with some new code lines, the sections you have seen before will no longer be highlighted:

```
public static void main(String args[])
{
    SimpleService myapp = new SimpleService();

    System.out.println ("Simple service starting...");

    myapp.init();
    System.exit(0);
}
```

We also use several styles in the text:

❑ Important terms, when first introduced, are highlighted as follows: **important words**

❑ Filenames and code within the text appear as: `SimpleService.java`

❑ Text in user interfaces, and URLs, are shown in this style: **File/Save As...**

❑ Keys that you may be required to press are indicated in italic, like so: *Ctrl, Alt, Ctrl-z, F12*

In addition:

▶▶ **FAST FORWORD**
These sections contain information about a background technology or concept with which you may already be familiar. If not, these boxes will give you a brief overview, and a pointer to further information.

These boxes hold information about quirks or bugs found in the early releases of a technology.

Important bits of information you shouldn't ignore come in boxes like this!

While this background style is used for information asides to the current discussion.

Customer Support

We always value hearing from our readers, and we want to know what you think about this book: what you liked, what you didn't like, and what you think we can do better next time. You can send us your comments, either by returning the reply card in the back of the book, or by e-mailing us at feedback@wrox.com. Please be sure to mention the book title in your message.

How to Download the Sample Code for the Book

When you log on to the Wrox site **http://www.wrox.com/**, simply locate the title through our **Search** facility or by using one of the title lists. Click on **Download** in the **Code** column or on **Download Code** on the book's detail page.

The files that are available for download from our site have been archived using WinZip. When you have saved the attachments to a folder on your hard-drive, you need to extract the files using a de-compression program such as WinZip or PKUnzip. When you extract the files, the code is usually extracted into chapter folders. When you start the extraction process, ensure your software (WinZip, PKUnzip, etc.) is set to **Use Folder Names**.

Errata

We've made every effort to make sure that there are no errors in the text or in the code. However, no one is perfect and mistakes do occur. If you find an error in one of our books, like a spelling mistake or a faulty piece of code, we would be very grateful for feedback. By sending in errata, you may save another reader hours of frustration, and of course, you will be helping us provide even higher quality information. Simply e-mail the information to **support@wrox.com** your information will be checked and if correct, posted to the errata page for that title, or used in subsequent editions of the book.

To find errata on the web site, log on to http://www.wrox.com/, and simply locate the title through our **Advanced Search** or title list. Click on the **Book Errata** link, which is below the cover graphic on the book's detail page.

E-Mail Support

If you wish to query a problem in the book with an expert who knows the book in detail then e-mail **support@wrox.com**, with the title of the book and the last four numbers of the ISBN in the subject field of the e-mail. A typical e-mail should include the following things:

❏ The **name**, **last four digits of the ISBN**, and **page number** of the problem in the **Subject** field.

❏ Your **name**, **contact information**, and the **problem** in the body of the message.

We **won't** send you junk mail. We need the details to save your time and ours. When you send an e-mail message, it will go through the following chain of support:

1. **Customer Support**

Your message is delivered to one of our customer support staff, who are the first people to read it. They have files on most frequently asked questions and will answer anything general about the book or the web site immediately.

2. **Editorial**

More in-depth queries are forwarded to the technical editor responsible for that book. They have experience with the programming language or particular product, and are able to answer detailed technical questions on the subject. Once an issue has been resolved, the editor can post the errata to the web site.

3. **The Authors**

Finally, in the unlikely event that the editor cannot answer your problem, they will forward the request to the author. We do try to protect the author from any distractions to their writing; however, we are quite happy to forward specific requests to them. All Wrox authors help with the support on their books. They will mail the customer and the editor with their response, and again all readers should benefit.

The Wrox Support process can only offer support to issues that are directly pertinent to the content of our published title. Support for questions that fall outside the scope of normal book support is provided via the community lists of our http://p2p.wrox.com/ forum.

p2p.wrox.com

For author and peer discussion join the P2P mailing lists. Our unique system provides **programmer to programmer**™ contact on mailing lists, forums, and newsgroups, all **in addition** to our one-to-one e-mail support system. Be confident that your query is being examined by the many Wrox authors and other industry experts who are present on our mailing lists. At http://p2p.wrox.com/, you will find a number of different lists that will help you, not only while you read this book, but also as you develop your own applications.

To subscribe to a mailing list just follow this these steps:

1. Go to http://p2p.wrox.com/

2. Choose the appropriate category from the left menu bar

3. Click on the mailing list you wish to join

4. Follow the instructions to subscribe and fill in your e-mail address and password

5. Reply to the confirmation e-mail you receive

6. Use the subscription manager to join more lists and set your mail preferences

early adopter

JXTA 1

P2P and Architecture Juxtaposition

A quiet revolution is underway. The endless cycle of re-inventing centralized client-server technology yet again under a new name with a new set of jargon is being broken. Peer-to-peer computing (P2P) has arrived, and there is no turning back. This is truly a grassroots revolution, an attempt to put the infrastructure of the Internet to radical new uses, driven by its users. It's about taking the communications infrastructure of the Net, and using it to communicate, directly, one user to another, peer to peer.

This book is about JXTA, a technology that will help us to participate in this revolution. However, before we start to develop applications with JXTA, we need to work out what sort of applications those are going to be, and that means looking at what kind of needs JXTA was designed to address.

Imagine a global content-sharing system, where amateur artists can share their creations with the world, closet poets can find an audience for their eclectic creations, garage bands can get their well-deserved exposure, and programming hobbyists can find a large population of ready and willing users for their applications. This system thrives only on the machines that are connected to it, and the content that is being shared on those machines – created by their proud owners. No centralized registration or control is required in this system: as long as there is at least one person who can create content, and one person who wants that content, the system continues to work.

Imagine an instant messaging system that can scale to millions of users, enabling any user anywhere to send messages and engage in interactive conversations with any other user. Imagine that a message sent from a PC will automatically be delivered to a cell phone if the recipient is currently on the road. This system will work without any centralized servers or registration. Once started, this system will never be turned off again so long as there are people somewhere in the world using it.

Imagine a tactical battlefield support system, where soldiers are using whatever data devices are available to communicate, exchanging intelligence or command information with their commanders and each other. This system will enable a spectrum of different devices, each potentially using a different method of data communication on different media (wireless, satellite, land-based line, laser, microwave), to participate in the exchange of data in a uniform way. Furthermore, this system will be self-organizing and confer survival properties by providing a virtualized network over any arbitrarily changing network topology. Should units or equipment become unavailable, the remaining peer groups will reorganize into different groups that can continue communications in a uniform manner.

Finally, imagine a new type of browser that doesn't only browse the web, but can be used to browse any content shared by anyone using those browsers. With it, you would have access to everything that is on the web today, plus the calendar stored on your PDA, the call list on your cell phone, your nephew's little league schedule on his school's PC, and the latest masterpiece created by your 9 year old daughter on her P2P enabled electronic Etch-a-Sketch!

These scenarios all ought to be possible, even using current networking technology. The Internet offers us the capacity to send a packet of data from any connected point in the world to any other. However, conventional wisdom, and conventional architecture, require you to temper the requirements stated above slightly. For example, the first suggestion – a global content sharing network – sounds like the idealized view of the World Wide Web when it was created. We know that the Web hasn't turned out that way, and the reason is that having the capacity to distribute content widely on the Web requires enormous individual resources, beyond those of the average garage band or poet. The instant messaging system has been attempted many times, but in almost every case has not been able to deliver on the promise of permanent availability in the absence of centralized services, or low cost scalability to tens of thousands of users.

Architects of networked systems have traditionally accepted that these failings are part of the structure of distributed applications, that there is no way to avoid these limitations. However, peer-to-peer architecture allows us to think again, and overcome those problems, enabling us to develop the applications we have described, and much more besides that we can't even yet imagine. Obviously, P2P is not quite the good old Internet that we are used to.

The Essence of P2P

What characteristics of these systems we have described set them apart from the systems we can develop with current architectures? Distilling the above examples down, we can see they all exhibit the following properties:

❑   The system is based on the interaction between peers

❑   There is zero reliance on centralized services and/or resources for operation

❑   They can survive extreme changes in network composition

❑   They thrive in a network with non-deterministic topology

❏ They can scale to a massive concurrent user base

We need to look at each of these in turn to better understand the potential of P2P.

Systems Based on Interaction between Peers

There is one thing common between mega-sites on the Internet (Yahoo, CNN, etc.), and the client-server or multi-tiered server architecture used in corporate intranets – they all depend on the existence of a set of powerful and robust servers in order to handle all their users. Figure 1 illustrates this centralized architecture.

Figure 1

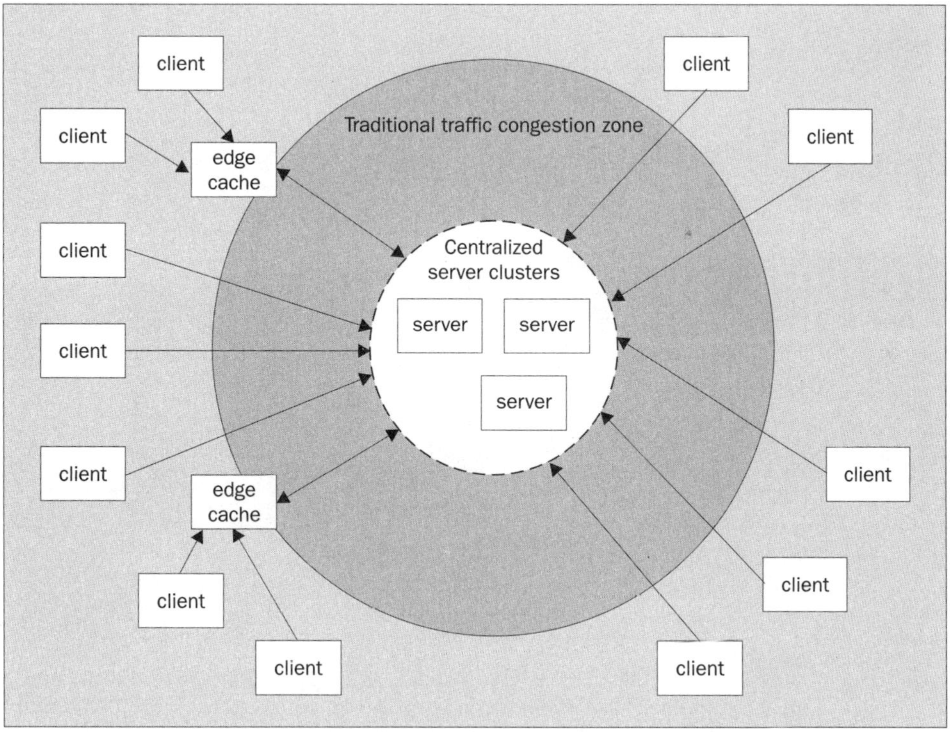

Even if clustering or other local distributed technology is used at the server site, it is still a group of centralized servers that must be up and running for the system to work. The client, regardless of whether it is a "fat" client or a "thin" client, will not be able to perform the work required without connecting to the centralized server.

Typically, the center of the network consists of mega-servers and a sophisticated data routing and caching infrastructure that ensures that the edge of the network (clients, web browsers) can access this centralized information in the most efficient way. In fact, this is pretty much the picture of today's Internet, without P2P applications.

The behavior of this sort of system is well known. As more and more users come on board, the computing power, storage, and bandwidth associated with these centralized servers must increase. Both the hardware and software components must be able to "scale" in order to support the increasing load created by the user base. Typically, as the scalability requirement reaches tens of thousands of users, the cost of the system enters the stratospheric range.

A P2P system relies solely on the interaction of peers. Because of the commonly accepted server-centric view of a network, sometimes this behavior is known as action "at the edge of the network". Figure 2 shows why this term was coined.

Figure 2

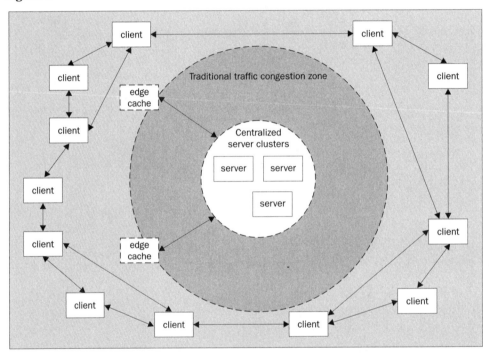

As Figure 2 shows, P2P is about clients talking to clients, without the servers in the middle. These P2P "clients", to distinguish them from the conventional clients, will be called peers from now on. Since peers interact directly with peers, this means that if we use conventional terms, each peer must assume both client functionality and server functionality; and indeed, we will see shortly that this is precisely the case.

By having each peer handle a portion of the processing that would have occurred on some mega-centralized server, it is possible in some applications to scale the overall throughput and performance with the number of peers concurrently connected to a network. This is the dream scenario for many practitioners of distributed and parallel computing.

Zero Reliance on Centralized Servers or Resources

A pure P2P system does not require the existence of any centralized servers or resources to operate. Therefore, a pure P2P system must not rely on any centrally administered naming or addressing system. This means that our favorite address resolution system, DNS, does not fit the P2P model too well. While the DNS tables are replicated onto many distributed servers, and in principle DNS is decentralized, the one central name hierarchy (which we rely upon to ensure that when we type www.wrox.com into our browser, our packets are really sent to Wrox's web server) is administered, at its root, by a central authority. What's more, we have all experienced the situation when all the name servers for a domain are down, and there is no way that we can access a web site by name. This is a fundamental flaw that a pure P2P system avoids – the downtime of a few peers cannot affect the operation of the entire system or network.

Instead, addressing systems in a pure P2P system must be completely decentralized. If there are a hundred thousand peers on the P2P network, any one peer should be able to locate and communicate with any other peer. Now, if most of the system was destroyed and there are only two peers left, they should still be able to locate each other and communicate.

Surviving Extreme Changes in Network Composition

The last scenario above illustrates the need for a P2P system to survive extreme changes in network composition. This is the premise of the battlefield application scenario that we mentioned earlier. Essentially, a properly designed P2P system should enable two peers to communicate with one another as long as there is some way to send data between them. In a large fully connected network of peers, there may be many choices when selecting the actual network protocol and medium to communicate between the peers. A good P2P system will implement some optimization measures to take full advantage of this, and select the most efficient – by distance, bandwidth availability, reliability, cost, or some other criteria. As the composition of the network changes, the original set of assumptions of the best way to get from peer A to peer B may no longer be true. A well-designed P2P system should constantly adapt to this change and select different combinations if necessary.

Thriving in a Network with Non-Deterministic Topology

In a P2P system, the former "clients" make up the network and do all the work. A client machine, as we are well aware, is typically not an always-on, super-robust, or highly redundant machine. This means that the machine may be switched on and off by the user at any time, it may malfunction and never reappear on the network, its disk and memory has no guaranteed backup or protection, and any content it holds should be considered volatile. At any moment in time, the overall topology of a P2P network is completely unpredictable. The set of nodes that makes up the network varies constantly with time as users log on and off the network, systems restart, and out-of-commission machines are removed from the network. With this non-deterministic and constantly changing network, a P2P system must guard against these unpredictable pitfalls and provide a reliable and robust (or at least predictably useful) service to the consuming peers.

Scaling to a Massive User Base

Being completely decentralized has its benefits. This means that scalability does not rely on beefing up any particular set of server hardware that all clients must use. By removing this centralized bottleneck, and designing applications that distribute the processing work effectively among the current set of peers, well designed P2P systems should be able to scale to a massive user base – limited only by the bandwidth available between the peers. In an increasingly broadband world, where even wireless devices are expected to be able to handle high bandwidth content in the near future, that's not a severe limitation.

In fact, instead of degraded performance and dismal throughput as the number of users increases, P2P systems can be designed in such a way that system performance and throughput *increases* as the number of users increases. This is certainly a desirable and attractive attribute!

Defining P2P

We still have not precisely defined what P2P is, but now, having examined some of the characteristics we think are desirable in such systems, we are in a position to do so.

When asking what P2P is, you will get very different answers depending on whom you ask. The ironic truth is – it really does not matter! Most people agree that, in a P2P system:

❑ Resources and bandwidth at the edge of the network should be fully utilized

❑ The crux of its functionality does not depend on centralized servers

❑ The is a non-determinism in its specificity, yet it can be fault-tolerant and exhibit graceful degradation because of the potential for high redundancy

❑ It is a dynamite technology awaiting its killer application

This last point perhaps is the most fascinating one of them all. Our understanding of P2P technologies and implementation is maturing rapidly, we realize that it holds tremendous potential, but we are too set in our ways to discover a killer application that can utilize the technology to its fullest potential. This is normal in the typical technology adoption curve; microprocessors belonged to the embedded controller category for a decade before the killer application – the PC as we know it today – was discovered. The first powerful microprocessors and high capacity RAM were sitting on the sideline before the killer application – the PC Spreadsheet and Database – legitimized their wide adoption. High-bandwidth network access technologies (such as early ISDN) sat dormant and under-adopted for decades until the killer application – the Internet – came along. If history contains any lessons, what P2P is exactly will only be defined by its killer application or applications. It is only when a technology matures that mainstream vendors will commit resource to fully exploit its various facets, and extract every drop of value added possible.

Bandwidth and Resources

In the mind of contemporary network engineers, P2P is about computing carried out in a fully distributed fashion, utilizing bandwidth and resources at the edge of the network, with the centralized backbone acting solely as a conduit that carries traffic from one edge of the network to another. It is today's fully centralized world turned inside out. Nevertheless, this may prove desirable, since today's centralized web experience means that bandwidth at the edge of the network, and the computing resources in an individual's computer, are badly under utilized. Today's traffic flow is highly asymmetric – modern high-speed Internet-access technology such as Asymmetric Digital Subscriber Line (ADSL), or even the asymmetric upstream and downstream speed of the V.90 56k modem standard, bear testament to this. Even in today's world, where interesting services and content seem to originate from fewer and fewer mega-servers, there is a great need to decongest the flow of such network traffic and move it to the edge. Edge caching technologies, as this class of heavily patented inventions are called, attempt to locate major caching resources at the edge of network, closer to the most frequent points of access. This technique efficiently offloads the centralized servers from serving the more static content, to private servers at the edge of the network. Innovations in custom content markup languages even enable a significant portion of active content to be cached at the edge of the network. While this architecture is certainly P2P-like, the fact that private servers are used makes it highly disputable whether these edge-caching systems can truly be classified as P2P systems. Figure 3 shows the similarity of typical edge caching technology to the P2P architecture we are discussing:

Figure 3

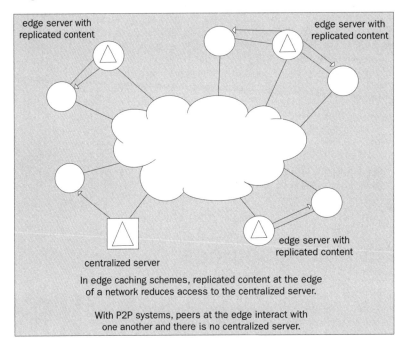

edge server with replicated content

edge server with replicated content

edge server with replicated content

centralized server

In edge caching schemes, replicated content at the edge of a network reduces access to the centralized server.

With P2P systems, peers at the edge interact with one another and there is no centralized server.

Enthusiasts and researchers in distributed and massively parallel computing have long worked with network architectures that employ P2P-style concepts. Most of the research and experimentation in this area, however, involves high speed interconnects between computing elements that can only be achieved via a custom electronic bus. However, as the PC-to-PC interconnection speed approaches the gigabits per second mark, and ever faster CPUs begin to catch up with the work of supplying data, the distinction between bus-based interconnections and network-based interconnectsions quickly blurs. This force may become the liberating agent that unleashes several decades of previously undeployed or shelved research into wide applications within a vast market. Formerly only the domain of a few, fundamental principles and novel concepts in the fields of massively-parallel and distributed computing can now be readily applied on today's high-speed networks. When transposed into the world of computing resources interconnected via high-speed networks, many concepts in these specialized domains map to the "action at the edge of the network" that is a feature of modern P2P computing. The Search for Extra-Terrestrial Intelligence, SETI, for example, has managed to use the world's PC resources to help it perform searches for extraterrestrial intelligence by distributing a screen-saver. One can readily argue that modern technology hotbeds such as Jini and JXTA are the by-products of this phenomenon. Unarguably, some of the component technologies within Jini and JXTA benefited tremendously from prior research in massively-parallel computing and distributed search algorithms. Despite this head start, the particular way in which these technologies are adapted to present day requirements is unique in the history of systems design – and must be judged on its own merits.

The Case for P2P

Some view P2P as the result of evolution; as an inevitable stage that we must go through; as a temporary stopping place in our species relentless drive towards greater and greater efficiency. Let's explore their rationale for a moment, and we can decide for ourselves if P2P is indeed an inevitable step.

Striving for Greater Efficiency

Efficiency is an unstoppable force, because of its unbreakable tie to financial saving. On the surface, P2P is obviously an efficiency improvement, because it is about the more efficient use of computing resources and the more efficient use of formerly underutilized bandwidth. What is less evident, however, is the associated social undercurrent. P2P is also consistent with increasing the efficient utilization of human intellectual resources – and the ephemeral interaction between individuals in our society. From the way software is developed – nuclear physicist by day turns hacker by night and contributes to open source P2P software systems – to the success of online auction services, people on PCs are connected and disconnected with each other just long enough to perform some mutually beneficial and satisfactory exchange. In these ways, P2P reflects the way we have changed – the way we have become more efficient in the age of the Internet, constantly seeking ways to remove sources of friction between supplier and consumer. This efficiency revolution is already claiming some casualties. If media distribution can be performed instantaneously, and at extremely low cost, traditional, inefficient means of doing the same thing are simply left awaiting their eventual demise. We have certainly seen this begin to be played out in the music distribution industry, as traditional distribution companies unleashed their legal and financial fury upon the P2P e-distribution startups. As constituents of the society and the market-at-large, incidents such as these also remind us that there is a heavy price to pay, in terms of progress, if we relent in our constant drive for greater efficiency.

Computing for the World on a Massive Scale

Scalability is a tough issue that plagues designers of conventional client-server or multi-tier server systems. It is typically limited by both software architecture and maximum expandability of server hardware platforms. While there exists scalable mega-server hardware today that can handle a worldwide base of frequent users, the cost of such hardware is prohibitive and out of the reach of most small to medium size businesses. P2P systems, since they leverage the computing power that exists on the networked peers, have the potential to massively scale without the same limitations as centralized solutions. Of course, the specific scalability of any P2P application will depend on the design. Typically, the type of applications that P2P systems excel in is quite different from those that use conventional client-server services – therefore the ability to scale massively under these different conditions may be akin to comparing apples and oranges. As an example, ad-hoc file sharing and instant messaging applications can definitely scale better using P2P architecture rather than centralized servers; on the other hand, relational database servers are still the domain of centralized mega-servers (or server clusters).

The Allure of Organic Growth

Pioneer systems such as Napster, Gnutella, Morpheus, Jabber, IRC, and so on give P2P an air of legitimacy because of their grassroots origin and proven success. At the very least, they have illustrated that P2P style design has a legitimate role in handling large file sharing and messaging systems. Another aspect that is common in all of these systems is the organic, almost viral growth of the user base. In each of these products, the system becomes more attractive to users as more and more users join the network. For file sharing services, it means an increasing selection of files and higher replication redundancy – resulting in a higher probability of finding what you want. For instant messaging systems, a larger user base means more people that you can chat with and a larger diversity of interests and viewpoints.

Is P2P Inevitable?

Well, it is time to ask the question again; is P2P inevitable? Much of the answer will depend on how the technology captures the imagination of the world's system design engineers. For decades, distributed and massively parallel computing studies have created experimental systems based on ideas that have since languished in libraries on university campuses. Will P2P provide a foundation to realize some of these ideas, allowing them to be put to productive use?

If only we could foretell the future. If hype was any indicator of success, then P2P would be worth betting on, but we all know that's not the case. As system designers, we must examine what P2P has to offer, and make up our own minds whether it provides us with a useful approach to a problem. If the lessons we learn from experimentation with P2P are taken on board in the systems we design, then even if the industry analysts, technology pundits, or soothsayers are not quite on-the-money with their predictions, P2P will make an important contribution to the way we design future systems and change the way we look at networking software design.

Adding Value with P2P

Regardless of whether P2P is inevitable, there are some added bonuses that building a system on P2P principles bring to the table, which are markedly different from any other component of conventional design. We will explore a few of the most attractive valued-added advantages here.

Harnessing Non-Determinism

There is a certain amount of non-determinism inherent in P2P systems. For one thing, the composition and topology of the network is non-deterministic. The devices that make up the network may join or leave the network at any time.

One important hazard, to beware of when working with P2P systems, is that we may need to toss all that we think we know about system and software testing and verification out of the door. Non-determinism really throws a kink into setting qualification standards for the testing and verification of a P2P system.

When we discuss JXTA later, we will find out that, on a specific test trial, a perfectly healthy and functional JXTA system may actually do nothing, have no peers communicating with each other, and exhibit no productive output. Yet, such a system can be deemed fully valid, and completely operating according to specification.

Take a more practical example, a peer-to-peer file and music service such as Gnutella. Someone using Gnutella in North America and/or Europe may boast the ability to retrieve any old favorite piece of music at any time through the system. Yet, on the very same system, someone living in South Africa may not be able to find any music at any time of day no matter how frequently they try. The system is the same, the software used and connectivity is the same, but the user experience can vary greatly. This is characteristic of most P2P systems.

Fault Resilience and High Availability

P2P systems can potentially display high availability and fault resilience properties. How, you may ask, can a system that has a potentially non-deterministic topology ever be fault resilient and exhibit high availability? The answer is due to one simple concept: Redundancy.

By replicating the available services or resources, one can provide some guarantee on the availability of a service or resource. In typical P2P system design, this redundancy is a necessary aspect used to hedge against the non-deterministic changes in network topology and composition. The same mechanisms, when used in a network that has deterministic topology, can be used to add fault-resilience and high availability features.

Breaking Free of "Big Brother"

Some P2P advocates would like to think of P2P as not simply an architecture, but as a movement favoring de-centralization, and therefore a source of momentum away from (possibly sinister) centralized control, be it commercial or governmental. There is nothing inherent in P2P systems that dictates they must not contain a centralized component, or that they don't work in unison with a network of centralized systems. As we move forward in technical history, it is highly likely that we will go through a period of time where hybrid centralized and P2P styled systems will work together and complement one another. Therefore, while this "breaking free of big brother" spirit may be relevant in the case of destabilizing movements such as Napster, this is rather moot in the reality of practical P2P.

The Future of P2P

How is P2P likely to affect all our lives? Well, as we have discussed before, if it is indeed revolutionary, the revolution is definitely quiet. The school of thought that says P2P is a part of an "evolutionary" process instead of a revolution also has very valid basis. Regardless of which camp we side with, one thing is for certain: P2P systems will not wipe out conventional systems overnight.

Juxtaposition Not Displacement

P2P, the new kid on the block, does not stand a chance of displacing client-server or multi-tier server computing in the near future. The decades of lead-time that these existing architectures have, and our mature understanding of their properties, enable us to utilize them to get the work done. On the other hand, with the present phase of rapid development and experimentation in the P2P scene, it will only be a matter of time before we achieve the same mature understanding and experience with this technology.

In the meantime, however, P2P will work in conjunction with today's mega-server-dominated networks. Working in perfect juxtaposition, P2P can and will add value to the client-server systems that we know and love today.

In due time, as both software engineers and users become more and more familiar with what P2P brings to the table in terms of additional functionality, breakthroughs will almost certainly occur. Problems that are deemed difficult to solve via the conventional network architecture and resources may be natural or easy for P2P systems. As more and more of these problem domains are discovered, P2P computing will stake its own ground in computing.

In fact, this is exactly what the network engineers envisioned – that P2P will be the equalizing force for the asymmetrical bandwidth requirements of centralized server systems – and that the additional bandwidth usage will be applied to production use.

The Juxtaposed Universe

What will the immediate future, where P2P systems work in harmony with centralized server solutions, look and feel like? Let us explore a few aspects of the way we work that lend themselves naturally to this sort of hybrid implementation.

Fostering the Way We Already Work Together

The way people work together, in teams or in groups, is mirrored perfectly by the hybrid system. Established bases of expertise (such as a group of doctors) and reliable source of information (such as a respected news agency) require a static and consistent presence, and potentially a centralized store of information that can be viewed collectively as virtual asset.

P2P systems augment the world of permanent connections with some transient ones. Through P2P-based technology, expertise in subject matter can be "traded" or "bartered" between providers of service and those who require the service – in an instant. There need not be a history of cooperation before the trade, nor does there need to be any follow-up or royalty after.

A Universe of Shared Resources

Anything that can be digitized can be shared through a P2P network. This is a fantastic possibility for some, and a nightmare for many. This literally means that the differential playing fields of the information haves and have-nots can be leveled, enabling knowledge and creativity to flow freely between anyone who can afford the bandwidth. This might help special interest groups, communities, governments, countries, or even the world to become more productive and more efficient.

Unfortunately, established legacy economic models place great value on the infrastructure that distributes the content from the creator to the final consumer – and the P2P style of thinking threatens to potentially wipe out the value of that infrastructure overnight. This is the core reason why established players the in conventional distribution industry are reacting with unprecedented alarm in some situations.

Hopefully, the fear will subside through example and understanding. In fact, traditional content providers stand the best chance of being pioneers in leveraging the power of the P2P-style computing system to expand the reach and distribution of their content to new areas and markets that were formerly unreachable. Much rethinking has to be done with respect to what constitutes a profitable business model, and trial and error will no doubt cause some casualties along the way. However, at the end of the day, the original promise of P2P to realize a "worldwide flat-contentscape" should respectively bolster and weaken the coffers of content and distribution players.

Unbounded Roaming Worldwide – Any Device/Any Time

A peer in a P2P system can be as sophisticated and powerful as a super computer, or as common and simple as a digital watch. If a universal set of protocols is established and used by all P2P devices, they will be able to communicate and share information/resources with each other in a meaningful way. This utopian view of P2P computing is certainly not yet realized yet, but is definitely within the realm of possibility in the near future.

Relevant Information Gravitates Towards Interested Users

Incorporating the latest research results in distributed search technology, P2P systems have the potential to enable "natural" information flow – from those who create it, to those who need or want it. This is quite unlike the conventional chaotic scenario, with all information available to everybody. With sophisticated relevancy tracking and judicial use of past access history and user rating, a P2P-based content management system could ensure that popular items of contents (to a specific group of users) are replicated more frequently – or are easier to obtain within that group.

When the number of services available through the P2P network reaches a critical mass, all our daily computing needs can potentially be satisfied via shared resources over the network. This might include:

❑   Content and information that we seek

❑   Specialized services that we use daily

❑ Computing resources that we need to get work done

❑ Storage capacity that we use to store our personal data

We have already had a taste of this possibility, where personalized portal sites have become many web users' preferred "home stop" for their daily computing needs. P2P promises to offer the same set of features or more some day in the future, potentially without the commercial buy-in required by today's portal sites.

JXTA: Realizing P2P

The P2P description so far consists mainly of many high concepts, concepts that at first appear to be extremely difficult (if not impossible) to implement. It would be a pity, and a waste of talent, for each P2P software vendor to reinvent their own version of these concepts. The sad fact is, almost all current P2P (or partially P2P) applications roll their own P2P network and protocols – committing major design and development resources.

It must be possible, then, to abstract some common functionality that is required to realize a P2P system, and put it in a library of sorts. By "factoring out" this set of fundamental behaviors of P2P systems, they can be reused by any designer of P2P systems – freeing them from worrying about the nitty-gritty details, and enabling them to concentrate on the important thing: application details.

JXTA is born from this spirit. Project JXTA is a Sun Microsystems originated, open source development project. JXTA is short form for Juxtapose, and reflects the world that JXTA is being born into – where traditional client-server architecture systems live harmoniously with JXTA-enabled P2P systems.

Building a P2P Interaction Model

In arriving at the JXTA model of operations, the team of engineers at Sun Microsystems examined the existing P2P systems and attempted to extract their common elements. Their goal was to factor out the common tasks that every P2P system must perform – and which can be tedious to code/design repeatedly.

The factoring, however, must be done (as much as possible) in a way that does not dictate how the resulting P2P system must work. In other words, JXTA must be irresistible to developers – because it is easier to build on top of JXTA than to roll your own P2P system – but not be restrictive, or limiting in the applications that may be built on top of it.

Several major abstract concepts are so pervasive throughout the JXTA P2P interaction model; they deserve a brief mention here:

❑ Discovery

❑ Communications

❑ Peer Groups

- ❑ Sharing of resources
- ❑ Group services
- ❑ Flexible endpoints
- ❑ Interoperation

Discovery

In a JXTA world, peers are addressed using a decentralized addressing scheme. This means that an IP address for a peer is meaningless over the long term in the JXTA network. Instead, two peers can "discover" one another using JXTA mechanisms without being fixed to any physical address on any physical network transport. Discovery is dynamic, and occurs just before the peers begin communications.

To go one-step further, if one of the peers should change physical network address during communication, JXTA will re-discover, and resume communications! This is a powerful tool to guard against the dynamic and non-deterministic nature of the underlying physical network.

In other words, in JXTA, discovery is how two peers with no fixed physical address locate each other.

Communications

After the peers find each other, they will carry out the work they set out to do. Inevitably, this requires communication between the peers. Since the actual physical network characteristics and composition may change during the course of this communications, we cannot fix the means of communications. For example, HTTP-based communications may suddenly become unavailable between two peers because of a rebooting firewall node between them. JXTA provides a high-level virtual abstraction for the communications channel (called a pipe) that will switch the physical means of moving messages between peers automatically (and adaptively) in these cases.

In other words, in JXTA, the pipe implementation ensures that you can get a message from peer A to peer B as long as there is some (JXTA-supported) physical means to do so.

With these two pervasive concepts in mind, we can examine some other concepts factored out by the JXTA designers, and which form the basis for the components within the JXTA operational model.

Peer Groups

In every P2P system, entities (or peers) interact with each other to communicate, perform computing chores, and/or share resources. This sort of interaction is always carried out with some purpose in mind – or a cause if you will.

While it is possible to treat the entire connected world of computing entities as one huge network, practicality in terms of search time and management makes it unfeasible. Some partitioning is necessarily to make implementation manageable. This partitioning comes in the form of groups of entities, all coalescing dynamically to interact for the common cause. These groups can be created or disbanded at any time, and their membership can fluctuate depending on the number of entities desiring to interact for the cause. Any specific entity may belong to lots of these groups at the same time, interacting independently within each.

More concretely, a group of entities may coalesce in a group to talk about today's news. Another group may coalesce to share an expensive photo printer. Yet a third group may coalesce to engage in a network-based combat simulation game. At any time, any individual entity may be talking, printing photo, and playing the combat simulation all simultaneously – by belonging to these three groups.

Groups in JXTA are a pure partitioning mechanism. The members of a group share the same set of resources, and the group boundary is the discovery boundary when looking for peers.

Sharing of Resources

One unifying view of the "common cause" that we referred to earlier, when entities gather in groups, is to share resources. The group that coalesces together to print is sharing the printer. The group that coalesces together to talk about today's news is sharing a service that tracks members and relays their messages. The group that coalesces together to play a game is sharing a service that tracks players, score, and individual activities. In many ways, we can say that P2P systems use client-server architecture in a microcosm. Indeed the services shared in groups of peers are reminiscent of client-server interaction. The unique difference, however, is that in most cases the shared "service" runs on one of the peers – physically one of the clients. In this way, a peer that hosts a "service" is sharing yet another one of its precious resources – CPU cycles – with the group.

The Concept of Group Services

Group services are services that are reliably available in a group. There is a need for certain services to be "always" available as long as a group is functioning. This necessitates some measure of guaranteed high availability. High availability comes at a cost; the cost is that it must be redundantly implemented across a number of members. As long as one of the members in the group still has an instance of a service running, that service will be available to the group.

Communications with Flexible Endpoints

Client-server computing is full of fixed endpoints. For example, the IP address relating to www.wrox.com is always the same address (or set of addresses). In P2P systems, since the composition of the peers involved constantly changes, there is a need to perform communications through flexible endpoints. Another way to view flexible endpoints is to say that the very same peer may be located via very different means (different physical network, different physical address) at different points in time. For example, I may be using my notebook computer docked (with its own IP address on the Internet) between 9a.m. and 5p.m. in the office, but my notebook will only be accessible via a citywide packet network outside of those hours.

Delaying the binding process between a "peer" and its associated physical address as late as possible can create flexible endpoints. The latest time possible is just before a message is sent to the peer.

This late-binding approach is also very useful for services that JXTA applications use. Instead of having "FTP server at 26.333.22.11", literally a fixed address and a fixed instance of the service, we connect to a "Pipe service at pipe ID <some UUID>". This allows the pipe to be "bound" at the latest possible moment in time. This literally means that you will not know to whom (which peer) exactly you will connect for the pipe service until you actually make the connection. In a P2P world, this is entirely acceptable. As long as the service that you end up binding to (at the time of connect) can perform the work you required, it really doesn't matter which peer (or peers) you may be contacting to get the work done. In fact, this gives JXTA-based systems a means of achieving some measure of fault tolerance.

Members Must Interoperate

Early phases of many technology adoption cycles are plagued with proprietary incompatible systems that "get the job done". In most systems, the ability to interoperate must be designed-in at an early stage of a project. Retrofitting an existing proprietary system to be interoperable is often a labor-intensive and ultimately futile exercise.

JXTA in Perspective

In this book, we will not fuss over the precise definition of what is a P2P system, except for setting the background state-of-the-art within these few pages. Our focus will be on *one* particular implementation of a P2P platform (bases upon which P2P systems are built); that has the potential to become the major P2P platform utilized worldwide. Below is a partial list of the unique attributes that set JXTA apart from its closest so-called "competitors":

❑ It is designed from day one to be independent of the actual physical transport used – TCP/IP, wireless packet network, HTTP-based polling behind a firewall, etc. can all be used with satisfactory results

❑ It is designed from day one to be interoperable – any device capable of sending information over the actual physical transport will have a way to interoperate with this P2P system

❑ The software base is completely open source; private interests are invited to exploit, deploy, and actively market technology/devices based on the software – with no financial obligation to remunerate the community that developed and maintains it

❑ It is well conceived, and designed, leveraging decades of design experience in distributed networks and massively parallel computing

❑ It is currently being worked on by some of the brightest software engineering minds across the world

❑ There are current efforts to create JXTA implementations in Perl, GNU C, Ruby, and other languages; these implementations will be compatible with the Java reference implementation

While it is uncertain when and where the first killer application for P2P may come from – and therefore who will ultimately define the "true" meaning of P2P computing, JXTA, having a full stacked deck, stands a good chance of being the place where exciting future action will occur.

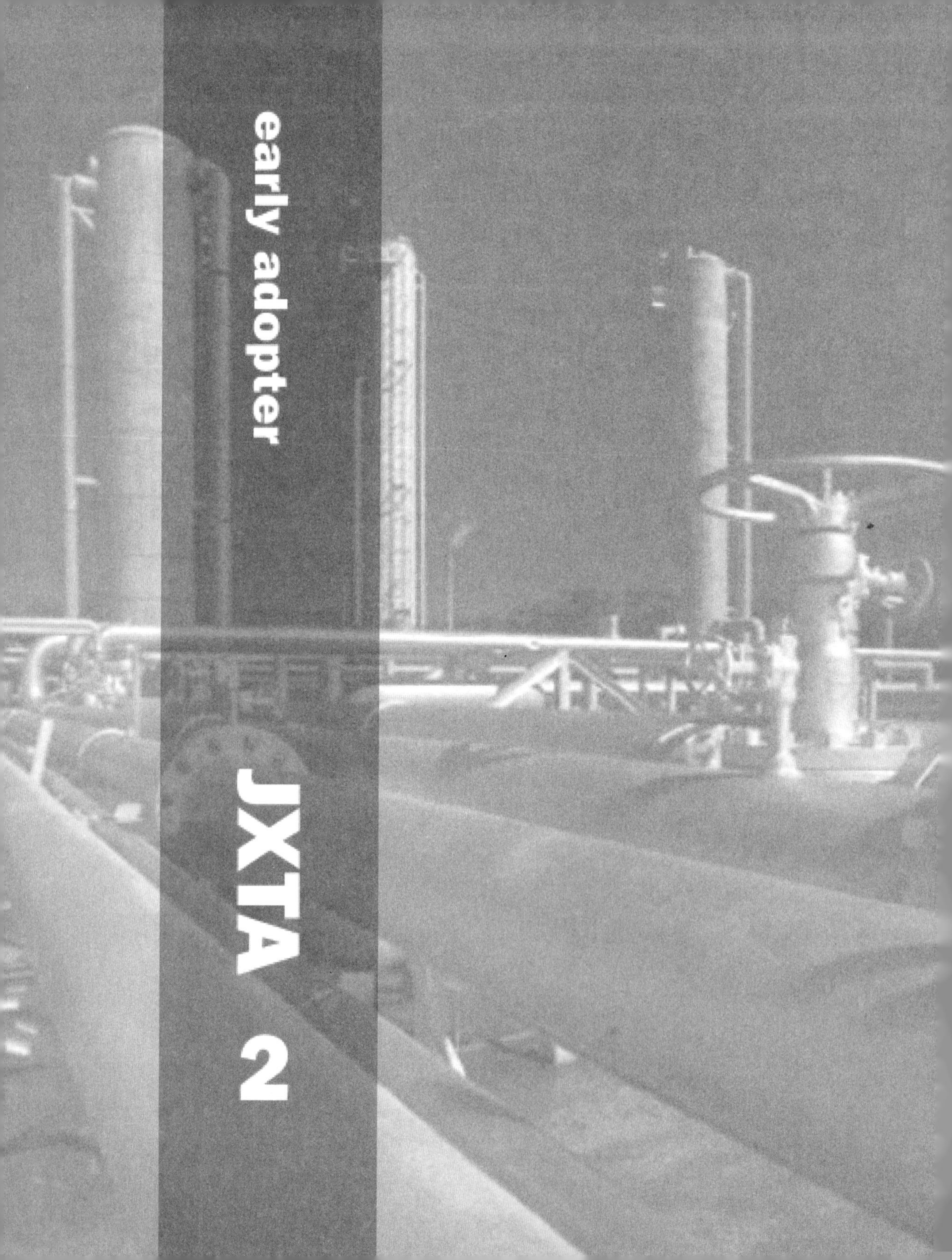
early adopter
JXTA 2

JXTA Basics

In this chapter, we will discuss the conceptual and physical foundations of JXTA, including coverage of the mid-level component view that is exposed through a set of programming APIs. We will also take a peek behind the scenes to see how JXTA accomplishes much of the P2P grunge work.

Before our in-depth discussion, let us first get a taste of what JXTA is all about. We will download and install the required executables, and try out a P2P chat directly from the JXTA command shell application.

A JXTA Preview

JXTA is an open source project, being actively developed by the JXTA community at http://www.jxta.org/.

You will always be able to find the latest binaries and sourcecode for JXTA at this site. Furthermore, you may sign up for participation in any of the ongoing projects. There are mailing lists at this site that are of interest to all JXTA developers, and P2P practitioners in general.

Downloading and Installing JXTA

Before we start working with JXTA, we must first download and install a working instance of the reference implementation. Currently, the only implementation of JXTA available is written completely in Java. There are also implementations in C, Perl, Ruby, and other languages that are actively being worked on by JXTA community members. In this book however we will only cover the Java reference implementation, with our example programs written in 100% pure Java code. This section will assist you in locating the latest version of JXTA to install.

Stable and Daily Builds

To download the latest version of the JXTA platform (and associated services and applications) go to the download section of the www.jxta.org web site. At any point in time, there will exist two complete branches of images that are archived and ready for direct download, these are:

1. The latest stable build

2. The daily build

Thus far in JXTA history, the release frequency of the stable build is paced at about 1 to 2 months apart. This can mean that there may be a lot of changes in between builds. If you would like to develop upon a stable platform, and do not mind revamping your code (sometimes involving major changes) later, you can use the latest stable build. During this initial rapid development period of JXTA, many application developers will need to track the evolution by building against the most recent daily build. The jxta-dev mailing list on www.jxta.org can be used to track ongoing platform API changes.

In fact, it is possible to retrieve any previous versions of JXTA at any time through its version control system. The version control of JXTA builds is achieved using the open source project **CVS**. You can download the CVS command-line client, or a Microsoft Windows client, from www.cvshome.com. All previously registered versions of any source file in the JXTA project may be retrieved using CVS. Build versions are synchronized by build labels and, by selecting a build label, the source and binaries of any previous version in history can be retrieved. If you are already familiar with CVS you can easily access any branch of development using the client tool. However, if you're not familiar with CVS, you can use the browse link on the JXTA project web page to access the web interface to CVS. This web interface will allow you to click your way through the different versions of development online.

Deciding what to Download

There are various choices of download for either the daily build or the stable build.

JXTA community members from all around the world are continually developing project JXTA. It is a fast moving project and changes to the platform occur regularly. To provide consistency throughout this book we will use the JXTA stable build 39e, dated 11-21-2001, in our examples. As indicated in the previous section it is possible to retrieve all the previous versions of JXTA using CVS.

Here are some of the available choices of files to download at the time of writing:

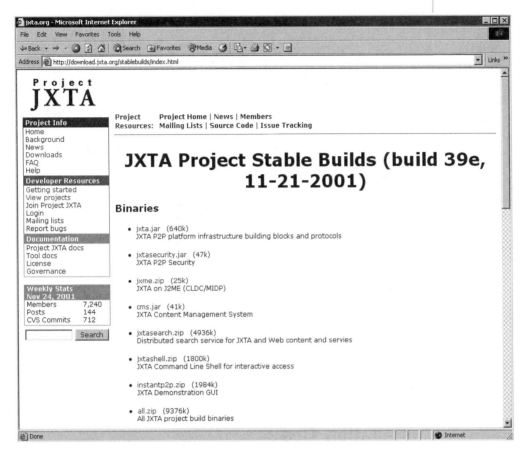

Download Choices

To experiment with JXTA, you should download the JXTA shell distribution. This distribution can be downloaded as an archive of JAR files, or as a self-installing archive for the Microsoft Windows platform.

Here is a description of some of the download choices:

Archive	Description
jxtashell	A JXTA application that provides a command shell, similar to that offered by UNIX and Microsoft Windows. The shell enables a user to experiment with JXTA without actually writing any code.
cms	The Content Management Service is a peer-group service that is optional. This service can be used to share content (that is files) between peers in a peer group.
ip2p	Instant P2P is a non-trivial sample application for JXTA that includes chat and file-sharing capabilities. It also serves as a showcase for new JXTA features and applications.
jxta-search	An optional distributed search service that can be installed to provide a high performance and scalable distributed search mechanism within a JXTA network.

For our initial experiment, download the jxtashell.zip bundle from the stable build selection of the site.

Source Distribution

Being an open source project, all source files for the platform are available. You may consider downloading some of the source distributions to learn how things are achieved by JXTA. Should you wish to work on replacing or contributing to the platform core itself, you will need the Apache Ant tool at http://jakarta.apache.org/ant/index.html to build the sourcecode.

Installation Tips

To ensure a smooth installation, make sure that you have the following:

❑   JDK 1.3.1 or later installed and tested

The jxtashell.zip file that you have downloaded is a bundle that includes:

2. The JXTA command shell application

3. The JXTA platform itself

If you extract the jxtashell.zip archive file, all of the Java executable binaries are bundled in JAR files within the lib subdirectory. Here is a brief description of these executables:

Executable Name	Description
jxtashell.jar	The actual command shell executable, including the default set of commands. The shell can be dynamically extended with custom user commands, as we shall see in the next chapter.
jxta.jar jxtasecurity.jar jxtaptls.jar minimalBC.jar cryptix-ans1.jar cryptix32.jar beepcore.jar log4j.jar	The JXTA core, or more frequently referred to as the JXTA platform. It includes support for the component view of the API, all of the core services, various transport drivers, secured transport via Transport Level Security (TLS), and more. This set of JAR files includes runtime support for the platform in the form of other open source project binaries.
cms.jar cmsshell.jar	The JXTA content management system and associated shell extension. This is an optional group service (at the time of writing) that can be installed.

The JXTA platform will be started when you run the JXTA command shell application (or any other JXTA application). We will see how to achieve this programmatically in later chapters.

The JXTA platform will display a configuration window (the GUI configurator) when you run a JXTA application, such as the command shell, for the very first time. You can use this GUI configurator to configure the specific instance of the JXTA core. Configuration information is written to files and system-created subdirectories under the directory in which you have started the application. This means that you can create multiple instances of a JXTA application, each having a different platform configuration, simply by creating and starting the application from different directories, as illustrated below:

Figure 1

In the case here, test1 and test2 are two separate instances of the JXTA command shell. Since the configuration information is written into different directories, test1 and test2 can have completely different platform configurations.

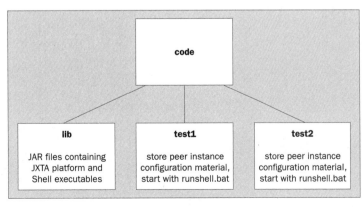

For testing purposes, we will install multiple instances of JXTA peers on the same physical networked machine. We will also be running these instances simultaneously. To simulate multiple independent peers, we will make sure that each instance has a different physical endpoint (for example, a different IP/port combination on the TCP or HTTP contact).

If you are fortunate enough to have a large network of machines to test on, you can configure machines across two TCP/IP subnets to test the P2P nature of JXTA.

Configuring the JXTA Core

The configurator interface will be displayed when you first start the JXTA platform, or anytime the platform needs to be reconfigured. Primarily, the following information must be entered or configured:

❑ A peer name that is unique

❑ One or more transports that the physical node supports (such as TCP, HTTP)

❑ Any startup rendezvous that is already known

❑ Any endpoint-router service that is already known

❑ Whether the peer should attempt to use a router service or not

❑ Proxy information required when connecting out from a firewall

Security information including a login name and password; this is used to create and access unique public/private key pairs that enable Transport Level Security (TLS) operations (for authenticated encrypted connections)

The first configuration screen that you will see is shown here:

Under most situations, you need only enter a unique peer name here. This screen is all you need if you are configuring a single instance of JXTA, on a single physical machine, to access the Internet. The configurator will determine the IP address automatically, use a default port, and configure both TCP and HTTP transports (at the time of writing, these are the only two functional default transports).

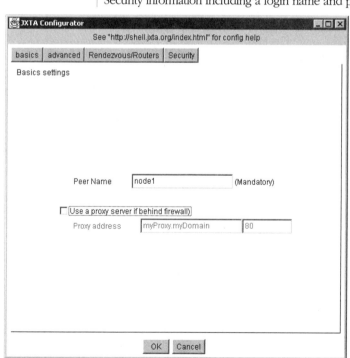

If you are behind a non-transparent firewall that uses a proxy out to the Internet, you can configure the proxy host and port on this basic setup screen as well.

If you need to configure multiple instances of JXTA on the same physical machine – as we will want to do in our experiment, we must proceed to the **advanced** configuration page – as illustrated below:

For most of the samples within this book, you can manually specify the TCP transport details. Make sure you have entered in the hostname of your machine, and have selected a different port number (differ by 2 port numbers – for example 9701 and 9703) for each instance. Disable the HTTP transport (as it is slightly more verbose and will slow down testing) if you are testing on the same host.

If you are behind a firewall and wish to access the network outside of the firewall,

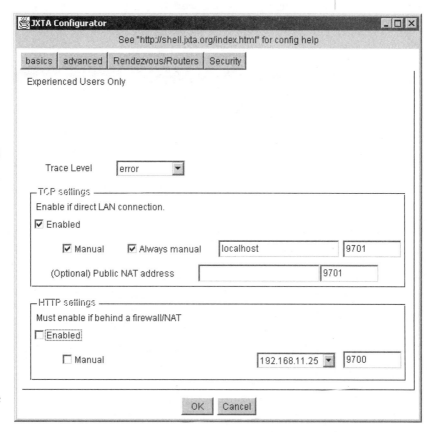

however, you must configure the HTTP transport for proper relay service operation.

Networks and Firewalls

There is one thing in common with Network Address Translation-based (transparent) or proxied (non-transparent) firewalls; JXTA peers behind the firewall can only connect to peers outside the firewall, but those peers outside the firewall will not be able to connect directly to peers inside the firewall. In order for peers within the firewall to receive messages, a message relay service must be used. A peer behind a firewall contacts a relay service (typically on a router node, but almost always also a rendezvous node) to register itself for message relay. The relay service, which will be covered in detail later on within this chapter, will queue any messages for its registered client and allow the client to poll for messages on a regular basis.

We will see a little later that rendezvous peers are peers that run the rendezvous service, assisting in the propagation of distributed queries, while routers are peers that run the routing service, assisting in routing of messages between peers.

Currently, only the HTTP transport supports a relay service. Therefore, if you are behind a firewall and wishes to access the wide area network (i.e. other JXTA peers on the Internet), you must enable the HTTP transport and configure some rendezvous and/or routers.

The rendezvous and routers configuration screen is shown below:

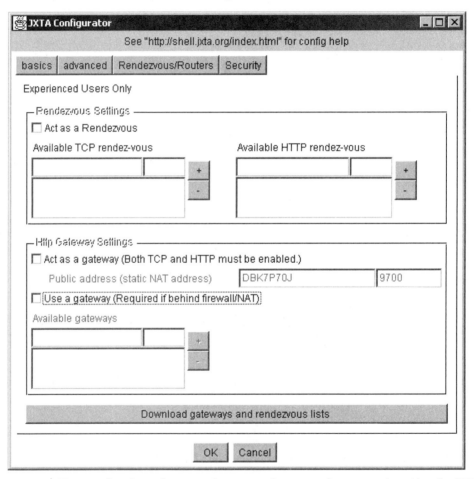

You can directly configure any known rendezvous and routers, using either the TCP or HTTP transport. The Download gateways and rendezvous lists button enables automated update from a site where the JXTA community maintains the latest available list of public rendezvous and routers. This is essential if you would like to access all the current peers available on the Internet-wide JXTA network.

Note that there is an option to act as a rendezvous or router. You can use this option to set up your own rendezvous network or routers for JXTA experimentation. You can also use this option to elect the peer to become a router or rendezvous ithin the larger Internet-wide set of JXTA peers.

> *The current version of this configuration screen uses "router" and "gateway" as interchangeable terms.*

Security Setup

The very last setup screen is a mandatory one and relates to security:

This screen allows you to enter a user name and password for accessing the key ring (a storage for public and private keys) used in the end-to-end TLS implementation. We will have more to say about TLS later, for now simply:

2. Select a user ID of your own choosing

3. Select a password of at least 8 characters

4. Remember and keep in a safe place this user ID and password

You will be prompted to enter this security information only the very first time you configure the platform. On subsequent startups, you will simply be prompted for the entry of the user ID and password for validation.

Trying out a JXTA talk Session

We will now proceed to start the JXTA instant messaging application called **talk** (modeled after the UNIX `talkd` server) via the JXTA shell.

Setting up Two Independent Peers on the Same Machine

For our experimentation with the shell, perform the following configuration.

❑ Go into the `lib` directory of the code distribution for this chapter

❑ Copy all of the JAR files in the `lib` directory of the JXTA shell into the `lib` folder of the source code distribution for this chapter

❑ Change directory to the `test1` directory of the sourcecode distribution

❑ Run the `runshell.bat` script file to start an instance of the shell and configure this shell as shown below:

Configuration Page	Description
Basics	Peer name: node1
	(Do not configure proxy)
Advanced	Enable the TCP transport, set the host manually to localhost, and the port manually to 9701
	Disable the HTTP transport
Rendezvous/Routers	Disable: Act as Rendezvous
	Disable: Act as Gateway
	Disable: Use a Gateway
	(Do not enter any rendezvous or router information)
Security	Enter a user ID and password of your own choosing, make sure your password is at least 8 characters in length, and keep this information in a safe place

Change directory to the `test2` directory of the code distribution
Start the `runshell.bat` script file to start another instance of the shell and configure this shell as shown opposite:

Configuration Page	Description
Basics	Peer name: node2
	(Do not configure proxy)
Advanced	Enable the TCP transport, set the host manually to localhost, and the port manually to 9703
	Disable the HTTP transport
Rendezvous/Routers	Disable: Act as Rendezvous
	Disable: Act as Gateway
	Disable: Use a Gateway
	(Do not enter any rendezvous or router information)
Security	Enter a user ID and password of your own choosing, make sure password is at least 8 characters in length, and keep this information in a safe place

This configuration will set up two independent peers on the same physical machines, looping back on the TCP transport and will enable us to experiment with JXTA on a single machine.

Familiarizing Yourself with the JXTA Shell

When a JXTA shell instance starts up, it will display the welcome screen, as illustrated:

We can enter any shell commands at this time, and the output will be displayed on the console. For instance, the following command will list all the currently known commands:

JXTA> **man**

The man command can be used to display usage information relating to individual shell commands, as shown here:

```
JXTA Shell - 1                                                    _ □ ✕
=================================================
========= Welcome to the JXTAShell  Version 1.0 =========
=================================================

The JXTA Shell provides an interactive environment to the JXTA
platform. The Shell provides basic commands to discover peers and
peergroups, to join and resign from peergroups, to create pipes
between peers, and to send pipe messages. The Shell provides environment
variables that permit binding symbolic names to Jxta platform objects.
Environment variables allow Shell commands to exchange data between
themselves. The shell command 'env' displays all defined environment
variables in the current Shell session.

The Shell creates a Jxta InputPipe (stdin) for reading input from
the keyboard, and a Jxta OutputPipe (stdout) to display information
on the Shell console. All commands executed by the Shell have their
initial 'stdin' and 'stdout' set up to the Shell's stdin and stdout pipes.
The Shell also creates the environment variable 'stdgroup' that
contains the current JXTA PeerGroup in which the Shell and commands
are executed.

A new Shell can be forked within a Shell. The 'Shell -s'
command starts a new Shell with a new Shell window. The Shell can
also read a command script file via the 'Shell -f myfile'.

A 'man' command is available to list the commands available.
Type 'man <command>' to get help about a particular command.
To exit the Shell, use the 'exit' command.
JXTA>
```

JXTA> **man
<commandName>**

For example, the following command prints out information about the Shell command:

JXTA> **man Shell**

We will examine many of the commands in the JXTA shell in the next chapter. However, you can always use the man command at any time, to find out information about a specific shell command.

Starting a talk Session

Now, to try out the JXTA talk application, we need to enter some commands in the JXTA shell. Using the shell instance on node1, type in the following (the shell response is included in italicized font):

JXTA> **talk -register node1user**
......
User : node1user is now registered

JXTA> **talk -login node1user**

Using the shell instance on node2, type in the following (the shell response is given in italics):

JXTA> **talk -register node2user**
......
User : node1user is now registered

JXTA> **talk -login node2user**

```
JXTA> talk -u node2user node1user
found user's advertisement attempting to connect
talk is connected to user node1user
Type your message. To exit, type "." at begining of line
```

Now type the message that you wish to send to the other node, for example as shown below:

```
hello
```

Note that at node1 we have now received a real-time instant message from node2user.

```
talk: from node2user to node1user
Message: hello
```

We can consummate the connection with the command:

```
JXTA> talk -u node1user node2user
found user's advertisement attempting to connect
talk is connected to user node2user
Type your message. To exit, type "." at begining of line
```

Now type the message that you wish to return, as below:

```
hello back!
```

Have a look at the shell instance for node2 and you will see that the above message has been received and is displayed in the shell. Having performed the above steps, you can see how easy it is to carry out a simple peer-to-peer conversion between the two nodes by typing in your messages at the JXTA shell prompt.

Enabling P2P Instant Messaging Across Diverse Terrain

What we have accomplished in this preview is to start and work with the JXTA talk application. This application makes use of the JXTA platform to perform peer-to-peer instant text messaging. While we have used loop-back on a single machine to make the experiment simple, the same steps can be used to:

1. Start a conversation between yourself and any other peer out on the Internet-wide JXTA network

2. Start a conversation between yourself on a PC, and a target JXTA peer running on any other device (for example PDA cell-phones, pocket PCs, two-way pagers, etc.)

The discovery and communication processes can work right through firewalls with the proper platform configuration. In fact, it can be used to communicate with peers behind their own firewalls (often called 'traversal of double firewalls'). Furthermore, the discovery of the target peer is completely decentralized – meaning that it can be carried out over the JXTA network at any time without reliance on some specific server(s) being available.

This preview has given us a glimpse of the JXTA shell, and what the JXTA platform can do. Let us now turn our attention to *how* the JXTA platform does its work.

JXTA: The Basic Concepts

JXTA is an interoperable substrate (layers of APIs and protocols) for building P2P systems. By focusing on the plumbing, rather than the shape or forms, the designers of JXTA are attempting to isolate the basic components and encapsulate the functionality that is part of every P2P system. The pieces aim to be a "P2P systems construction kit", making it easy to create your own P2P system, but without getting in the way and dictating how you *must* do things. This is a high priority goal in the design of JXTA.

> *JXTA has been developed to facilitate the creation of P2P services, applications, and systems without dictating specific policies or restricting the approaches to the design of such systems.*

As P2P applications developers, only we can be the judges to determine if JXTA has achieved its goal.

This chapter examines the components and the layers that make up JXTA. At the lowest level, JXTA is really a set of interoperable protocols. These protocols enable JXTA peers to:

1. Locate peers, services, and resources (discovery)

2. Send messages between peers over virtual channels called **pipes** (communications)

3. Obtain information on other peers

4. Share services and resources

5. Interact using a P2P topology over a diverse physical network topology

6. Join and leave peer groups

Layered on top of these protocols are components within the JXTA platform that are realized via APIs. Many of these components are individual concepts that do not necessarily lend themselves to the classic layering. However, as we examine the components that are within the JXTA platform, we will realize that they are a means to an end – and that end is to create heterogeneous communicating peers that interoperate over a set of common protocols. This will encourage the adoption of JXTA as the preferred basis for P2P application, service, or system implementation across systems with heterogeneous and diverse requirements.

Interoperability is a high priority goal in the design of JXTA.

> *JXTA is designed to be interoperable on the protocol level, enabling applications and services to be created using any programming language on any operating system or hardware platform. It is the aim of the JXTA community to preserve this interoperability throughout JXTA's longer-term evolution.*

Finally, JXTA must be implementable across a diverse world of devices, and a myriad of networking and communications transports. It is not being designed to minimize dependency on any specific characteristics of any device and/or networking transport. For example, if JXTA required a connections-based transport, it would be completely useless for incorporating wireless PDAs into a P2P network – if the PDA utilizes a packet-based digital broadcast network that does not support connections. In order to become the P2P glue that enables all current and future devices to participate, over most of the current and future network transport scenarios, JXTA is designed to be as flexible and tolerant as possible to the differences in these configurations/transports.

> *JXTA is designed to be transport agnostic, and assumes only a minimal asynchronous one-way message passing transport. There is no requirement for reliability, quality of service, or bi-directional capability. JXTA also does not require a peer to implement any of the protocols that it does not use – enabling even clients with minimal computing capability to participate in the P2P network.*

With these design goals in mind, we are now ready to examine how these design goals are realized through the core components and concepts of JXTA.

JXTA Core Components and Concepts

To understand why multiple levels of abstractions exist within JXTA, we need to consider what JXTA is really doing for us. Namely, it provides us with a view of a "network" where the conventional notion of a network fails us.

In more fancy P2P terms, it provides a completely non-centralized way for peers to communicate and share resources with one another.

In other words, JXTA works with no assumption of a centralized directory naming and addressing system such as DNS for the Internet (although the current reference implementations use the TCP and HTTP transport, which supports DNS). JXTA works over a network where individual peers are being turned on, turned off, rebooted, removed, or replaced constantly. JXTA works over a network where a peer can roam and take on the form of a new physical network endpoint at different point in time. For example, my notebook computer may be on at the office TCP/IP network from 9am to 5pm, and on a radio packet-switched network the rest of the time.

To accommodate these feats of magic, the JXTA designers have examined the design of many P2P or P2P-like systems and factored out some common attributes that are built into JXTA.

As one can imagine, dealing with a constant change of network topology, and the non-deterministic mapping between peers and real network endpoints is not a trivial programming exercise. If JXTA were to expose just this layer of communications as its API it would make the implementation of P2P systems with JXTA much more difficult and possibly have a considerable impact on the success of the JXTA platform.

Therefore, it is vital to simplify the API programming model. JXTA accomplishes this by providing a mid-level component view to application and service programmers. This view consists of components at the JXTA core's highest level of abstraction – and it is a simplistic view.

Figure 1

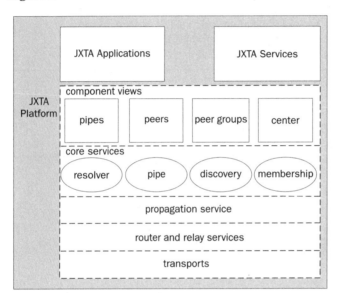

The figure here shows the two levels of abstraction (components and core services) as well as the network virtualization layers that the JXTA platform is composed of. Our coverage will proceed in a top-down manner.

JXTA Components

The highest level of abstraction in the JXTA core is a component-based view that has very simplistic operational semantics. It is a view created for the application developer, to ease the task of designing and programming P2P applications and services. This view should provide the most straightforward bridge to JXTA for developers who are already familiar with current client-server programming models.

The JXTA platform is layered and the components that are visible at this level are:

1. Peers

2. Pipes

3. Services

4. Peer Groups

In fact, this is the view that we can take when designing most JXTA-enabled applications or services. At this level, JXTA is a network that consists of peers communicating with one another via communications channels called **pipes**. Let us take a look at the idiosyncrasies of each of these components, and see how JXTA's lower-level requirements correspond to these restrictions.

Peers

Peers are the fundamental entities in a JXTA system. Some observable properties of peers are:

1. They are universally unique entities within the JXTA network that communicate with one another

2. They may be consumers of services

3. They may also offer services of their own

Without restricting the mapping into real-world entities, which will inevitably restrict the type of applications that JXTA can be used to create, peers in JXTA are represented by only one single unique ID – the **Peer ID**.

In P2P applications we can conceptually map a specific machine or device to a peer (and maybe even an individual behind a machine to a peer in the near future). However, this is not required by JXTA, and is completely application-dependent.

A unique property of peers in JXTA is that a peer can be associated with one or more physical networking endpoint – and these endpoints can change dynamically.

This obviously satisfies our requirement that an individual peer may "roam" around different physical networks, and therefore dynamically move from one physical network endpoint to another, while maintaining the same peer identity within the JXTA network. Imagine the complexity in implementing this "virtualization" of peer identity across multiple dissimilar network transports – and you will begin to appreciate how the elegant design of JXTA shields us from the great complexity of the implementation underneath.

Pipes

We already know that JXTA peers communicate with one another, but we have not yet said how. Any conventional means of communication that designates a communication channel with fixed endpoints and some sort of centralized address management scheme (such as TCP sockets) will not be useful. Instead, JXTA peers communicate through pipes. Pipes as communication channels must satisfy the following requirements:

1. The transport endpoint at each end may (physically) change at any time (for example from TCP to HTTP to BEEP to wireless packet to Bluetooth, etc.)

2. Even the most restrictive supporting transport (for example some analog paging network, or smoke signal) can be used to implement it

To satisfy these very tough requirements, JXTA pipes are special in the following way:

1. Either end of a pipe is not "bound" to a physical endpoint until just before communications occur, and may be rebound during operation as many time as necessary

2. The very basic JXTA pipes are unidirectional, unreliable, and asynchronous. These basic pipes are called "unidirectional pipes"

To achieve bi-directional communication between two peers will require the creation of two separate pipes (and the potential binding and rebinding of four pipe endpoints during operation). More specifically, JXTA does not provide any guarantee that the establishment of a pipe in the opposite direction is even possible. "Unreliable" means that messages sent over pipes are not guaranteed to be delivered and may be arbitrarily lost. "Asynchronous" implies that multiple messages sent through the same pipe may arrive at the other end out-of-order. Taken together, this means that JXTA pipes may deliver multiple copies of the same message, or that all message sent may be lost. This sounds very severe, but is absolutely essential to ensure that the lower-level requirements are all satisfied by the model.

In any specific application of JXTA, since the application designer will have a priori knowledge of the network topology, its idiosyncrasies, and traffic patterns that the application needs to work with, less restrictive and more reliable means of communication can be provided. This is an excellent example of how JXTA can be "juxtaposed" onto more conventional system designs.

Even though they share the same name as UNIX pipes, JXTA pipes are not an in-memory data structure; they are also not files on the disk, but are simply a label or name (actually a unique ID embedded in an XML document called an **advertisement**) that has no physical manifestation until it is used. JXTA pipes are therefore virtual in every sense of the word. The action of committing the pipe advertisement to a "physical pipe endpoint" is called binding, and it is performed during run time. In fact, either end of a JXTA pipe can be dynamically bound to a different "physical pipe endpoint" at a different point in time.

The unidirectional nature of the basic JXTA pipe means that to communicate through a pipe, the sender of the message must first bind to the "input pipe", and the receiver of the message must have independently bound to the "output pipe" associated with the other end. When you have the possession of a pipe advertisement, you are ready to bind to that pipe. During binding, you have the option of asking for the input or the output end of the pipe. You should ask for the input end if you wish to write to the pipe, or ask for the output end if you wish to read from the pipe

Since communication/transport endpoints are properties associated with peers (although the mapping is flexible and subject to change), pipe endpoints are also associated with peers. One can view the act of binding a pipe as resolving the endpoint of a pipe to a peer(s). In order to preserve pipe semantics, once bound, each end of the pipe is responsible for maintaining the binding. This means that each may independently rebind should network topology changes necessitate such an action.

This means that with JXTA we can provide multiple redundant implementations of a service, each hosted on a different peer, and advertise only a single pipe that will automatically "fail over" and rebind to another peer should the currently bound peer disconnect or die. In fact, this dynamic mapping between pipe endpoints and peers is exploited within a peer group by the JXTA platform itself.

JXTA pipes can be of two different types:

1. Unidirectional pipe

2. Propagate pipe

A unidirectional pipe is established between one input endpoint and one or more output endpoints. A propagate pipe supports multiple input endpoints. Essentially messages are propagated between the multiple endpoints at the receiving peers (each supporting an input endpoint). The two types of JXTA pipes are illustrated below:

Figure 2

We can see from this diagram why unidirectional pipes are sometimes called "many-to-one" pipes, and the propagated pipes are sometimes known as the "many-to-many" pipes. The initial release of the Java reference implementation supported only unicast pipes. A separate experimental project called JXTA-wire was used to test out implementations of the "many-to-many" propagate pipes. At the time of writing, the propagate pipe functionality has just been fully incorporated into the JXTA core platform, and can now therefore be viewed as an integral part of the platform.

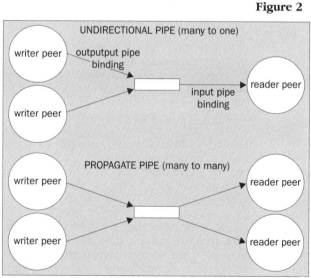

Again, if we have specific knowledge of our application behavior or the specific network topologies used, we can readily create higher-level variants of these pipe types including bi-directional pipes or reliable pipes. However, the JXTA specification does not mandate them, and the JXTA core platform need not support them natively.

Services

Given that we have a mechanism for peers to communicate with each other (pipes) over a P2P network, we can now allow one peer to perform useful work on behalf of another. This can be viewed as the establishment of many temporary client-server relationships between peers. Obviously, any particular peer can be a client as well as a service to any other – faithful to the P2P nature of the network.

A Service in JXTA (called a Network Service in the JXTA specification) is therefore:

1. Hosted by a peer

2. Performs useful work on behalf of a remote peer

This definition is almost the same as the definition of a "server" in the conventional client-server architecture. The JXTA specification has purposely left the definition of a JXTA service wide open. This is done to accommodate the large variety of possible interaction between peers, and to facilitate the migration or juxtaposition of conventional servers into the JXTA network.

The way that a service gets started and shuts down is not specified by JXTA. For example, in a world where P2P systems are working in harmony with traditional client-server systems, conventional web services can become JXTA services via a simple gateway. If the JXTA specification dictates how services must be started up or shutdown, this bridging/gateway opportunity may be lost. The control of the service lifecycle is, of course, an implementation-specific concern.

Now, if the service in question actually use a JXTA pipe as a communications mechanism, it is called a JXTA-enabled service. Note that this means that an "out of JXTA band" means of communicating between a peer and a service is definitely allowed within the JXTA framework. For example, a juxtaposed solution may use JXTA's discovery mechanism to locate services, and then use TCP/IP sockets to actually access the services once located.

Thus far, we have only been talking about services that are associated with a peer. Like the conventional client-server architecture, services associated with a single peer (called **peer services**) suffer from the same availability problems of traditional services – if the peer hosting the service becomes unavailable, the service is no longer available.

In order to accommodate a network of peers that may come and go at any time, JXTA defines a type of redundantly implemented service that can be uniformly accessed by peers – called a **peer-group service**. Before we can understand how the peer-group service works, we must take a look at what a JXTA peer group is.

Peer Groups

Peer groups, as their name suggests, are groupings of peers. In JXTA 1.0, they represent:

1. A security domain within which membership can be authenticated and managed

2. A grouping within which member peers can shared common services

3. A partitioning of the potential universe of network endpoints to limit the propagation of distributed queries

In other words, peer groups are a partitioning of peers over a P2P network. A peer can have membership in as many peer groups as it desires it can also choose to have a different identity within each group. Note that a peer has a unique identity in the JXTA universe, represented by the Peer ID. This identity does not change regardless of which group it is currently in, or how many group memberships the peer may have. In this way, the peer group concept appears to be at a higher level (almost application) than the rest of the components that we have described so far.

Peers can freely create, discover, join, or monitor peer groups, subject to restrictions enforced by any security system that may be operating (if any).

By default, all peers are deemed to belong to a "world peer group". In other words, all peers in a JXTA network are members of the "world peer group". The current JXTA implementation creates a subgroup under this world peer group called the **NetPeerGroup** by default. The NetPeerGroup consists of all the peers that can be reached via discovery over the currently supported transports on the network. In many situations, operating within this default group is sufficient for an application as the number of peers in the network may be limited in the first place, and membership tracking is not necessary.

A JXTA service can be associated with a peer group, and we learned earlier that a peer group is a grouping within which member peers can share common services. Services that are associated with a peer group (instead of an individual peer) are called **peer-group services**.

Peer-Group Services

Peer-group services are services that are associated with a peer group. Typically, instances of a peer-group service are running on multiple peers within the group (frequently one instance per peer). This helps with the high availability of the service. The service will be available as long as at least one service instance is still running within the group. Most peer-group service designs incorporate some aspect of information sharing between the redundant running instances, making a rebinding to a different instance as transparent as possible.

Other Components and Concepts

JXTA consists of peers, entities that dynamically bind to network endpoints, communicating with one another over dynamic virtual communications channels called pipes. Pipes are asynchronous, unidirectional, and unreliable channels that are dynamically bound to peers. Communicating peers can make use of each other's resources by each providing a service to be accessed by others. Services that use a JXTA pipe for input are called JXTA-enabled services. Peers can join peer groups to enjoy secured access or authenticated access to resources, to share a set of services, or to limit propagation of JXTA messages. Services can be associated with a peer group instead of a single peer, providing high availability for services when multiple peers in the peer group host service instances.

This is an adequate summary of the component view of how a JXTA network operates. There exists, however, an additional concept that can be useful in many JXTA applications – but is not essential for the usage or operation of the JXTA core platform.

Codats

Codats are individual pieces of binary information in the JXTA network that are identified by a unique ID. The word "codat" refers to "CODe or DATa". JXTA codats are atomic entities of independently identifiable content. For example, an MP3 file is a codat, a ZIP file is a codat, an AVI media file is a codat, and a compiled Java class is a codat. JXTA codats are very useful in applications that manage or share content. The ability to uniquely identify content is vital in JXTA-enabled systems where content may be widely replicated, and where textual names associated with the content may be ambiguous or sensitive to differences in locale.

This concludes our examination of the component view of the JXTA platform. Now, we will look under the hood and see how this view is implemented.

Platform Core Services

The second level of abstraction in JXTA consists of the platform core services that together implement the component view at the top level. It will give us a glimpse into how JXTA actually works. All of these services are peer-group services in JXTA. More specifically, one instance of each of these services can be running on each instance of the JXTA platform. In JXTA 1.0, the core services include:

Service	Description
Discovery	This service allows peers to discover each other. It is also used to discover peer groups, services, pipes, etc. The discovery is performed via a propagated remote query for specific advertisements.
Pipe	The pipe service enables peers to bind to pipe endpoints. It also manages pipes created by the peer and facilitates the passing of messages through the pipe(s).
Resolver	The resolver service is a façade, if you will, for propagating distributed requests, and forwarding responses to pre-registered handlers. In a generic sense, it provides a propagation service to query requests within a peer group. Specific services register with the resolver service to handle certain requests, when the resolver service receives these requests, it will then call the registered service to process it.
Access	This is a security service. Although not well developed in JXTA 1.0 (since more practical research needs to be done in distributed or non-centralized trust networks), it can be used to control access to any service or resource access based on a credential supplied.
Membership	This is not part of the reference implementation. The protocol used by this service, however, is part of the JXTA 1.0 specification.
Monitor	This service enables a peer to be monitored for uptime, traffic on each incoming and outgoing channel, and other information relating to status.

Together, these services present the component view that we have discussed previously. Unlike any peer or peer-group service that you may write on the application level, one very special property of these core services is that their on-the-wire communications protocols are the specified protocols of JXTA itself. We will cover these protocols in-depth later.

JXTA Messages and Advertisements

When peers communicate with each other, it is JXTA messages that are being passed between them. JXTA messages can be either text or binary format for communication, depending on the transport involved. For example, while HTTP transport typically uses the most interoperable XML-based text format messaging, the TCP transport can use a more bandwidth-efficient binary message format.

Each message used in the text-based format is actually an XML document (without the formal document declaration and document element). This is called a **structured document** in JXTA lingo. The unique property of a structured document, other than that it can be easily parsed an manipulated across many platforms and using many different programming languages, is that it can be extended by simply adding more tagged elements to the document. In fact, payloads are added to messages by inserting a structured document fragment associated with a tag. This tagged structured document can then be easily recovered at the receiver's end.

Advertisements are a special type of JXTA messages. Advertisements, as the name suggests, advertise the existence of a resource. Some pre-defined advertisements in JXTA include:

Advertisement	Description
Peer Advertisement	Describes a peer, associated with a unique Peer ID and a peer name (may or may not be unique), the peer group that the peer belongs to, and also all the transport endpoints associated with the peer.
Peer-Group Advertisement	Describes a peer group, the unique Peer-Group ID, a peer-group name (may or may not be unique), and service advertisements for all the peer-group services associated with the group.
Pipe Advertisement	Describes a pipe, providing its unique Pipe ID and an optional name. It also provides the Peer ID associated with the pipe instance.
Service Advertisement	Still valid as a concept, describes a service and means of accessing the service (. a pipe). It can either be a standalone (peer service), or part of a peer-group advertisement (peer-group service). This advertisement has been superceded by a combination of the `ModuleClass` advertisement, `ModuleSpec` advertisement, and `ModuleImpl` advertisement.

Runtime "Binding" is Equivalent to a Distributed Query

JXTA advertisements are propagated and cached via a network of rendezvous (described in detail later). This means that most peers in a JXTA-based P2P network will cache advertisements that they encounter, and will respond to distributed search queries if a matching advertisement can be found.

Every advertisement has an expiration date, after which the advertisement should be removed from any cache. This is necessary because of the dynamic composition of a P2P network. Stale advertisements can waste a lot of system resources in terms of storage and retries (caused by bad information in the advertisement).

We now know that expiration time is a mechanism to keep the cached set of advertisements within a P2P network current. Now, carefully re-examine the advertisement table above, and notice the following:

1. A pipe advertisement contains a unique Pipe ID and the peer that hosts the pipe

2. A peer advertisement contains a unique Peer ID and the network endpoints that are associated with the peer

Now, given we have a Pipe ID, and we want to "bind" to the pipe, what we need to do is to perform a distributed query for pipe advertisements that contain this unique Pipe ID. Any advertisements found in this distributed query will contain a mapping between the Pipe ID and the peer that actually hosts the pipe – resolving the pipe to a peer.

Given a Peer ID, if you actually want to contact the peer via a network transport, say HTTP, you must resolve the peer's current network endpoints. This again is equivalent to a distributed query to find the peer advertisement associated with the given Peer ID.

At this point, we must descend several levels and get right to the physical network underneath in order be make these higher-level concepts understandable. In JXTA, a **network transport** is a supported network protocol stack on a peer. For example, TCP is a network transport, HTTP is a network transport, BEEP is a network transport, and a cellular phone network or a wireless packet network can be a network transport. A **transport endpoint** is a physical address on a network transport at any moment in time. For example, an IP address plus port number is a transport endpoint for the TCP transport. A URL can contain the transport endpoint for an HTTP transport, and a cellular phone number can be the transport endpoint for a cellular phone network transport. Therefore, a pipe binding operation involves:

1. Resolving a Pipe ID to a Peer ID

2. Resolving a Peer ID to a transport endpoint

In practice, here is how binding is used to facilitate pipe communications between a service peer and a client peer:

1. A service peer wanting to receive requests from clients first creates a pipe; it does so by creating an advertisement and publishing it (making it available all over the peer group via the rendezvous network)

2. The service peer then binds to the pipe's input end (obtaining a transport endpoint at that time) and waits for messages

3. A client peer wanting to communicate with the service peer will query for pipe advertisements (previously published), and the rendezvous network will locate and respond with the advertisement

4. The client peer then binds to the pipe's output end (obtaining a transport endpoint at the time) and sends the message

In each case, we can see that coupling the expiry data mechanism with a way to conduct distributed queries among the peer group we can dynamically bind a pipe to a peer, and a peer to its network endpoints.

Note that this mechanism works in a completely non-centralized manner. It will also work without dependency on any specific network nodes. This binding mechanism will work over any transport that is supported by JXTA.

Mechanism of Operations

In fact, all of JXTA's core services work via one of the following mechanisms:

1. Sending messages between peers

2. Propagating distributed queries throughout the peer group, and processing any response

3. Propagating advertisements throughout the peer group

The following table documents the mechanism used by each of the core services:

Core Service	Mechanism of Operation
Discovery	Propagates distributed queries throughout the peer group, and processes any response. Also propagates advertisements throughout the peer group (in a remote publish operation).
Resolver	Propagates distributed queries throughout the peer group, passing the response to registered handlers.
Pipe	Propagates distributed queries throughout the peer group, and processes any response.
Membership	Sends messages between peers using pipes.
Monitor	Sends messages between peers using pipes.

The above table hints at the similarity between the discovery service, the pipe service, and the resolver service. In fact, we will discover later that the pipe service and the discovery service both uses the resolver service to perform its work.

Another very important point to note here is that almost all of the core services depend on the following to function:

1. Query propagation

2. An advertisement caching network

These are precisely the functions of the next layer of network services.

The Virtual Networking Layer

All of JXTA's core services depend on the services in the virtual networking layer to:

1. Propagate queries throughout a peer group

2. Provide a network of nodes that cache advertisements

A service called the **rendezvous service** is the centerpiece of this layer. This layer can be called a virtual networking layer because it rides on top of a network that is composed of peers in a peer group – and not on physical network transports.

In other words, lower layers must:

1. Find and maintain routes between peers

2. Resolve peers to physical network endpoints

The Rendezvous Service

So what is this elusive rendezvous service? The following figures illustrates how this rendezvous service works.

A rendezvous service propagates queries among a network of rendezvous. Rendezvous within this network are all connected to one another (although this may not be by a direct physical connection). Each Rendezvous caches and maintains any advertisement that it encounters that has not yet expired.

Figure 3

In the diagram, we can see that a peer may send its rendezvous (any one in the network) a query for an advertisement. First, the rendezvous will check to see if the advertisement can be found in the cache locally; if so the advertisement is returned and the query is not propagated further. Now, if the query cannot be satisfied by this rendezvous, it will

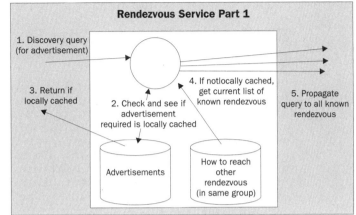

propagate (broadcast within constraint) the query to all the rendezvous that it knows about, therefore acting as a client to those rendezvous. The diagram below shows what happens next.

Figure 4

Now, if an advertisement exists in the peer group that satisfies the distributed query, one of the rendezvous in the network will respond. When this happens, as is shown in the figure here, the rendezvous that propagated the query will cache the advertisement (so future queries can be responded to immediately) and then responds to the client (or an upstream rendezvous).

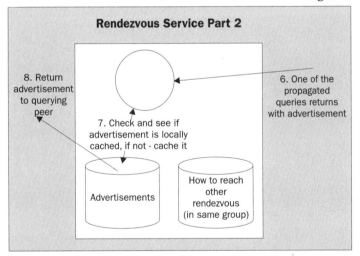

In this way, rendezvous nodes propagate queries throughout the peer group via the rendezvous network, and propagate advertisements backwards towards the requests that they match. Any peer within the network can be configured to become a rendezvous, or a rendezvous can be started on any peer at any time – completely consistent with the operation of a P2P network.

Peers only need to reach one rendezvous node to gain the benefit of query propagation (thus allowing all the core services to operate over the entire peer group).

At the time of writing, the Rendezvous service is undergoing transformation to become a more general "propagation service". Other than the name change, the propagation service offers JXTA peers a general means to propagate arbitrary JXTA messages (not just distributed queries or responses) throughout the peer group to interested recipients.

Rendezvous Becomes the Propagation Service

Propagation is performed by piggybacking on the network of rendezvous already in place. The propagation service allows clients to obtain a time-limited lease on a connection over which to send propagated messages and/or receive propagated messages. The rendezvous code has been modified to recognize incoming propagated messages and re-broadcast those messages to all the known rendezvous in the network and clients with unexpired lists. This enables any peer in the peer group to send and receive propagated messages (as long as it has a connection to a rendezvous/propagation service). Note that a propagated message has an embedded structured document that is used by the propagation service to control the time-to-live of the propagated message and to detect potential propagation loops.

The figure below illustrates a network of rendezvous, and contrasts how the new propagation service works.

Figure 5

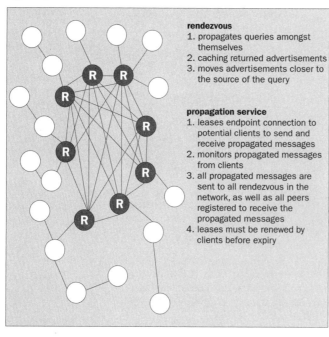

rendezvous
1. propagates queries amongst themselves
2. caching returned advertisements
3. moves advertisements closer to the source of the query

propagation service
1. leases endpoint connection to potential clients to send and receive propagated messages
2. monitors propagated messages from clients
3. all propagated messages are sent to all rendezvous in the network, as well as all peers registered to receive the propagated messages
4. leases must be renewed by clients before expiry

Note how the use of rendezvous/propagation service greatly reduces the propagation traffic within a P2P network. In practice, one can often ensure that configured rendezvous are peers that enjoy high bandwidth connectivity – thus enhancing the performance of the P2P network.

Routers and Relays – Paths Between Peers

Routers and propagation services are key services that enable JXTA to work over a variety of HTTP and TCP/IP-based transports.

The core function of a router is to be able to send JXTA messages from one endpoint to another. In order to do this, the router must maintain information about the endpoints that it can reach and how to get there (in terms of the intermediate endpoints that the message must be passed through).

Router Service

A router service maintains route information between peers. It caches route information locally, but collaborates with other router service instances to find routes between peers. A route consists of a set of gateways (or intermediate peers) moving from the source to the destination, where each peer is resolved to its physical transport endpoint during the routing of a message. When a route is used to forward messages, it is entirely possible – thanks to the ever-changing topology of typical P2P networks – to cause the message to be suddenly unroutable. In this case, the router services involved must attempt to rediscover a new route to send the message back on its way. The JXTA router service has a unique property in that it is both a peer group service and an endpoint transport implementation.

The Service/Transport Duality of the JXTA Router

Once upon a time, not too long ago in JXTA history, the rendezvous (propagation service), router, and transport were concepts and code modules that were not very cleanly separated. Design review and public pressure has necessitated the componentization of these concepts. The most important motivation for this modularization is to satisfy the need to enable third parties to create their own transports.

It is not uncommon in system-level design, especially in networking or operating system work, to have tightly coupled modules that provide no convenient means of external interfacing. One can find evidence of this in almost all modern-day operating systems – such as in the innards of Linux and Microsoft Windows. The main reason for such tight coupling is:

1. Simplicity of internal coding

2. Elimination of additional layering for highest possible performance

Internal to JXTA, we can observe an artifact of such factoring. It represents the "tug" between:

1. The need to componentize the JXTA platform

2. The need to provide a transport interface open to third parties, and to a lesser degree an alternative router implementation

3. The need to maintain high performance, or at least future tenability, within the router logic

Some may see all this rationale as justifications for a big code kludge. You can be your own judge of this. But the JXTA router sits at a very interesting location in the internal platform architecture. The location reflects its two principal roles:

Role	Description
Service	Like the resolver service, and the propagation service, the JXTA endpoint router is a service that propagates queries among a network of endpoint routers. In fact, it is this network of endpoint routers that propagate routing information among themselves. Each endpoint router also caches any routing information that it sees, and has the ability to rediscover a route should it become invalid. Peers that are not endpoint router themselves can make use of the service of a discovered endpoint router to route its messages.
Transport	Using the internally cached routing information, combined with the results from queries, the JXTA endpoint router provides a virtualized "point-to-point" transport "driver" for the endpoint service. This means that the endpoint service will see direct single-hop routes between peers when it works with the endpoint router transport. To the endpoint service, the endpoint router looks just like a TCP transport, or HTTP transport, etc.

This is illustrated in the figure below:

Figure 6

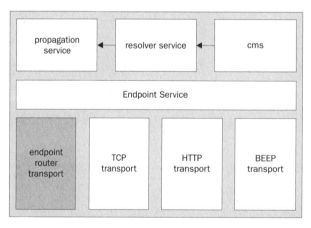

We can see in the figure that the endpoint router is a transport. In this way, we see a very conventional layering where platform core services are on top of the endpoint service, and the endpoint service in turn works with a series of "direct connect" transports including TCP, HTTP, BEEP, and the virtualized endpoint router transport. The diagram also shows a typical scenario: some non-core services such as the Content Management Service (CMS) makes use of the core services such as the Resolver Service to simplify and unify its own coding logic.

The service role of the endpoint router is illustrated below:

Figure 7

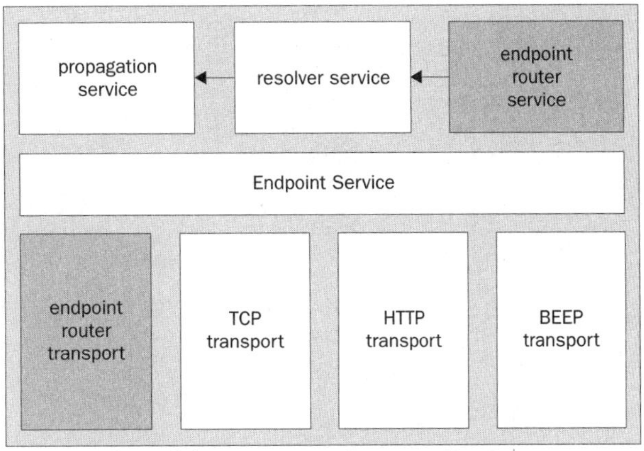

Here, we see the endpoint router service making use of the core resolver service to propagate its own routing queries among other endpoint router peers. Much of this routing information is cached, and made use of by the lower layer "transport" component of the endpoint router.

How does the endpoint router deal with the possibility of recursion? It may attempt to virtualize routing using the already virtualized router transport. The answer is quite simple: since both the service role and the transport role are realized within the same code module, a flag is set to ensure that routing service queries are never transmitted over the router transport. Not a perfectly clean design, but it should perform well.

Relay Service

Not every transport supports or requires the use of a relay service. The relay service is used for network nodes participating in a JXTA network that cannot be connected to directly. Some of the reasons why a relay service may be needed are:

1. Using an HTTP transport, but the network node is behind a firewall (we can only connect out from the firewall, not back in)

2. Using some other unidirectional transport, such as an analog pager network

The figure below shows how the relay service helps with the delivery of messages to and from a peer behind a firewall:

Figure 8

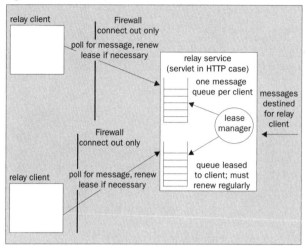

We see in the diagram that the relay service manages leases on the message queues that it maintains on behalf of clients. This is necessary since clients may disappear and never returns on a P2P network, for any reason or no reason at all. The lease-based expiry mechanism will ensure that the resources utilized by the queue will eventually be reclaimed should the corresponding client peer become defunct. Any "live" clients of a relay service must regularly renew the lease to ensure that its queue on the relay service does not expire prematurely. The router on the relay service node will claim that it "knows how to route the message to its client". Other routers will forward messages destined to a relay service's client to the node containing the relay service.

In practice, the client will occasionally poll its queue on the relay service for messages – and renew the lease on the queue if necessary. In this way, for transports that require the relay service, it is an integral part of the router-level logic.

The New Age Communications Stack

At this point, we have seen the entire communication stack that the JXTA platform entails. The following figure shows a summary of the stack:

Figure 9

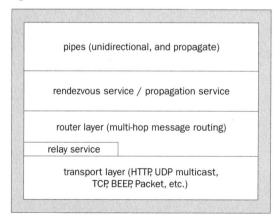

Pipe binding (mapping into peers) relies on the rendezvous/propagation service to perform the distributed queries. The rendezvous, in turn relies on a router layer that maps paths between peers. The router service is both a service and a transport. The relay service is a part of the router, and provides queuing services for peers that cannot be connected to directly.

The way in which JXTA virtualizes a network against a changing and decentralized addressing network is best visualized by the 3-dimensional figure below:

Figure 10

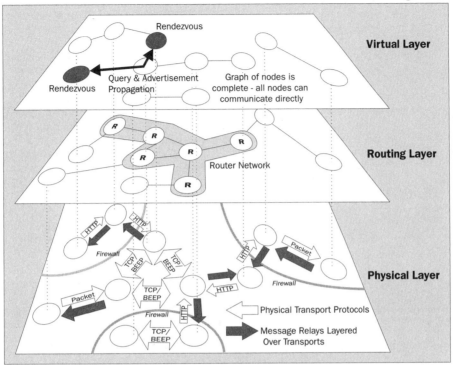

We can see in this figure that even though the underlying network transport connecting the peers together may be intermittent and unreliable, the JXTA platform layers ensure that a virtual mesh is established between all peers in the network – allowing every peer within the P2P network to communicate with every other without dependency on any centralized server or addressing scheme.

The JXTA Interoperability Level: The Protocols

The JXTA protocols are the basis for JXTA's unique interoperability. Any platform that supports a common transport, such as TCP/IP, and has the ability to transmit and receive XML-based messages over that transport can interoperate. This means that JXTA services and clients can be created on almost any current operating system, using almost any programming language.

This means that JXTA protocols are defined:

1. Independent of specific transports

2. Independent of programming language and operating system

3. Independent of specific security mechanisms

JXTA clients or services need not implement all of the protocols below as the specification allows a client or service to implement only the protocols that it actually uses in application.

It is worthwhile to spend some time understanding these protocols because of one simple reason: These protocols *define* JXTA.

Everything else that we cover in this book including APIs, applications, programming tricks, and architectural details, are all implementation details specific to the Java reference implementation of the JXTA protocols. The protocols that we will cover in detail in this small section define what JXTA is currently all about. We will therefore take a detailed look at them, and explain the elements and details that make them important as we go along. This will go a long way towards our understanding of JXTA in the later exploration of the reference implementation.

Figure 11

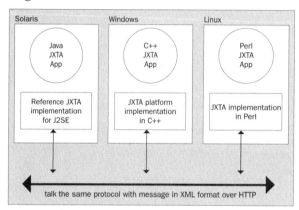

The figure illustrates this very important and unique interoperable level of the JXTA architecture.

The figure above illustrates how applications written using different programming language, running on different operating systems, can all interoperate with each other via JXTA's interoperable protocol layer.

Implicit Assumption of these Protocols

There is an implicit assumption in the following protocols – it is also the fundamental assumption of the operational model of JXTA itself – that messages are passed between JXTA peers on a transport that supports the JXTA protocols. While sounding trivial, one must bear in mind that certain transports, such as a paging network, may not support bi-directional connection and/or communications. This means that devices operating on these restrictive transports cannot directly implement some of these basic protocols.

> *Our discussion of the following protocol is based on the Protocol Specification 1.2 Dated June 22, 2001. Refer to the section at the end named* 'Subject to Extreme Changes'. *This is the only steady frame-of-reference available at the time of writing. Wholesale protocol changes are planned and will take effect after this 1.2 specification. JXTA is a rapidly evolving project. While the specific details may change (such as the exact document format), the rationale behind them and the insights that we will gain in the analysis following should remain the same.*

Peer Discovery Protocol

The peer discovery protocol, as its name suggests, enables one peer to discover others. The protocol is not just restricted to the discovery of peers, but also allows discovery of anything that can be associated with a peer, including peer groups, pipes, services, or content. In fact, the discovery protocol can be used for anything that can be associated with a published advertisement. The JXTA protocol specification describes only the specific advertisement types mentioned, but an actual JXTA implementation or application can easily add to this set.

Discovery is performed within a group context. However, all peers belong to the world group and therefore the initial discovery is always done in this context. Once a peer has joined a specific peer group, future discovery is performed in the context of that group only. This shows that one of the notions relevant to a peer group in JXTA is discovery boundary.

The Peer Discovery Protocol works as illustrated below:

Figure 12

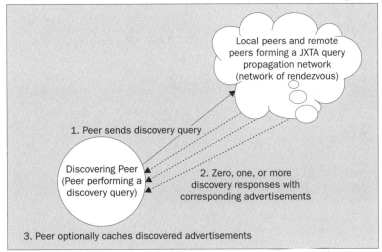

1. Peer sends discovery query

2. Zero, one, or more discovery responses with corresponding advertisements

Discovering Peer (Peer performing a discovery query)

Local peers and remote peers forming a JXTA query propagation network (network of rendezvous)

3. Peer optionally caches discovered advertisements

In the diagram above, the peer discovery message that is sent out from the discovering peer is in the following format:

```
<?xml version="1.0" encoding="UTF-8"?>
<jxta:DiscoveryQuery>
 <Type> Advertisement type </Type>
 <Threshold> Max advertisements in response </Threshold>
 <PeerAdv> My own peer advertisement </PeerAdv>
 <Attr> An attribute to query </Attr>
 <Value> The value desired for the attribute </Value>
</jxta:DiscoveryQuery>
```

The advertisement type is coded, with 0 signifying peer advertisements, 1 signifying peer-group advertisements, and 3 signifying general (content) advertisements. The threshold field indicates the maximum number of replies wanted from each responding peer. To facilitate responses, the <PeerAdv> element contains our own peer advertisement. This further propagates our advertisement during the query process, allowing the rendezvous to cache our peer advertisement.

If the above query sounds like a distributed search for advertisements to you, you've grasped the essence of JXTA.

Any peer that receives the query can respond to the query if it has an advertisement that matches the discovery criteria, subjected to the threshold limit specified. The response to a discovery advertisement is in the following general format:

```
<?xml version="1.0" encoding="UTF-8"?>
<jxta:DiscoveryResponse>
  <Type> Type of advertisment </Type>
  <Count> Count </Count>
  <PeerAdvertisement> Peer advertisement </PeerAdvertisement>
  <Attr> Attribute </Attr>
  <Value> Value </Value>
  <Response Expiration="expiration time">
    Advertisement response
  </Response>
  <............>
  <Response Expiration="expiration time">
    Advertisement response
  </Response>
</jxta:DiscoveryResponse>
```

Note that the responding peer may actually have (cached locally) many advertisements that match the query. This response format enables the responding peer to send many such advertisements within a single message. The number of bundled advertisements is indicated by <Count>, and it should always be less than or equal to the value of the <Threshold> element specified in the query. Note that the responding peer itself is identified by the <PeerAdvertisement> element. The <Attr> and <Value> element pair corresponds to the criteria specified within the original query. Each of the advertisements found is bracketed by a <Response> element and this element also sets the expiration time for the response. The expiration time is vital since the response can be propagated throughout the peer group and be cached in multiple peer locations. If the expiration time is not set, all the peers ever active in the history of time will have their stale entries cached throughout the peer group. This is clearly not a desirable situation. A reasonable expiry time ensures that the network will only cache the most recently available set of peer advertisements.

In normal operating circumstances, a peer should only respond to the discovery message if it has the type of advertisement that the discovering peer is seeking. There is one special case, however, where the peer discovery query has both the <Type> and <Threshold> fields set to 0.

This is a special "discover all peers" query. All peers receiving this message are expected to respond with all the peers that they know about (peers currently in their cache that have not yet expired). When this special "discover all peers" query is sent to a rendezvous peer, all the peers that the rendezvous knows about will be returned and this is why connecting to a rendezvous is essential when working with JXTA over a wide area network such as the Internet.

The query dispersion pattern of discovery messages can be described as follows:

1. The discovery peer sends the discovery message to each immediate neighbour (connection hop = 1)

2. The discovery peer sends the discovery message to each known propagation service

Of course, if the peer is caching some advertisements itself, the peer's own cache should be the first place where the discovery process should look.

In fact, the above dispersion pattern is exactly the same as the pattern for many of the query/response protocols to follow, such as the peer resolver and pipe resolver. This will result in the factoring out of this common functionality (for the Java implementation anyway) into a generic resolver service for handling the required query propagation within the peer group.

Peer Resolver Protocol

The Peer Resolver Protocol is the protocol that enables the creation of the **generic resolver service** that we have mentioned. In fact, it is the very under-pinning of JXTA peer-group services (recall that a peer-group service can have multiple simultaneous instances executing within a peer group – potentially creating a high-availability service).

The Peer Resolver Protocol enables peers to send generic queries against "handlers" that are registered within a peer group. Note that these "handlers" are associated with the peer group, and not a specific peer. Within the Java reference implementation of this protocol, interested peers register their handler with the resolver service – the resolver service is then responsible for calling an available instance of the handler to process the query by distributing the query throughout the peer group. There could be as many as one handler per peer in a group associated with a specific handler name and the resolver service does not guarantee that any specific handler will be invoked to process the query.

The Peer Resolver Protocol is the protocol that enables the resolver service to perform its magic – making it possible for resolvers written in, say C on UNIX, to interoperate with their Java counterpart. The figure overleaf illustrates the message flow of the Peer Resolver Protocol.

We can see that a single query may result in zero or more responses from the query propagation network. The resolver service is responsible for forwarding the responses to the corresponding registered handlers for processing.

Figure 13

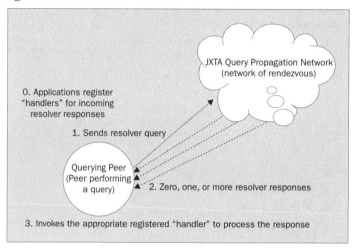

The resolver query message has the following format:

```
<?xml version="1.0" encoding="UTF-8"?>
<jxta:ResolverQuery>
  <Credential> Credential </Credential>
  <HandlerName> Name of handler </HandlerName>
  <QueryId> Incremental Query ID </QueryId>
  <Query> Query string </Query>
  <SrcPeerId> Peer ID of requester </SrcPeerId>
</jxta:ResolverQuery>
```

Note that the querying peer is supplying a credential as an opaque field. This credential can be used by a security subsystem to validate that the query peer does indeed have access privilege to the handler being invoked. JXTA itself does not specify how this validation may be performed, it only provide the "hooks" necessary for such an implementation.

As mentioned earlier, the query is done against the name of a handler, and not against a specific peer. The <QueryId> element is used by the querying peer to track outstanding queries. Recall that a query within a P2P network may:

1. Yield a response immediately

2. Yield a response sometime in the future

3. Not yield any response at all

This is all part of the non-determinism inherent the JXTA system. As a result, a peer can have tens or even hundreds of outstanding queries pending response from the network at any time. The `<QueryId>` element enables a querying peer to correlate the incoming responses against the pending queries that it has. The `<Query>` element contains an arbitrary string that is meaningful only to the handler itself. Since the resolver service is performing a generic function, the content of this field is dependent on the actual resolution that is being performed – for example, discovery and pipe binding queries that are both clients of the resolver service will have very different query strings.

Finally, the `<SrcPeerId>` element identifies the querying peer uniquely within the peer group. Note that while it identifies the peer, it does not identify the physical endpoint that a peer is at. The generic resolver service is responsible for mapping the peer into an endpoint for forwarding the response of the query back to the source peer.

When a peer hosting the handler responds to the query the response message will have the following format:

```xml
<?xml version="1.0" encoding="UTF-8"?>
<jxta:ResolverResponse>
  <Credential> Credential </Credential>
  <HandlerName> Name of handler </HandlerName>
  <QueryId> Query ID </QueryId>
  <Response> Response </Response>
</jxta:ResolverResponse>
```

Note that the `<QueryId>` element is returned, since it is vital in helping the querying peer to correlate responses from multiple outstanding queries. The credential returned may be the same as the incoming credential, or it may be a new credential granted for future access – JXTA does not specify how it must be used. The name of the handler is also returned. The `<Response>` element, as expected, is as handler specific as the original query string.

Peer Membership Protocol

While the set of messages defined in the Peer Membership Protocol is quite comprehensive in supplying a framework upon which membership of a peer group can be tracked and managed, in practice it is not frequently used. In fact, there is some discussion in the JXTA community about the possibility of potentially removing the Peer Membership Protocol from the JXTA specification at a future date.

The reason for this debate is the rather vague role of the peer-group membership concept in typical P2P networks. A survey of contemporary P2P-style applications such as Napster, Gnutella, and Morpheus indicates that the concept of peer-group membership may be best contained at the application level, rather than on a system and infrastructure level. In other words, there is a fear that implementing peer-group membership at the platform level may actually reduce the utility of JXTA as a generic foundation for building all sorts of P2P applications.

Having said that, JXTA 1.0 has the Peer Membership Protocols included – and we will describe them here. When a peer starts, it is deemed to belong automatically to the peer group called the "world group". Other than this special world group, a peer will need to use the discovery protocol to discover other peer groups, and use the Peer Membership Protocols to become a member of another group.

More specifically, a peer needs to use the Peer Membership Protocols to:

1. Find out how to join a group

2. Request to join the group by authenticating with the required credential

Other than group joining, the protocol also provides a mechanism for these other operations:

1. To renew an existing membership

2. To cancel an existing membership

The following figure illustrates the message flow involved in this protocol.

Figure 14

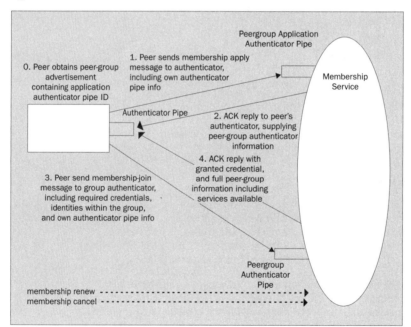

In the above diagram, we can see that a peer wishing to join a group must first obtain the advertisement for the group. This advertisement can be obtained readily using the discovery protocol – querying specifically for peer-group advertisements, or probing a specific peer for the group(s) it belongs to via the Peer Information Protocol.

Once a peer has an advertisement, it can begin to obtain information on how to join the group. This is done via a `MembershipApply` message to the membership application authenticator service (part of the membership service) for the group – which is a JXTA-enabled peer-group service. Being a JXTA-enabled peer-group service, the membership application authenticator's Pipe ID is readily available within the group advertisement. The. The fact that these protocols actually use pipes, a higher-level abstraction than endpoint services, again reinforces that they could be considered application-level (and application-specific) protocols rather than platform core protocols – a point that is passionately debated. `MembershipApply` message has the following format

```
<?xml version="1.0" encoding="UTF-8"?>
<jxta:MembershipApply>
 <Credential> URI </Credential>
 <SourcePid> Source Pipe ID </SourcePid>
 <Authenticator> Authenticator pipe adv </Authenticator>
</jxta:MembershipApply>
```

The peer seeking membership application information supplies its credential (JXTA credentials are in URI format), and also a Pipe ID to identify itself. The membership authenticator service can authenticate the identity of the peer using the credentials before giving further information on how to join the group. The content of the `<Authenticator>` element is a specific pipe that the source peer will use to receive membership authenticator messages. This is the pipe through which the membership application authenticator service will be replying with an acknowledgement message. The format of the acknowledgement message contains detailed instructions on how to join the group. The acknowledgement message format is:

```
<?xml version="1.0" encoding="UTF-8"?>
<jxta:MembershipAck>
 <Credential> URI </Credential>
 <SourcePid> Source Pipe ID </SourcePid>
 <Membersship> Membership pipe adv</Membership>
 <PeerGroupAdv> Peer group advertisement </PeerGroupAdv>
 <PeerGroupCredential> URI </PeerGroupCredential>
</jxta:MembershipAck>
```

The credential supplied from the peer-group membership application authenticator can be used to authenticate the authenticator (for example via public key encryption) or any other security measures deemed appropriate by the application. The source Pipe ID is returned. The `<PeerGroupAdv>` element is the payload of the message and contains additional information on the peer group – specifically the membership authenticator pipe. The `<PeerGroupCredential>` element contains the credential granted by the application authenticator service to the requesting peer – for joining the peer group.

To join a group, the join message must be sent from the peer to the membership authenticator of the group (note carefully that this is a membership authenticator – and not the membership **application** authenticator). This is the format of the membership-join message.

```
<?xml version="1.0" encoding="UTF-8"?>
<jxta:MembershipJoin>
 <Credential> Credential of requestor </Credential>
 <SourcePid> Source Pipe ID </SourcePid>
 <Membership> Membership pipe Advertisement </Membership>
 <Identity> Identity </Identity>
</jxta:MembershipJoin>
```

Note that the credential supplied must be the same as the one returned by the authenticator in the acknowledgement message that is sent back by the membership application authenticator. The `<SourcePid>` is used to identify the peer. The `<Membership>` element specifies a pipe that the membership authenticator should send the response to. If authentication is successful, the membership authenticator will respond with an acknowledgement message. In this message is a full group advertisement giving more information on the peer-group services that are available in the group. It also contains a granted credential that must be used when accessing group resources in the future. Note that the peer requesting to join can specify an alternative identity that is used only within the group. This identity is only meaningful to the underlying membership tracking system and not to JXTA itself.

Two other messages are defined for the Peer Membership Protocol, they are:

1. Membership renewal request

2. Membership cancellation request

Here is the format of the renewal request; it enables a peer to update its credential for security systems that require it.

```
<?xml version="1.0" encoding="UTF-8"?>
<jxta:MembershipRenew>
 <Credential> Credential </Credential>
 <SourcePid> Source pipe Id </SourcePid>
 <Membership> Membership pipe Adv </Membership>
</jxta:MembershipRenew>
```

Note that the fields are almost identical to the membership application request. The membership service will then send back an acknowledgement message with the new credential if the renewal is accepted.

The membership cancellation request has the following format:

```
<?xml version="1.0" encoding="UTF-8"?>
<jxta:MembershipCancel>
 <Credential> Credential </Credential>
 <SourcePid> Source pipe Id </SourcePid>
 <Membersship> Membership pipe Adv </Membership>
</jxta:MembershipCancel>
```

Pipe Binding Protocol

The Pipe Binding Protocol is also known as the Pipe Resolver Protocol. The Pipe Binding Protocol is used whenever a pipe advertisement is "realized" into a pipe instance. More specifically, a pipe advertisement is resolved to a specific peer that is hosting the pipe service, mapping the other end of the pipe.

The message flow of the pipe binding protocol is illustrated below:

Figure 15

Notice the similarity to the Peer Resolver Protocol. In fact, the Pipe Binding Protocol uses the Peer Resolver Protocol to get its work done. The local instance of the `PipeService` is responsible for handling the messaging between peers. Once a pipe is resolved or established, the

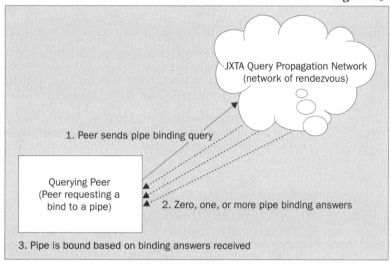

`PipeService` at each end of the pipe will be actively attempting to establish and re-establish the pipe against a constantly changing non-deterministic network topology. This can involve the repeated rebinding of the pipe.

The pipe-binding query has the following format:

```
<?xml version="1.0" encoding="UTF-8"?>
<jxta:PipeBindingQuery>
 <Credential> URI </Credential>
 <Peer> Optional Peer ID </Peer>
 <Cached> true or false </Cached>
 <PipeId> Pipe ID to be resolved </PipeId>
</jxta:PipeBindingQuery>
```

The querying peer supplies a credential, usually granted from the membership service. The pipe resolver instances that receive the query can use the credential to grant or deny access according to the security policy in place. The optional <Peer> element is use only when the requesting peer wants to specify a specific peer who should reply to this query. The <Cached> element controls whether the reply can come from cached information that is potentially stale. The <PipeId> element contains the payload of the request, which is the pipe to be resolved to a peer ID.

Since the query is performed via the resolver service, the query message is propagated among the rendezvous via the underlying propagation service. In effect, this is a distributed search for a pipe service instance.

Now, a peer that decides to answer this query will respond with a `pipe-binding` answer message. This message is in the following format:

```
<?xml version="1.0" encoding="UTF-8"?>
<jxta:PipeBindingAnswer>
 <Credential> URI </Credential>
 <PipeId> Pipe ID resolved </PipeId>
 <Peer> Peer ID </Peer>
 <Found> true or false </Found>
</jxta:PipeBindingAnswer>
```

The exact usage of the credential will depend on the security system in use. The Pipe ID resolved will enable the querying peer to correlate multiple pending responses. The <Peer> element contains the payload of the resolution, which is the Peer ID of the peer hosting the pipe that is being resolved.

The <Found> element is significant only if the querying peer has specified a peer that must answer to the query. It indicates that the pipe being resolved at the specific peer is either working (contains "true") or no longer exists (contains "false").

Endpoint Routing Protocol

The Endpoint Routing Protocol is used by the endpoint router service/transport. In the previous section we discussed the interesting duality of this service. Within the service, routing information is cached and takes the following form:

```
<?xml version="1.0" encoding="UTF-8"?>
<jxta:EndpointRouter>
 <Src> Peer ID of the source </Src>
 <Dest> Peer ID of the destination </Dest>
 <TTL> Time to live </TTL>
 <Gateway> Ordered sequence of gateway </Gateway>
 <.................>
 <Gateway> Ordered sequence of gateway </Gateway>
</jxta:EndpointRouter>
```

The above XML document maintains a route between two peers where the source peer is referred to by the <Src> element and the destination peer by the <Dest> element. The <TTL> element indicates the length of time that the route will be valid. The <gateway> element specifies a series of intermediate peers that a message must travel through to get from <Src> to <Dest>.

During the normal operation of endpoint routers query requests are propagated among themselves (all the endpoint routers within a peer group). The router-query message has the following format:

```
<?xml version="1.0" encoding="UTF-8"?>
<jxta:EndpointRouterQuery>
 <Credential> Credential </Credential>
 <Dest> Peer ID of the destination </Dest>
```

```
<Cached>
   true: if the reply can be a cached reply
   false: if the reply must not come from a cache
</Cached>
</jxta:EndpointRouterQuery>
```

The `<Credential>` element, as usual, depends on the security system that is currently in deployment (if any). The `<Dest>` element specifies the destination of the route being queried. The `<Cached>` element specifies whether the querying peer wants to restrict the response only to dynamically discovered routes (guaranteed to be valid at the time of response) or if a cached route is desired.

Only peers that have a route to the requested destination will respond. The response message is in the following format:

```
<?xml version="1.0" encoding="UTF-8"?>
<jxta:EndpointRouterAnswer>
 <Credential> Credential </Credential>
 <Dest> Peer ID of the destination </Dest>
 <RoutingPeer>
   Peer ID of the router that knows a route to DestPeer
 </RoutingPeer>
 <RoutingPeerAdv>
   Advertisement of the routing peer
 </RoutingPeerAdv>
 <Gateway> Ordered sequence of gateway </Gateway>
 < .................>
 <Gateway> Ordered sequence of gateway </Gateway>
</EndpointRouterAnswer>
```

In this response, we can see that the series of gateway peers is copied form the stored routing information. The querying peer can use the destination Peer ID to coordinate multiple pending queries. The `<RoutingPeerAdv>` element contains a description of the routing peer that can be used to route a message to the destination peer.

Peer Information Protocol

The Peer Information Protocol is typically used in conjunction with the discovery protocol. It can be used to obtain status information on a remote peer, and also to get a map of the services running on that peer.

The `Ping` message is always sent to the endpoint found within a discovered peer advertisement. The format of a `Ping` message is:

```
<?xml version="1.0" encoding="UTF-8"?>
<jxta:Ping>
 <Credential> Credential </Credential>
 <SourcePid> Source Peer Id </SourcePid>
 <TargetPid> Target Peer Id </TargetPid>
```

```
 <Option> type of ping requested</Option>
</jxta:Ping>
```

The format of a PeerInfo message, which is the response to a Ping message, is shown below:

```
<?xml version="1.0" encoding="UTF-8"?>
<jxta:PeerInfo>
 <Credential> Credential </Credential>
 <SourcePid> Source Peer ID </SourcePid>
 <TargetPid> Target Peer ID </TargetPid>
 <Uptime> Uptime </Uptime>
 <TimeStamp> Timestamp </TimeStamp>
 <PeerAdv> Peer Advertisement </PeerAdv>
</jxta:PeerInfo>
```

Subject to Extreme Changes

In this very early stage of JXTA's developmental life, even this interoperability layer is subject to changes. In fact, changes are on the way as JXTA developers discover the limitations of the initial 1.0 protocols. Our discussion of protocols so far has centered on the post 1.0 evolution of the JXTA protocols. In due time, a revised official protocol document will become available that will incorporate all of the changes that are made to this protocol.

Core to the proposed changes are ones that address:

Recent Changes	Rationale
Breaking up service advertisements and group advertisements into many smaller advertisements	Large advertisement size in practice for original group and service advertisements, leading to inefficient usage of bandwidth
Standardization on spelling and upper/lower case on advertisement tags, especially those relating to tags that are not yet documented in a protocol document evolution	Interoperability is not possible without this; many mysterious bugs have surface because of it

This does beg one question: how will we go about building interoperable platforms if the layer of interoperability continues to change?

For now, the answer appears to be: make sure that all interoperable platform creators are "in" on the changes. This means that the owners of all the interoperable platforms must be a closely-knit group. Clearly this will not last for a long time, and will likely disappear as soon as commercial interest and competitive forces set in.

The other approach currently adopted to hedge against changes is to provide an archive of all previously stable releases – each implementing a previously frozen state of the protocol specification. Theoretically, interoperable platforms can then be tested and benchmarked against these stable releases. While this "best practice" works well for matured, and slowly evolving operating systems it is disastrous for a young and rapidly evolving technology like JXTA. For one thing, all of the latest and greatest applications based on the reference implementation are guaranteed to be updated to the latest edition of the protocol – taking advantage of its additional features. This leaves the creators of interoperable platforms on other OS and programming languages no choice but to keep changing and updating their own code. This may become significantly more difficult as the design of the platform increases in complexity. The only audience that this approach is useful for are those who can create both sides of the interoperable equation – those who essentially embed the protocol interoperability into their own product line.

This extreme change cycle is indicative of a rapidly evolving (and improving) product,. where research is given substance by the implementers of actual code and systems – and feedback from developers osmoses back into the design of the system. This is the current culture of the JXTA community.

Until the JXTA community comes up with a workable process of control over protocol evolution, the interoperability element of JXTA will remain a relatively "weak" feature of the product. Since interoperability on a protocol level is the differentiator for JXTA and sets it apart from other products this issue needs to be addressed with vigor in the immediate future.

The JXTA Java APIs

With a basic understanding of what JXTA is composed of, we are ready to examine the API that is provided in the reference implementation for working with these components and concepts.

APIs are Specific to Implementation

Unlike the protocols that we have covered in the previous section, APIs are by nature specific to an implementation. In fact, JXTA programming APIs may even be different depending on the programming language that the implementation is bound to. For example, there is no requirement that a C++ API for JXTA should bear any resemblance to the Java Reference API.

Throughout this book, we must understand that we will be working with the J2SE reference implementation of JXTA. While our JXTA creations will remain interoperable with other JXTA application that may be written in other programming language on other operating systems, the code that we write in Java will only be usable on those system that support J2SE.

The Java JXTA reference implementation exposes APIs at multiple levels of the communications stack. The following figure reveals the layers of the stack, and how they correlate to specific interfaces available via the API:

Figure 16

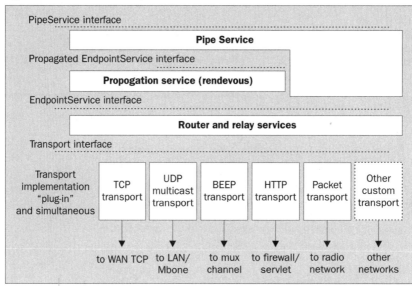

We can see that there is programmatic access at each and every layer within the stack. This not only allows us to use the stack at the various levels, but also enables the adventurous developer to replace implementations of core components with a custom version.

Platform-level system programming is out of the scope of this book as is replacing platform components. When programming JXTA services and applications, typically we will only use a few of the most common API packages. We will take a quick look at these packages and some of the classes and interfaces within them.

Discovery via the net.jxta.discovery Package

A peer on the JXTA network must obtain the various advertisements of peers, peer groups, pipes, etc. in order to operate properly. Unless the advertisements are hard-coded by design, or available via some persistent storage, they must be discovered dynamically during run time. The figure overleaf shows how this discovery process works.

Figure 17

The peer wishing to perform discovery formulates a query, and then sends it first to all peers that are in the local area network (one hop away). The same query is also sent to all the rendezvous that the peer knows about for propagation. This means that the discovery query dispersion pattern consists of all peers one hop away, plus all the known rendezvous.

Interfaces and classes within the net.jxta.discovery package can be used to perform this dynamic run-time discovery. Of course, underneath, a distributed

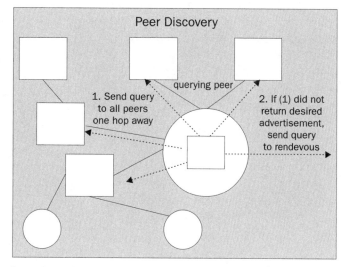

search for JXTA advertisements throughout the rendezvous network is actually occurring (as we have learned earlier). Here are the classes and interfaces that we will work often with:

Class or Interface Name	Description
net.jxta.discovery. DiscoveryService	This interface can be used to interact with a discovery service instance (a peer group service). It can be used to publish advertisements (locally or remotely). It can also be used to query for advertisements (locally or remotely). Locally cached advertisements can be flushed using this interface.
net.jxta.discovery. DiscoveryListener	When discovery is performed remotely (remote query for advertisements), one can register a listener with the discovery service. If new advertisements are discovered, the registered listener will be notified. This interface is implemented by a JXTA application that is interested in discovery events. It is used in conjunction with the net.jxta.discovery.DiscoveryEvent class.
net.jxta.discovery. DiscoveryEvent	This event is sent to registered listeners of a discovery service. It can be used to retrieve the associated net.jxta.protocol.DiscoveryResponseMsg, which contains any new advertisement discovered.

For example, we can use the following code fragment to perform the discovery of a pipe advertisement with the name of WROX-SERV:RequestPipe.

```
import java.util.*;
import java.io.*;
import net.jxta.protocol.DiscoveryResponseMsg;
```

```
import net.jxta.discovery.DiscoveryService;
import net.jxta.discovery.DiscoveryListener;
import net.jxta.discovery.DiscoveryEvent;
import net.jxta.peergroup.PeerGroup;

public class MyService implements DiscoveryListener
{
  ...
  public void performDiscovery(PeerGroup group) {
    DiscoveryService disco = group.getDiscoveryService();
    Enumeration enum = null;
    ...
    try {
      // Local discovery in the cache
      enum = disco.getLocalAdvertisements(DiscoveryService.ADV
        , "Name", "WROX-SERV:RequestPipe");

      ... Process locally cached advertisements if found ...

      disco.getRemoteAdvertisements(null
         , DiscoveryService.ADV, "Name"
         , " WROX-SERV:RequestPipe ", 1, this);
      ...
    }
    catch (Exception ex) {...}

  } // End of method performDiscovery

  // Implementation of discovery listener
  public void discoveryEvent(DiscoveryEvent evt)
  {
    DiscoveryResponseMsg dmsg = evt.getResponse();

    if (dmsg.getResponseCount() > 0) {
      Enumeration enum = dmsg.getResponses();
      ...Process the discovered advertisements...
    }
  }

} // End of class MyService
```

We can see in the code fragment above how local discovery (in the cache) is done via the getLocalAdvertisement() method. Remote discovery may return much later asynchronously, and the use of the DiscoveryListener interface will enable us to deal with this asynchronous behavior in a reasonable way. We can also see how to obtain the DiscoveryResponseMsg from the DiscoveryEvent; this provides us with direct access to the advertisements just discovered.

Advertisement Access with the net.jxta.protocol Package

There is one activity that we will find ourselves doing frequently when programming JXTA applications – working with advertisements. In a JXTA application, we will be creating, publishing, and searching for advertisements. The net.jxta.protocol package contains a set of abstract classes that enables us to work with these advertisements in an implementation independent way. The Java reference implementation has classes that actually implement the advertisements, but they all derive from this set of abstract classes. The methods of the abstract classes allow us to access the individual elements of an advertisement directly.

Class name	Description
net.jxta.protocol. PeerAdvertisement	Refers to a peer advertisement; provides methods to access type, name, description, Peer ID, peer-group ID, and a service parameter table that is typically used during configuration.
net.jxta.protocol. PeerGroupAdvertisement	Refers to a peer-group advertisement; includes methods to access fields including type, name, peer-group ID, description and module spec ID.
net.jxta.protocol. PeerInfoAdvertisement	Refers to a peer-info advertisement; provides access to traffic channels information and associated traffic, timestamp of the advertisement, uptime of a peer, and the Pipe ID of both the requesting and destination peer.
net.jxta.protocol. PipeAdvertisement	Refers to a pipe advertisement, enable us to access its name, type, and Pipe ID.
net.jxta.protocol. EndpointAdvertisement	Refers to an endpoint advertisement, a part of a peer group advertisement. Enables access to endpoint addresses, advertisement types, keywords, names, and transport advertisements.
net.jxta.protocol. ModuleSpec Advertisement	Part of what used to be a service advertisement but now broken up to reduce transmitted size. Enables access to name, type, creator, description, module spec ID, parameters, spec URI, and version fields.
net.jxta.protocol. ModuleClass Advertisement	Part of what used to be a service advertisement but now broken up to reduce transmitted size. Enables access to name, type, description, and module class ID.
net.jxta.protocol. ModuleImpl Adveritsement	Part of what used to be a service advertisement; provides access to type, code, description, module spec ID, parameters, provider, URI, and compatible implementation info.

We can create an advertisement using a factory class, net.jxta.document.AdvertisementFactory. This enables us to create and access advertisements using Java code without working directly with the underlying implementation classes. This classic Factory design pattern is illustrated overleaf:

Figure 18

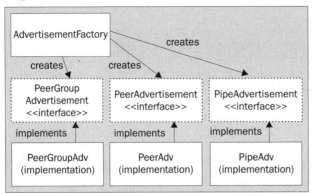

We can see that the `AdvertisementFactory` class knows how to create every type of platform advertisement, and it supplies a `static` method for creating them. The advertisement that it creates is backed by an implementation of the corresponding interface. In practice, the platform will register the factory methods with the `AdvertisementFactory` class during startup. The user of the `AdvertisementFactory` will never have to know about the implementation-specific way of creating an advertisement because this design pattern hides the intricate details.

For example, here is a simple code fragment showing how we would create a pipe advertisement and set its name:

```
import net.jxta.protocol.PipeAdvertisement;
import net.jxta.document.AdvertisementFactory;
...
PipeAdvertisement pipeAdv =
    (PipeAdvertisement) AdvertisementFactory.newAdvertisement(
    PipeAdvertisement.getAdvertisementType());
...
  pipeAdv.setName("WROXSERV:RequestPipe");
```

Note that we only have to supply a type to `AdvertisementFactory` to create a new advertisement; the type can be obtained conveniently via the `getAdvertisementType()` method available with every advertisement implementation (because it is part of the interface that it must implement).

Message Manipulation with the net.jxta.endpoint Package

The `net.jxta.endpoint` package is typically used in manipulating JXTA messages via the interface:

Interface Name	Description
net.jxta.endpoint.Message	Provides generic access to the elements, namespace, and source and destination addresses of a message. Can also be used to add elements to and remove elements from the message.

For example, here is a code fragment showing how we work with the elements of a message. In this case, we know an incoming message has an element tag named WroxTag, and we are extracting the XML document embedded within this tag.

```
import net.jxta.endpoint.Message;
import net.jxta.endpoint.MessageElement;
...
public void processMessage(Message inMsg) {

  MessageElement embeddedMsg = inMsg.getElement("WroxTag");
  if (embeddedMsg != null) {
   ... process the embedded message element ...
  }
...
```

The net.jxta.endpoint package also contains classes such as net.jxta.endpoint.EndpointService and net.jxta.endpoint.EndpointListener that will be useful for the implementation of peer-group services (services that have multiple active instances within the peer group).

Working with the Pipe Service: the net.jxta.pipe Package

Writing JXTA applications and services is about sending messages through pipes. The net.jxta.pipe package provides interfaces and classes that we will need when working with pipes. Here are some of the interfaces and classes that we will work with frequently within this package.

Class Name	Description
net.jxta.pipe. PipeService	An interface used to interact with a pipe service implementation. Can be used to create input and output pipes and register listeners with the created pipe. Of course, pipe "creation" is actually a binding or resolving process – based on a pipe advertisement – which we have described previously.
net.jxta.pipe. InputPipe	An interface used to interact with an input pipe. It can be used to poll for a message from an input pipe when a listener is not used.
net.jxta.pipe. OutputPipe	An interface used to interact with an output pipe instance. It can be used to send messages over the output pipe.
net.jxta.pipe. InputPipeListener	An interface implemented by a JXTA application in order to receive input pipe message arrival events.
net.jxta.pipe. OutputPipeListener	An interface implemented by a JXTA application interested in output pipe events – usually the completion of pipe binding.

Class Name	Description
net.jxta.pipe. PipeMessageEvent	A class used in conjunction with InputPipeListener signifying the arrival of a message on the input pipe. Can be used to retrieve the message that has been received.
net.jxta.pipe. OutputPipeEvent	A class used in conjunction with an OutputPipe (registered during the output pipe creation). Can be used to access the output Pipe ID and the OutputPipe instance itself after successful binding/resolving.

The usage of these classes and interfaces should be obvious from their descriptions above. One can use the polling method, or use the listener interface to work with the pipes. The listener interface is significantly more convenient and less error prone to work with, and should be used whenever possible. Here is an example, showing how to create an input pipe and process incoming messages:

```
import net.jxta.endpoint.Message;
import net.jxta.pipe.PipeMsgListener;
import net.jxta.pipe.PipeMsgEvent;
import net.jxta.pipe.InputPipe;
import net.jxta.pipe.PipeService;
import net.jxta.protocol.PipeAdvertisement;

public class MyService implements PipeMsgListener
{
  private InputPipe myPipe = null;

  public void BindPipe(PipeAdvertisement pipeadv, PipeService pipeserv)
    throws IOException {
    ...
    myPipe = pipeserv.createInputPipe(pipeadv, (PipeMsgListener) this);
    ...
  }

  // implementation of PipeMsgListner
  public void pipeMsgEvent( PipeMsgEvent ev) {
    Message inReq = ev.getMessage();
    ... start working with incoming message...
  }
}
```

In the `BindPipe` method above, we use the pipe service to bind to an input pipe. We supply `createInputPipe` service with the advertisement of the pipe to be bound, and an implementation of the `PipeMsgListner` (which is the class itself). Upon receipt of incoming pipe messages on this input pipe, the callback `pipeMsgEvent` method will be called by the platform. We can retrieve the incoming message using the `getMessage()` method of the `PipeMsgEvent` class and start processing the message.

JXTA Demystified

In this chapter, we have examined the basic components of JXTA, and appreciated how they are implemented on top of interoperable protocols across multiple configurable transports.

We discussed where to find the JXTA downloads, and how to determine what files to download and install. We have also learned how to configure the JXTA platform for peers that are either on the Internet or intranet, and how to use the JXTA shell to perform basic interaction between peers.

We have seen the most frequently used API packages within the Java reference implementation, as well as how to perform discovery of peers, peer groups, and pipes, how to create and work with advertisements, how to manipulate XML-based JXTA messages, and how to create and work with JXTA pipes.

We now have a minimal required comfort level with JXTA, and can now proceed to experiment with the components. One of the easiest ways to experiment with JXTA, without even writing any code, is via the JXTA shell. This is the subject matter of the next chapter.

In the next chapter we will look in more detail at how the JXTA shell can be used to interact with the JXTA platform at a high level. In particular, we will look at the range of JXTA shell commands that are available, how these shell commands can be used, and how we can implement our own custom commands and install them into the JXTA shell.

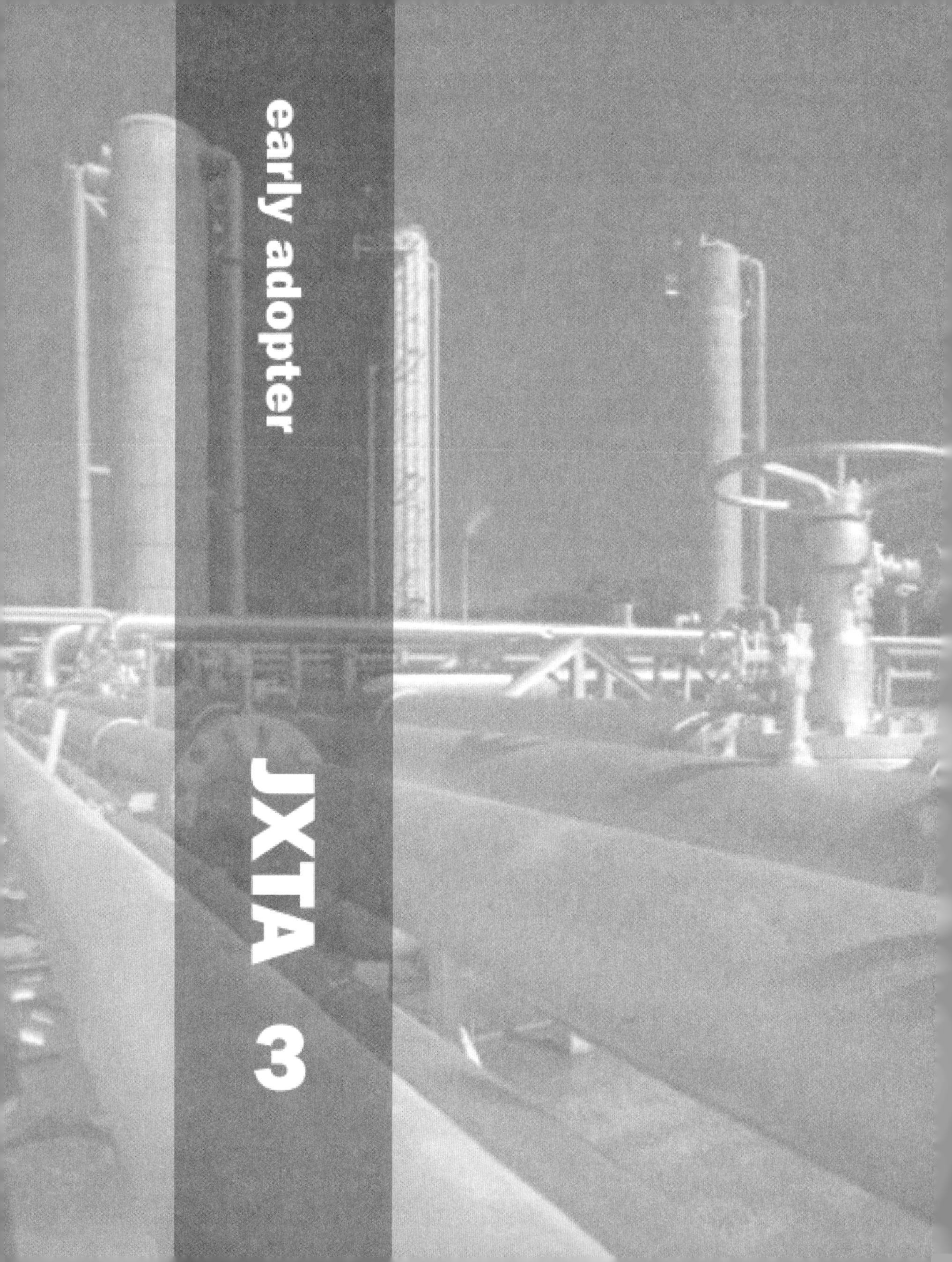
early adopter
JXTA 3

Taming the JXTA Shell

The reference implementation of JXTA comes with a default application. This is a command shell that allows you to interact with the JXTA platform, by issuing commands against it directly. The JXTA shell provides a textual command-line interface. We worked briefly with this application in the *JXTA Preview* section of the last chapter.

The JXTA shell is highly versatile. It provides a way to experiment with the components view of JXTA, without having to code actual JXTA clients or services. We will be able to perform discovery, create advertisements, publish advertisements, bind to pipes, send and receive messages using pipes, etc – all without writing a single line of code.

Architecturally, the JXTA shell is a bona fide JXTA application; it sits on top of the JXTA platform and makes use of the JXTA platform API just like any other. The JXTA shell does not take advantage of any special provisions provided by the platform layer. Figure 1 illustrates where the JXTA shell fits into the JXTA architecture.

Figure 1

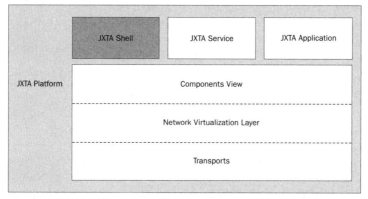

One can deduce from this diagram that it is completely possible to replace the JXTA shell with a shell of our own creation – or an application-specific version. This is certainly true. However, anticipating that programmers and experimenters will want to customize and enhance the JXTA shell, the designers have already incorporated two ways of doing so within the JXTA shell's functionality:

❑ The ability to run batched shell scripts

❑ The ability to add additional customized commands, on a binary executable level, without restarting the shell

These two mechanisms provide flexible extensibility for the command-line processor. We can simply create custom shell scripts and/or install custom commands into the JXTA shell.

In this chapter, we will become very familiar with the JXTA shell. We will look at the following topics:

❑ The internal architecture of the shell

❑ Shell variables and redirection

❑ Built-in commands

❑ Working with the JXTA components view via the shell

❑ Emulating multiple peers on a single networked machine using the JXTA shell

❑ How to write JXTA shell scripts

❑ Extending the JXTA shell with our custom commands

This is an essential step in mastering JXTA. The interactivity provided by the JXTA shell will enable us to experiment with various aspects of the JXTA component model quickly and easily, without tedious coding and debugging. Other than being an excellent learning aid, the skills and techniques that we acquire with the JXTA shell will stay with us throughout our JXTA development career because the JXTA shell is also an excellent mechanism for testing and debugging our JXTA applications and services.

The Proven Value of a Shell

Operating system designers have long realized the value of a command shell as user interface. A command shell enables users to interact with the operating system through an interactive, easy-to-use user interface. Querying the system's state, and issuing commands, are simply accomplished using such an interface.

The Unix and DOS Command Shells

MS-DOS, and versions of UNIX before X-Windows became widely available (and affordable) used command-line shells exclusively. MS-DOS's (in)famous command line user interface is architecturally a shell, and of course UNIX has long being blessed with shell variations such as the Bourne shell, bash, csh, the Korn shell, etc. Users who are familiar with these operating systems, and there is certainly a sizable population who are also developers, particularly in Java, will be right at home with a command shell. Many features of the underlying operating system, or its API, are made available through commands in these shells. In addition, these shells can also be used to access the file system, and launch applications.

By leveraging this familiarity with command shells, the JXTA shell designers are able to provide a relatively painless means of transferring a developer's existing skills to a P2P platform. The JXTA shell looks familiar, feels familiar, and is very inviting to hardcore developers.

A Parade of Shell Commands

The JXTA Shell offers a wide variety of commands, covering almost every aspects of the components view of JXTA. There are commands for:

- ❑ Data management
- ❑ System management
- ❑ File access
- ❑ Advertisement management
- ❑ Peer group management
- ❑ Peer management
- ❑ Pipe management
- ❑ Message manipulation
- ❑ Pipe communication
- ❑ Configuration and information

There is even a built-in JXTA application with its own service and client. We will examine these commands and cover their most typical usage in the following pages. You may want to start a shell instance from the `test1` directory that we set up and used in Chapter 2, and follow along to try out the commands.

Data Management Commands

Data within the shell is stored and handled via environment variables. The following data management commands all relate to the manipulation and examination of environment variables, and the formatting and processing of textual output to the console window.

set

Faithful to DOS and UNIX Bourne-family shells, the `set` command is used to give an environment variable a value. For example, we can easily create a new environment variable to refer to the standard input pipe:

```
JXTA>set myinput stdin
```

The first argument is always the name of the variable being set, and the second a reference to the object we want to set it to.

setenv

As the C-shell equivalent of the `set` command, this is an alternative syntax to give an environment variable a value.

env

The env command displays the current set of environment variables and their value. Note that all environment variables refer to objects (an advertisement, pipe, etc.). The env output displays only the type (Java class) of the object, and not its content. Use the `cat` command to display the content of any environment variable of interest. If you ran the `set` command given above, then used env, you'd see the following line in the output:

```
JXTA>env
...
 myinput = Default InputPipe (class net.jxta.impl.shell.ShellInputPipe)
...
```

cat

The cat command is used to display the content of environment variables. Environment variables can be used to refer to all sorts of objects, but the `cat` command does not know how to display all of them. Currently, `cat` can be used to display:

- structured documents

- advertisements

- messages

- strings

to display the value of a variable, use the syntax:

```
cat <var>
```

where `<var>` is the name of the environment variable you want to examine.

An optional -p switch, specified before the name of the environment variable, can be used to pretty-print the output. For example, you can view the local rendezvous service' Module Implementation Advertisement (MIA) immediately after the shell startup using the following commands:

First, send the `search` command (we'll look at this shortly):

```
JXTA>search
```

Then print out the MIA, which will be stored in the variable `adv0`:

```
JXTA>cat adv0
```

You should see the entire advertisement displayed, with output similar to this:

```
<?xml version="1.0"?>

<!DOCTYPE jxta:MIA>

<jxta:MIA xmlns:jxta="http://jxta.org">
    <MSID>
        urn:jxta:uuid-DEADBEEFDEAFBABAFEEDBABE000000060106
    </MSID>
    <Comp>
        <Efmt>
            JDK1.4
        </Efmt>
        <Bind>
            V1.0 Ref Impl
        </Bind>
    </Comp>
    <Code>
        net.jxta.impl.rendezvous.RendezVousServiceImpl
    </Code>
    <PURI>
        http://www.jxta.org/download/jxta.jar
    </PURI>
```

```
<Prov>
    sun.com
</Prov>
<Desc>
    Reference Implementation of the Rendezvous service
</Desc>
</jxta:MIA>
```

If you use `cat -p adv0` instead, the XML brackets will be removed and the tags displayed as fields:

```
jxta:MIA :
    MSID : urn:jxta:uuid-DEADBEEFDEAFBABAFEEDBABE000000060106
    Comp :
        Efmt : JDK1.4
        Bind : V1.0 Ref Impl
    Code : net.jxta.impl.rendezvous.RendezVousServiceImpl
    PURI : http://www.jxta.org/download/jxta.jar
    Prov : sun.com
    Desc : Reference Implementation of the Rendezvous service
```

grep

Search for a string pattern in a shell object, similar to the `grep` utility in UNIX. However, the `grep` command currently has a couple of restrictions:

❑   it may not be able to access the content of all shell objects, and can mostly operate on structured documents or advertisements only

❑   it does not support regular expressions

A `grep` command that doesn't support regexes may sound like a bit of a whacky concept to a UNIX user. Nevertheless, you will still find regular use for this command. For example, in a Module Implementation Advertisement referenced by the environment variable `adv0` (which, if you're following along so far, you should already have), if we want to find only the line containing the ModuleSpec ID, we can use the command:

```
JXTA>grep urn adv0
    urn:jxta:uuid-DEADBEEFDEAFBABAFEEDBABE000000060106
```

Note that it is anticipated that support for regular expressions will be added in the near future.

more

Allows output to be paged. The `more` command works in the same way as its DOS/UNIX counterpart – use a pipe character (|) to channel the output of any shell command into the `more` pager, and the output will pause as each page is written to the console:

```
JXTA>cat adv0 | more
```

wc

The wc command is a word count tool. It counts the lines, words and characters in an output stream. For example, we can use the following command to count the words in the standard console input (note that we terminate the input with a single line containing only a period (.)).

```
JXTA>wc
this is the first line
and this the second
.
        2       9       43
```

System Management Commands

System management commands are concerned with starting and stopping shell instances, and loading modules into the shell.

Shell

Note the capital "S" at the start of the command! This command can be used to start a new instance of the shell. The new instance will become the active shell, and the old shell will be suspended. The new shell instance will inherit all the environment variables of the parent shell.

The Shell command has two optional parameters that can be specified after
the command:

❏   [-f filename]: execute the script file

❏   [-s]: fork a new shell console in a new window

If you would like to open the new shell instance in a new window, and have both instances available, you can use the Shell -s syntax.

Shell -f <filename> can be used to start a new shell and execute a batch file with shell commands upon starting.

exit

This command is used to exit the current shell. Shells can be nested, and exit is used to exit from the innermost nested shell. Inner shells inherit environment variables from outer shells. Here is an example (we've omitted some of the irrelevant lines you'll see if you execute these commands yourself):

```
JXTA>setenv testvar stdin
JXTA>env
...
testvar = Default InputPipe (class net.jxta.impl.shell.ShellInputPipe)
...
JXTA>Shell
=========================================================
======== Welcome to the JXTAShell  Version 1.0 =========
=========================================================

The JXTA Shell provides an interactive environment to the JXTA
...
JXTA>env
...
testvar = Default InputPipe (class net.jxta.impl.shell.ShellInputPipe)
...
JXTA>setenv testvar stdout
JXTA>env
...
testvar = Default OutputPipe (class
net.jxta.impl.shell.ShellOutputPipe)
...
JXTA>exit
JXTA>env
...
testvar = Default InputPipe (class net.jxta.impl.shell.ShellInputPipe)
...
```

We can see how the inner shell inherited the value of testvar, but that changes in the inner shell do not affect the values of the variables in the outer shell.

clear

This command will simply clear the command line screen of text.

help

This command simply prints a message, letting you know that man, and not help is the command to look for help under the JXTA shell.

man

Displays the manual page (man page) on any JXTA command. This command is based on its UNIX cousin. If you execute the command without any argument, a list of all available commands, each with brief one-line description, will be displayed.

To obtain more detailed help on any specific command, use the syntax:

```
man <command>
```

history

Like its UNIX cousin, the shell keeps a running history of all the commands that have been issued. If you just type the command:

JXTA>**history**

The queue of commands will be displayed, with each command numbered. In fact, the queue is referred to by an environmental variable called History.

To re-execute a previous command, simply use the syntax:

!<num>

where <num> is the number beside the command listed in the history queue. You can also use the up and down arrow key on the keyboard to cycle through commands.

Unlike the familiar UNIX shell environment, all nested shells in JXTA shares the same history list. This can cause occasional confusion.

instjar

The instjar command is used to install custom JXTA shell commands from a specially constructed JAR file. Simply specify the names of any JAR files you want to load after the command. After the execution of the command, the custom commands residing in the JAR files will be available from the JXTA shell.

You can always find out which JAR file(s) have already been installed by issuing the command without any arguments, for example:

JXTA>**instjar**
0 doccmd.jar

uninstjar

The uninstjar command is used to remove JAR files that may have been previously installed. Once uninstalled, the custom commands in these JAR file will become unavailable from the JXTA shell.

version

This command can be used to find the version of the shell, and the build date and version number of the JXTA platform.

File Access Commands

JXTA itself does not explicitly deal with files. However, one convenient way to store information in structured documents (such as JXTA advertisements and messages) is to store them on disk. JXTA's shell provides commands to store the value of environment variables to disk and to retrieve a file and assign it to the value of an environment variable.

exportfile

Create a file from a structured document referenced by an environment variable. This command has the following syntax:

```
exportfile -f <filename> [<env>]
```

Since advertisements are structured documents, this command can be used to persist any discovered advertisement on permanent storage. For example, the following command will write a discovered advertisement to disk and name it discover.adv:

```
JXTA>exportfile -f discover.adv adv0
```

importfile

Create an environment variable that contains the content of a file. The file is assumed to contain a structured document. For example, we can import the advertisement we wrote to disk on the last example as a structured document, into the variable called mydisc, using:

```
JXTA>importfile -f discover.adv mytest
JXTA>cat mytest
.. display of advertisement..
```

Advertisement Management Commands

Advertisements are what we publish when we want to make a service available on the JXTA network, and what we find when we perform discovery operations. The shell provides several commands for creating, publishing, and discovering advertisements.

mkadv

This command will create an advertisement. The syntax for the command is as follows:

```
mkadv -g|p [[-t <pipetype>] [-d <doc>] [<name>]]
```

The first argument specifies the type of advertisement that you want to create. The possible choices are:

Switch setting	Advertisement type	Notes
-p	Pipe	Can use the -t option to specify the type of pipe (default is point-to-point). Not yet supported at time of writing.
-g	Peer group	Creates an advertisement representing a clone of the current peer group unless a -d option is supplied (see below).

If you specify a -d argument, the environment variable supplied should hold a structured document that is an advertisement (for example, one read in using the importfile command). The advertisement will then be created using the structured document.

An optional name can be added to the advertisement (this becomes an element of the structured document). This name can be used in distributed queries to find the advertisement.

share

This command remotely publishes an advertisement, making it visible to the entire peergroup.

search

There is one single command in the JXTA shell that will send a user-defined remote query for advertisements. The syntax is used by many custom variants of this command (covered later) to search for specific advertisements for discovery purposes. The command is search.

This command performs discovery of advertisements (using the Peer Discovery Protocol), and either searches locally for them, or (if the -r switch is specified) sends the query onto the network of rendezvous for resolution. If you do not specify any additional criteria, the search will match any advertisement. Here are the possible criteria:

Switch	Description
-a <attribute>	Base the query on the value of a specified attribute (that is, on a specific element within an XML document). Specify the value that must match using the -v switch.
-v <value>	This switch is used to specify the value that an attribute-based query must match. Recognizes a trailing wildcard character, *.
-p <peerid>	Search for advertisements only at the specified remote peer.

These are the very same fields as in a Discovery Query Protocol message (as described in Chapter 2), which is the underlying mechanism supporting this command. You can also limit the response using:

Switch	Description
-n <number>	The maximum threshold value – limits the number of replies from any specific responding peer

Because the discovery service will by default cache any discovered advertisement that has not yet expired, sometimes we may want to clear this cache before starting a new discovery. There is a special "flush cache" switch for this purpose.

Switch	Description
-f	Flush the local cache

This `search` command, as we have been using it, will create a set of environment variables named adv?, where '?' is a number beginning at 0. Each adv? variable will be a reference to an advertisement that has been discovered.

If you use the `-r` command (to specify that a remote search should take place), the resulting distributed discovery is asynchronous in operation. This means the results will not be available immediately. You can subsequently check progress for any discovered advertisements by issuing the `search` command without any switches:

```
JXTA>search
```

When the JXTA shell first starts, it will publish a Module Implementation Advertisement (MIA) for each core service that is started with the peer, as well as an MIA that groups all of these advertisements for the default `NetPeerGroup` that it creates. We can find these advertisements, and display the peer group MIA using the search command:

```
JXTA>search
JXTA Advertisement adv0
JXTA Advertisement adv1
JXTA Advertisement adv2
JXTA Advertisement adv3
JXTA Advertisement adv4
JXTA Advertisement adv5
JXTA Advertisement adv6
JXTA Advertisement adv7
JXTA>cat -p adv6
jxta:MIA :
   MSID : urn:jxta:uuid-DEADBEEFDEAFBABAFEEDBABE000000010206
   Comp :
      Efmt : JDK1.4
      Bind : V1.0 Ref Impl
   Code : net.jxta.impl.peergroup.ShadowPeerGroup
   PURI : http://www.jxta.org/download/jxta.jar
   Prov : sun.com
   ...
```

Peer Group Management Commands

Peer groups, as we have seen, provide a way to subdivide the world of JXTA peers into collections that share a common purpose. When working with the shell, it often makes sense to limit the JXTA operations we are performing to a particular group. The shell provides commands that allow us to switch between groups, create new groups, and discover existing ones.

groups

The groups command is used to discover peer groups. It can be considered a special case of the search command, since it searches only for peer group advertisements. The switches are exactly the same as the search command, so see our earlier description of the search command for more details. The discovered groups are assigned to group? variables instead of the generic adv? variables.

mkpgrp

This creates a new peer group. Before you can create a new peer group, you need the associated peer group advertisement. The advertisement can be created using the mkadv -g command (covered earlier), or it can be a custom group advertisement (potentially loaded using the importfile command, and changed into an advertisement using the mkadv -d mechansim). The full syntax is as follows:

mkpgrp [-d <doc>] [-p] [-m <service>]   <name>

By default, the peer group created will be a clone of the default NetPeerGroup.

The -m switch will be used to specify a membership service to use, but is not implemented yet.

Unless you use the -p switch, a peer group advertisement for the newly created group will automatically be published remotely using the discovery service.

By default, the created group is assigned to an environment variable called PG#<group name>. In addition, you can store the result in an environment variable of your own by assigning it at creation:

JXTA>**mygrp = mkpgrp newgrp**

 For example, the following command creates a doppelganger of the NetPeerGroup called doppy.

JXTA>**mkpgrp doppy**
JXTA>**groups**
group0: name = doppy

join

This is used to join a peer group. You can join a peer group that you have created using the mkpgrp command, or you can simply supply a discovered peer group advertisement as an argument. The full syntax is as follows:

```
join [-d <adv>] [-c <credential>] [<name>]
```

As mentioned in our discussions in the previous chapter, a peer can have an identity in each group it joins, and the identity can be used to authenticate against the supplied credential.

If the join is successful, peer group information will be stored in the environment variable PG@<group name> (note the at sign, not a pound/hash character, representing a group you have joined).

leave

This is used to leave a peer group. Reset the current peer group for the peer to NetPeerGroup. The option -k can be used to stop the group (or at least the services associated with it) at the same time. The group information variable will change from PG@<group name> to PG#<group name>.

An env command can always be used to view all the groups that we can join – the PG#<group name> variables – and also identify the groups we have already joined, shown by PG@<group name> variables.

chpgrp

The chpgrp command can be used to change the current peer group of the peer (represented by the shell instance(s)) to another group of which we are a member. Simply specify the name of an environment variable containing such a peer group to perform the switch.

Peer Management Commands

Identifying our peers, and communicating with them, is of course the purpose of JXTA activity, so the shell naturally provides the ability for us to examine the members of peer groups.

peers

This command performs discovery for peers. It is, like groups, a special case of the search command and has identical syntax. See the description of the search command for more details. The discovered peers are stored in environment variables called peer?, where ? is a number starting from 0.

peerinfo

This command queries for peer information, via the Peer Information Protocol. By default, only cached `PeerInfo` messages will be queried, unless the -r switch is used. The -r switch will cause the query to be propagated through the rendezvous network. You may use the -peerid <peerid> option to specify a single peer for the query to target. Using the -l option returns detailed information on the local peer itself. As with the discovery commands, using -f will cause the local cache of `PeerInfo` messages to be flushed before the discovery operation begins. `PeerInfo` messages located by the command will be stored in environment variables called `PeerInfo?` where ? is a number starting at 0.

For example, we can view the `PeerInfo` for the local peer using the following commands:

```
JXTA>peerinfo -l
stored peerinfo0
JXTA>cat -p peerinfo0
jxta:PeerInfoAdvertisement :
   sourcePid :
urn:jxta:uuid-59616261646162614A78746150325033E27AFDD044C447BE99BFB0DA
840E3CB703
   targetPid :
urn:jxta:uuid-59616261646162614A78746150325033E27AFDD044C447BE99BFB0DA
840E3CB703
   uptime : -1004301734556
   timestamp : 1005309036
   traffic :
      in :
      lastIncomingMessageAt : 0
      out :
      lastOutgoingMessageAt : 0
```

Pipe Management Commands

To perform peer-to-peer communications, we need to be able to interact with pipes. We'll see how the actual communication is performed in the next section, but first we must learn how to create pipes ourselves

mkpipe

This command binds a shell input or output pipe to the pipe identified in the supplied pipe advertisement. The syntax is as follows:

```
mkpipe (-i|-o) <pipe advertisement>
```

The -i or -o switch specifies whether an input pipe or an output pipe should be created.

The Pipe Binding Protocol is used, and the pipe binding query will always be propagated throughout the current peer group. The resulting pipe is stored in an environmental variable called env? where ? is a number starting from 0 – if it is not explicitly assigned to a variable. For example, these are the commands to create a new pipe instance on this peer and bind to its input pipe:

```
JXTA> mypadv = mkadv -p myworkpipe
JXTA> mywp = mkpipe -i mypadv
JXTA> env

      . . .

mywp = InputPipe of myadv (class net.jxta.impl.pipe.InputPipeImpl)
```

Message Manipulation Commands

Before we can communicate between peers (that is, independent shell instances), we need to be able to create messages that have interesting content. There exists a set of shell commands for working with pipe messages. Let us take a look at these commands now.

mkmsg

This command creates a pipe message, which is actually a structured document. You can assign the result to an environment variable. By default, it will be assigned to an environment variable called env? where ? is a number starting from 0. The message created will have no payload content initially; we can use the put command to insert structured documents into the message later.

put

This command creates a new tag in the pipe message, and attaches the specified structured document to this tag. Essentially, a new XML element is created in the pipe message, containing the attached structured document. The syntax is:

```
put <msg> <tag> <document>
```

When the message arrives at the receiving end, the attached document can easily be extracted. It is typically used at the sending end of the pipe to attach payloads to the message.

get

This command extracts a structured document, associated with a tag, from a message into an environment variable. It is used at the receiving end of the pipe to extract data from the pipe message. The syntax is simply:

```
get <msg> <tag>
```

Pipe Communications

Now we know enough commands to join groups, create pipes, create messages, and attach data, we can finally cover the commands to send and receive messages through JXTA pipes.

send

This command will send the message specified to the output pipe specified. Its syntax is simply:

```
send <output pipe> <msg>
```

recv

This command can be used to receive a message from an input pipe into an environment variable. The syntax is as follows:

```
recv [-t timeout] <input pipe>
```

The -t switch can be used to specify how long (in seconds) the command should block waiting for incoming messages. If you do not specify the -t switch, the command will wait indefinitely for an incoming message. If you specify -t 0, then the command will check for messages and return immediately.

Configuration Management and Information

There are, finally, several additional commands that assist in configuring the peers, at the propagation/rendezvous level, and at the transport level.

peerconfig

This command enables reconfiguration of the JXTA shell peer instance. Once issued, the GUI configurator will be displaycd the next time the shell starts. This will allow you to configure the peer name, and transport information of the peer.

rdvstatus

This command obtains the rendezvous status of the peer. It will indicate whether the node is serving as rendezvous or not. It also displays all the rendezvous that it knows about (at the moment of query). The -v option can be used to provide a more verbose output.

rdvserver

This command dynamically starts a rendezvous service on this peer. In fact, it blocks the current thread of execution to run the server. Therefore, you must either use Shell -s to start another threaded instance of the shell before executing this command, or be content that the shell instance has turned into a standalone rendezvous service.

who

This command can be used to display the identity and credential information of the peer for the current peer group. This is an actual dump of a JXTA credential structured document. A -p option is available to print the information in "pretty print" format.

whoami

This command displays information from the peer's own peer advertisement. If the -g option is used, it will display information from the peer group advertisement for the current peer group. The -1 option can be used with it to view the Module Spec ID (associated with the set of services available in the group) of the peer group.

Application and Service in a Single Command

There also exists one shell command in the JXTA shell that is not really a command at all. It is a bona fide JXTA application (and associated JXTA service) disguised as a command. It is simply named talk. This is the same application that we tried briefly in the last chapter. Here, we will have a discussion in slightly more detail on this very important model application within the shell.

talk

Readers familiar with UNIX may be familiar with the UNIX talk command, and may also remember that it requires the use of a centralized server component called the talk daemon (or talkd). Under UNIX, the talk client command will not work without talkd running.

JXTA, being a P2P platform, cannot possibly have the same restriction. The solution is to have each and every peer run a service. This is exactly how the talk command works. The different "switches" of the talk command actually execute very different bodies of code. Here is a synopsis:

Switch	Description
-register <username>	This switch creates a "talk" advertisement, really the input pipe advertisement for a pipe that will be used to receive incoming messages. This advertisement is locally and remotely published (and cached).
-login <username>	This switch actually creates a JXTA service that will bind to the pipe of the advertisement and listen for incoming messages.
-logout	This stops the JXTA service that is listening for incoming talk messages.
-user <myusername> <username>	Here, the JXTA client logic is started, a propagated query is sent to look for talk advertisements from a peer with <username> in it (supplied by another user having called -register). Once located, the advertisement is used in binding to the output end of the pipe. Any message entered by this peer will be written to the output pipe.

To revisit how `talk` works, let us try it out. First, register the user (create the advertisement):

```
JXTA>talk -register snoopster
```

Now, we can verify that a new advertisement has been created.

```
JXTA>search -aName -v*snoopster
JXTA Advertisement adv0 (Search criteria: Attribute="Name"
Value="*snoopster")
JXTA>cat adv0
<?xml version="1.0"?>

<!DOCTYPE jxta:PipeAdvertisement>

<jxta:PipeAdvertisement xmlns:jxta="http://jxta.org">
    <Id>

urn:jxta:uuid-59616261646162614E5047205032503307C903F373F24876B4E2873E
E6DC142204
    </Id>
    <Type>
        JxtaUnicast
    </Type>
    <Name>
        JxtaTalkUserName.snoopster
    </Name>
</jxta:PipeAdvertisement>
JXTA>
```

In fact, this pipe advertisement has been published remotely. If you have another physical JXTA machine on the network, you may want to try the search command using the remote discovery option to see that the advertisement has indeed been propagated.

```
JXTA>search -aName -v*snoopster
```

Now, to bind to the pipe and obtain an input pipe, and to start a JXTA service listening to the pipe, we use the command:

```
JXTA>talk -login snoopster
```

Start another peer, using the `runshell.bat` command in the `test2` directory we set up in Chapter 2. In this new peer, register and login a user named bobby:

```
JXTA>talk -register bobby
......
User : bobby is now registered
JXTA>talk -login bobby
```

Finally, back in the first peer, we can now talk to bobby. The command to do this is:

JXTA>**talk -user snoopster bobby**

Figure 2 shows the operation of this talk application.

Figure 2

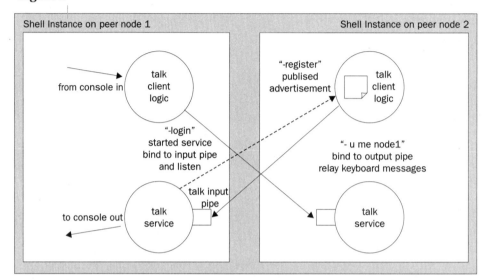

The simple talk service that is started when the -login switch is used will simply listen to the input pipe and print everything that comes through the pipe to standard output. Keyboard input is captured a line at a time by the client half of the application (started when the -user switch is used), and sent to the output pipe of the destination peer.

The talk command provides a great example of how the JXTA shell can be used to incubate ideas for new JXTA application or services. We can create a proof-of-concept implementation of a new application simply as custom JXTA commands, installed into the shell, and tested out using the shell – without investing time in designing a user interface. The shell can then be utilized as a harness to bootstrap development and testing, and allow the designer to work out the kinks before proceeding to create a full-fledged JXTA application or service.

This is the precise development approach that we will take with the application and service that we create in this book. In the next couple of chapters, we will be creating new JXTA services and applications by first incubating them in the JXTA shell.

Scripting with the JXTA Shell

At the current state of its evolution, sophisticated scripting with the JXTA shell is really not possible. It is not possible because:

❑ There is a lack of flow control

❑ There is no expression evaluation logic in the shell

❑ There is no support for a formal scripting language in the shell

❑ The existing shell commands are not consistent in their way of handling input and output

In the near future, these limitations may be addressed, and one may be able to create complete JXTA applications or JXTA services using the JXTA shell alone. In the meantime, some pioneering members of the JXTA community have used alternative Java-based shells (beanshell, rhino, jacl, etc.) to script JXTA commands with varying level of success.

As it stands today, the JXTA shell is limited to the batching of commands, with the assumption that all the commands will run successfully to completion (no testing or flow control logic). One major application for this batching capability is to create regression test suites for the shell commands themselves – the captured output can be compared to an expected output to ensure nothing is broken.

The Vital Role of JXTA Pipes

It is a good time now for us to experiment with the many concepts that we have discussed only in theory. Using the shell, we can gain some hands-on experience working with the component view of the JXTA platform. More specifically, we will experiment with the vital role of pipes in this section.

Without pipes, peers have no JXTA-supported way to communicate with each other. It is vital that we understand how pipes work since much of our JXTA programming will center on communications through pipes. In this section, we will use shell commands to construct a JXTA pipe, and then send a message between two peers through it.

Two Independent JXTA Shells

To try out this experiment, we must set up two independent instances of the shell. You can set it up on two machines on the same LAN, or follow the instructions to set it all up on one single machine.

The sourcecode download for the code in this chapter comes with a `pipetest1` and `pipetest2` directory that can be used for this purpose. The `runshell.bat` file can be used to start the shell (assuming that you have copied the latest JXTA shell build into the `lib` directory) on a Win32 system.

Configure the two shells as follows:

Instance 1	
peer name	node1
transport	TCP enabled, HTTP disabled
TCP address	manual – localhost port 9701

Instance 2:	
peer name	node2
transport	TCP enabled, HTTP disabled
TCP address	manual – localhost port 9703

This configuration ensures that there is no need to use rendezvous or gateways. It allows us to focus on the pipe manipulations.

Creating an Input Pipe

Now, we will create an input pipe on node1. First, create an advertisement, using the command:

JXTA>**myadv = mkadv -p wroxtestpipe**

You can view the content of this pipe advertisement via:

JXTA>**cat myadv**

The output should be similar to:

```
<?xml version="1.0"?>

<!DOCTYPE jxta:PipeAdvertisement>

<jxta:PipeAdvertisement xmlns:jxta="http://jxta.org">
    <Id>

urn:jxta:uuid-59616261646162614E504720503250332CC4D88AB19845949B2EBCEEA
AB6C49904
    </Id>
    <Type>
       JxtaUnicast
    </Type>
    <Name>
       wroxtestpipe
    </Name>
</jxta:PipeAdvertisement>
```

Publishing the Advertisement for Distributed Querying

Next, to publish this advertisement so other peers in the default group can see it, use the command:

```
JXTA>share myadv
```

Check to see that it is indeed shared, go to node2, and enter the following commands:

```
JXTA>search -r -aName -vwroxtestpipe
JXTA Advertisement search message sent
JXTA>search -aName -vwroxtestpipe
```

This looks for the advertisement that we have just created, specifically. You should get a response similar to:

```
JXTA Advertisement adv0 (Search criteria: Attribute="Name"
Value="wroxtestpipe")
```

Indeed, the advertisement can be found on node2. You can use the cat command and verify this new advertisement, adv0, is the same advertisement.

Receiving Pipe Messages from the Input Pipe

Back to node1; we need now to create an input pipe associated with the advertisement. Use the command:

```
JXTA>wroxpipe = mkpipe -i myadv
```

Now, the environment variable wroxpipe refers to the input pipe that we have just created. We are now ready to just wait for an input message, indefinitely on node1. Use the command:

```
JXTA>incoming = recv wroxpipe
```

This shell instance now will block waiting for an incoming message. This is similar to what you would do if you wrote a JXTA-enabled service that processed messages from its own pipe.

Binding to the Output End of the Pipe

Now, move over to node2. Assuming that you have used the search command previously, and that the published pipe advertisement is in environment variable adv0, we can bind to an output pipe by using the command:

```
JXTA>writepipe = mkpipe -o adv0
```

3

Creating and Populating a Pipe Message

The output pipe is now ready. We need to prepare a message that we will send over the pipe. First, create the message.

```
JXTA>mymsg = mkmsg
```

Next, add the payload to the message, in the form of a structured document. We have provided a customer.xml file in the pipetest2 directory for this purpose (if you're just doing this yourself without access to the code download, you can simply create your own).

```
JXTA>importfile -f customer.xml payload
```

The payload environment variable now contains the payload – a structured document that contains the customer information. We can see its content using:

```
JXTA>cat payload
```

You should get output similar to:

```
<?xml version="1.0"?>

<ShellDoc>
    <Item>
        <name>
            Jose Royale
        </name>
        <phone>
            0115298810020
        </phone>
    </Item>
</ShellDoc>
```

We must attach it to the message using the command:

```
JXTA>put mymsg customer payload
```

This will associate the payload with a customer tag. We can verify that the message now contains the payload:

```
JXTA>cat mymsg
```

We should now see:

```
Tag: customer
Body:
<?xml version="1.0"?>

<ShellDoc>
    <Item>
        <name>
            Jose Royale
        </name>
        <phone>
            0115298810020
        </phone>
    </Item>
</ShellDoc>
```

Sending the Message through the Output Pipe

Finally, we can send the loaded message over the pipe:

JXTA>**send writepipe mymsg**

Watching node1, the blocked `recv` command should complete, with the output:

```
recv has received a message
```

Verifying Receipt of a Message

The message is now in an environment variable called `incoming` (which we specified on the `recv` command line). You can `cat` the message to verify that. We will extract the payload, from the `customer` tag, using the command:

JXTA>**customer = get incoming customer**

Verify that the message was sent across the pipe between the two peers, using the command:

JXTA>**cat customer**

Your output should be similar to:

```
<?xml version="1.0"?>

<ShellDoc>
    <Item>
        <name>
            Jose Royale
        </name>
        <phone>
```

```
        0115298810020
      </phone>
    </Item>
  </ShellDoc>
```

This experiment shows how straightforward it is for peers to use pipes for passing messages around. We know that JXTA enables us to use pipe as a virtual channel of communications between peers. In the next experiment, we will see how JXTA creates this illusion – and begin to really appreciate the amazing work that JXTA is performing on our behalf.

Understanding Rendezvous and Routers

Figure 3

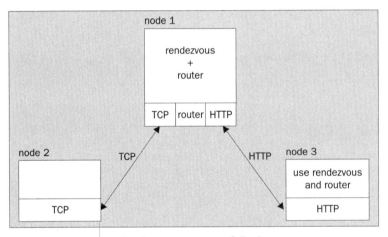

In the next test, we will experiment with the network virtualization layer of JXTA. We will see how the setup of rendezvous/propagation service and routers will affect the ability of peers to reach one another. In this scenario, we will simulate three nodes on a network using separate independent instances of the JXTA shell. Figure 3 shows the three peers that we want to similate.

In the diagram, note carefully that:

❑ node1 supports both TCP and HTTP transports, and is both a rendezvous (propagates queries) and a router (tracks paths between peers and routes messages)

❑ node2 supports only TCP transport, is not a rendezvous, has not been configured to use rendzvous nor routers

❑ node3 supports only HTTP transport, is not a rendezvous, but knows about node1 as the rendzvous

Essentially, node2 can connect to node1 via TCP transport, but not to node 3 directly. node3 can connect to node1 via HTTP transport, but not to node 2 directly.

To start our experiment, we must configure three instances of JXTA Shells as per the tables below.

Instance 1	
peername	node1
transport	TCP enabled; HTTP enabled
HTTP address	localhost port 9700
TCP transport endpoint address	localhost port 9701
Act as Rendezvous	checked
Act as Gateway	checked

Instance 2	
peername	node2
transport	TCP enabled; HTTP disabled
TCP transport endpoint address	localhost port 9703
Rendezvous	none configured
Use Gateway	not checked

Note that due to a minor GUI configurator bug, you will need to leave HTTP enabled until you uncheck the "**Use Gateway**" checkbox. After the "**Use Gateway**" checkbox is unchecked, you can then disable the HTTP transport.

Instance 3	
peername	node3
transport	TCP disabled; HTTP enabled
IITTP transport endpoint address	localhost port 9704
Rendezvous	HTTP configured at `localhost:9700`
Use Gateway	checked; configured at `localhost:9700`

Note that node3 has "**Use Gateway**" checked because HTTP transport cannot currently directly connect to a rendezvous without a router.

Make sure that the cm directory of each instance has been removed (to ensure there are no cached advertisements from previous experiments) before starting the shells.

The best way to do this is to use the directory structure provided by the chapter code distribution. Figure 4 illustrate this.

Figure 4

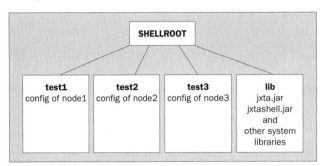

With the structure illustrated here, the JAR files are all kept in the lib directory, while each of the test1, test2, and test3 directories can contain the JXTAConfig, PlatformConfig, and the cm (cache/content management) directory of each instance. A runshell.bat batch file is already provided in each of the test directories for starting the shell.

Now, finally, we can start up all the shell instances.

Shell Commands to Validate Configuration

On node1, type in the command:

JXTA>**rdvstatus**

You should have a response similar to:

```
Rendezvous Connection Status:
_____


Is Rendezvous : [true]

Rendezvous Connections :

   [None]

Rendezvous Disconnections :

   [None]

Rendezvous Client Connections :

   Client name: node3
```

This shows that node1 is acting as a rendezvous, but currently is not connected to any other rendezvous, and has one single client – which is node3.

Next, type in the command:

JXTA>**whoami**

The response is similar to:

```
<Peer>node1</Peer>
<PeerId>urn:jxta:uuid-59616261646162614A78746150325033130EABE4BACA4948
AEED8028B6D8BBCE03</PeerId>
<TransportAddress>tcp://localhost:9701/</TransportAddress>
<TransportAddress>jxtatls://uuid-59616261646162614A78746150325033130EA
BE4BACA4948AEED8028B6D8BBCE03/TlsTransport/jxta-
WorldGroup</TransportAddress>
<TransportAddress>jxta://uuid-59616261646162614A78746150325033130EABE4
BACA4948AEED8028B6D8BBCE03/</TransportAddress>
<TransportAddress>http://localhost:9700/</TransportAddress>
```

The important thing to note above is that both TCP and HTTP `<TransportAddress>` are available for this node.

Type in the `rdvstatus` command on `node2`. The output should be similar to:

```
Rendezvous Connection Status:
_____

Is Rendezvous : [false]

Rendezvous Connections :

  [None]


Rendezvous Disconnections :

  [None]
```

Here, we see that `node2` is not a rendezvous; it is also not connected to any rendezvous. Now, try the `whoami` command on `node2`, and the response should be similar to:

```
<Peer>node2</Peer>
<PeerId>urn:jxta:uuid-59616261646162614A78746150325033A23AC4234EA54325
B515819D826A0D6703</PeerId>
<TransportAddress>tcp://localhost:9703/</TransportAddress>
<TransportAddress>jxtatls://uuid-59616261646162614A78746150325033A23AC
4234EA54325B515819D826A0D6703/TlsTransport/jxta-
WorldGroup</TransportAddress>
<TransportAddress>jxta://uuid-59616261646162614A78746150325033A23AC423
4EA54325B515819D826A0D6703/</TransportAddress>
```

We see here that `node2` has only the TCP `<TransportAddress>` and not the HTTP one.

Finally, try `rdvstatus` command on node3. The output should be similar to:

```
JXTA>rdvstatus

Rendezvous Connection Status:
_____


Is Rendezvous : [false]

Rendezvous Connections :

  Rendezvous name: node1

Rendezvous Disconnections :

  [None]
```

Here, it is clear that node3 is not a rendezvous itself, but is using a rendezvous on node1.

Try the `whoami` command on node3, and you should have response similar to:

```
<Peer>node3</Peer>
<PeerId>urn:jxta:uuid-59616261646162614A78746150325033FB2D319D3A934C6
D8A8B80F2E902F29403</PeerId>
<TransportAddress>jxtatls://uuid-59616261646162614A78746150325033FB2D
319D3A934C6D8A8B80F2E902F29403/TlsTransport/jxta-
WorldGroup</TransportAddress>
<TransportAddress>jxta://uuid-59616261646162614A78746150325033FB2D319
D3A934C6D8A8B80F2E902F29403/</TransportAddress>
<TransportAddress>http://JxtaHttpClientuuid-59616261646162614A7874615
0325033FB2D319D3A934C6D8A8B80F2E902F29403/</TransportAddress>
```

On node3, we have only an HTTP <TransportAddress>, but no TCP one available.

In the simple exercise above, we can see how we can use the `rdvstatus` and `whoami` commands to positively determine the transport and rendezvous topology of a set of peers (if they are running the shell, or have the shell embedded). Now that we are certain of the configuration, we can proceed further.

The Radius of Discovery

To experiment with peer discovery, try this command on each of the nodes:

```
JXTA>peers
```

Assuming you have removed any pre-existing cm directory before you tried this example, your results should be:

peer	result
node1	node1 only
node2	node2 only
node3	node3 only

This is not surprising since the peers command looks only locally for cached or local peer advertisements.

Now, try the command for remote discovery on each of the nodes:

JXTA>**peers -r**

This time, discovery is done locally as well as remotely. The result, subsequently, of running peers is:

peer	result
node1	node1, node2, node3
node2	node1, node2, node3
node3	node1, node2, node3

This may first appear to be amazing, since there is no physical connection between node2 and node3. However, this is the precise value of the network virtualization layers in JXTA, providing a logical mesh at the higher level (that is, for discovery).

Here's what happened. Between node1 and node3, there should be no surprise that there is a connection, since node1 is a preconfigured rendezvous for node3. But node1 is not a rendezvous for node2, so how did they find out about each other?

The secret lies in the TCP transport. For local area network discovery, the TCP transport uses UDP multicast – and in doing so node1 and node2 readily discover each other. Once node1 discovers node2, it caches the node2 advertisement (since it is a rendezvous). As a rendezvous for node3, it also responds to node3's remote discovery query with the newly discovered node2. This is how node3 learns about node2!

How Pipes Virtualize Connections Between Peers

Now that we see how propagation for advertisements provides complete coverage within our physically disjointed (on a transport level) topology, let us take a step further and see how messages sent over pipes can also be virtualized by these layers.

We will use the talk command to illustrate this. First, on node2, type in the commands:

JXTA>**talk -register joe**
JXTA>**talk -login joe**

This will create a talk pipe advertisement, publish it remotely, bind to its input pipe, and start a JXTA service to monitor the input pipe created.

Now, on node3, type in the commands:

```
JXTA>talk -register jill
JXTA>talk -login jill
JXTA>talk -u jill joe
```

The response, after some delay, should be similar to:

```
found user's advertisement attempting to connect
talk: user joe is not listening. Try again later
```

Or to try on node2, type in the command:

```
JXTA>talk -u joe jill
```

You will get the response:

```
found user's advertisement attempting to connect
talk: user jill is not listening. Try again later
```

This may seem a little frustrating, since in fact, we know that both joe and jill are listening (since we have issued the talk -login command in each case). What is happening here is that while the talk pipe advertisement has propagated throughout the network, thanks to TCP-based discovery and rendezvous propagation, there is no physical way for node2 to connect to node3 because node2 uses TCP transport only and node3 uses HTTP transport only.

Now, recall our discussion about the duality of the router, and how the router service also has a "transport driver" that provides a virtual direct connection between peers – by potentially weaving in and out of physical transport at each peer? Sounds incredible? Let's see it in action.

On node2, type in the command:

```
JXTA>peerconfig
```

Shut down and start the node2 peer again, and this time, reconfigure it as follows:

Instance 2	
peername	node2
transport	TCP enabled; HTTP disabled
TCP transport endpoint address	localhost port 9703
Available TCP Rendezvous	TCP localhost:9701 configured

This configures node2 to use node1 for rendezvous (using TCP transport only), as well as setting it up to use the router at node1 to virtualize paths to and from node2 itself to other peers.

Now, try the following commands on node2:

```
JXTA>talk -login joe
JXTA>talk -u joe jill
```

Lo and behold, node2 can now bind to the output pipe of node3! You get the following response:

```
found user's advertisement attempting to connect
talk is connected to user jill
Type your message. To exit, type "." at begining of line
```

On node3, you can now try:

```
JXTA>talk -u jill joe
```

You now get the following response:

```
found user's advertisement attempting to connect
talk is connected to user joe
Type your message. To exit, type "." at begining of line
```

What failed previously now works perfectly. Figure 5 shows the new topology.

Figure 5

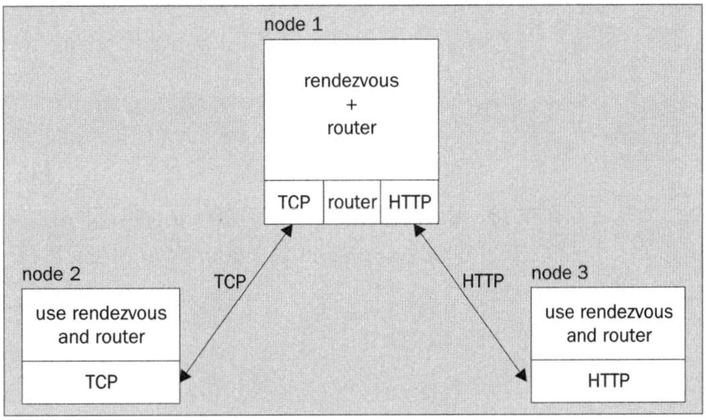

Thanks to the router at node1, the path between node2 and node3 has been "virtualized" at the network layer – by weaving from the TCP transport of node2 to the HTTP transport of node3 and vice versa! As well as TCP and HTTP, this can work with any other transports, for example between a packet network transport for wireless PDAs, and TCP for the Internet. This way, the

router acts as a relay service, which can enable participation even for peers that cannot be connected to directly (firewall, one way paging, etc.). One can clearly see the possibilities.

The magic of JXTA is to have the above miracle performed automatically and adaptively throughout the P2P network, all without any higher-level application intervention! In fact, the higher-level application enjoys a simple component view that just involves peers and pipes.

Extending the JXTA Shell

The JXTA shell can be extended with custom commands easily. The following section will reveal some motivation on why one may want to extend the shell, and then show how to do it with some real, working custom-command code.

While the JXTA shell comes with many built-in commands for working with the components of the JXTA platform, these commands are rather limited versions – and they often do not perform the exact function that we want them to. Developers and users would likely opt out of using the JXTA shell for development and testing if they were forced to work with only the included set of commands. Luckily, the JXTA community has taken a pragmatic approach to this problem, and decided that the best way to ensure the longevity of the JXTA shell is to:

❑   Provide an adequate set of basic commands to satisfy the largest audience possible

❑   Provide a simple extension mechanism for advanced users to add their own implementation of custom commands

Custom Commands to the Rescue

Custom commands enable advanced users to:

❑   Modify the behavior of existing commands (since sourcecode is available), creating versions of commands that better fit their specific requirements

❑   Create completely new commands addressing areas or operation that the shell command designer did not think of, or decided not to implement

❑   Adapt the JXTA shell to work with a specific P2P system that is built on top of JXTA

❑   Test new JXTA service and application code without creating complex user interfaces

❑   Create completely customized and embedded shells within an application

There are certainly many other possibilities. It should be obvious that the JXTA shell (and the code body that it encompasses) is much more than just a learning tool for JXTA newbies. Let's take a look at how we go about extending the shell and creating our own commands.

Basic Mechanism of Shell Extension

All of the shell's commands are part of the `net.jxta.impl.shell.bin` package. This includes commands such as `peers`, `groups`, `search`, etc. If you examine the sourcecode of the JXTA shell (available freely at jxta.org), you will notice that they are all individual Java source files under their own package with the same name. For example, `search.java` is in the `net.jxta.impl.shell.bin.search` package.

During run time, the JXTA shell uses introspection to enumerate all of these commands and make them available to the user. Any time the user types in a command, these commands are re-scanned to check if an implementation is available.

To extend the JXTA shell, we simply add our own command implementation packages under `net.jxta.impl.shell.bin`.

Figure 6 reveals how the JXTA Shell can be extended with our own custom commands.

Figure 6

In the diagram, we can see that our custom commands' classes must be "installed" into the `net.jxta.impl.shell.bin` package. This can be done in at least two different ways:

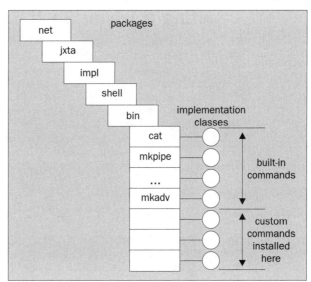

3

- ❏ Ensure that the Java VM running the JXTA shell has the JAR file(s) or directories containing our custom commands in its CLASSPATH. This will effectively merge the classes of the our custom JAR file with jxtashell.jar.

- ❏ Use the instjar command within the shell to install the custom commands. The instjar command uses Java's dynamic class loading capabilities to install the custom commands into place.

The second alternative is preferred, since it is directly supported by the shell itself, and does not require fiddling with the external Java VM's CLASSPATH. This makes it much less dependent on configuration and less prone to setup errors. Furthermore, it can be done at any time after the JXTA shell has already started – and commands installed with instjar can be easily uninstalled using the uninstjar command. This means commands can be installed, tested, and uninstalled as part of their development process, without repeatedly launching the shell.

All that remains now is for us to actually write some custom command implementation code.

Creating a Trivial Shell Extension

First, we will write a very simple shell extension in order to get to know the support system for writing new shell commands. Our simple shell extension is located in the package in the chapter code download called net.jxta.impl.shell.bin.date.date.java.

This extension provides a new JXTA shell command called date, and all it will do is print the current date and time. We use the java.text.DateFormat class from JDK 1.3 to pretty-print the date according to our default locale. The default instance of java.util.Calendar class is used to obtain the current time. Combining the functions of these two classes, we can print the current date using the line:

```
println(DateFormat.getDateTimeInstance().format(Calendar.getInstance().
getTime()));
```

We'll see that line in context in a moment, but naturally, we have to build some infrastructure in order to actually incorporate it into a shell command. First, notice that as expected, it resides in the net.jxta.impl.shell.bin.date package.

```
package net.jxta.impl.shell.bin.date;
```

We need to import the classes we need for date operations, as well as the package containing shell support classes.

```
import net.jxta.impl.shell.*;
import java.util.Calendar;
import java.text.DateFormat;
```

Every shell command is a subclass of ShellApp; this is required. net.jxta.impl.shell.ShellApp is an abstract class that provides a lot of environment information and support to the shell command implementation. Here are some commonly used methods of ShellApp that can save the custom command implementer a lot of work:

Method Name	Description
getEnv()	Gets the shell environment, including read and write access to any environment variable
getGroup()	Gets the current group of the peer represented by the shell
getReturnVariable()	Provides access to the environment variable on the left-hand side of an assignment

Typically, the logic of the command is implemented in the startApp() method of the class. The startApp() and stopApp() methods are actually part of the net.jxta.impl.Module interface that is implemented by every JXTA service or application.

```
public class date extends ShellApp {

  public date() {
  }
```

Here, we simply print the current day and time when the command is called. println() calls an inherited method that writes to the application's default output stream, as provided by the shell.

```
public int startApp (String[] args) {
  println(DateFormat.getDateTimeInstance()
                   .format(Calendar.getInstance().getTime()));
  return ShellApp.appNoError;
}

public void stopApp () {
}
```

One other method that is frequently overridden in a shell command is getDescription(). This command is used by the man command, to obtain a short description for the command.

```
public String getDescription() {
    return "Returns the current date and time.";
}
```

The help() method provides detailed usage help to a user when they use the command man date.

```
  public void help() {
      println("NAME");
      println("   date - get the current date and time");
      println(" ");
      println("SYNOPSIS");
      println("   date");
      println(" ");
      println("DESCRIPTION");
      println(" ");
      println("   'date' prints the current date and time to stdout.");
      println(" ");
      println("EXAMPLE");
      println("   JXTA>date");
      println(" ");
  }
}
```

As we can observe, writing a custom shell command is quite easy, we need only:

❑ Make sure our class is in the package
net.jxta.impl.shell.bin.<command name>, and called
<command name>

❑ Inherit from net.jxta.impl.shell.ShellApp

❑ Implement the logic of the command in startApp() and any other helper methods

❑ Use the helper methods available in the ShellApp abstract class whenever necessary

❑ Optionally implement help methods such as getDescription() and help()

Compiling the Custom Command and Creating the JAR File

You will find the sourcecode to the date command under the src directory of the distribution. We have also supplied a batch file (for Win32 systems) to compile the code and create a JAR file with it. The file is called makedate.bat and contains:

```
set SHELLROOT=..
javac -classpath %SHELLROOT%\lib\jxta.jar;%SHELLROOT%\lib\jxtashell.jar
-d %SHELLROOT%\classes net\jxta\impl\shell\bin\date\*.java
cd ..\classes
jar cvf ..\custcmds\datecmd.jar net\jxta\impl\shell\bin\date\date.class
cd ..\src
```

This will create a datecmd.jar file, containing the custom command, and place it into the custcmds directory of the distribution.

Run this `makedate.bat` file from the `src` directory to compile the code and create the required JAR file.

Installing the Custom date Command

The `datecmd.jar` file contains our customized `date` command, and is a very convenient packaging for delivering or sharing custom shell commands that we create. Anyone who gets a copy of the `datecmd.jar` file can also use our `date` command.

To install the JAR file into an instance of a JXTA shell, first start a JXTA shell from the `custcmds` directory of the distribution. Use the `runshell.bat` command to do this. then configure the shell to run locally, and at the command line install the JAR file using:

```
JXTA>instjar datecmd.jar
```

Testing the Custom date Command

We can finally try out this custom command:

```
JXTA>date
Nov 11, 2002   12:30 am
```

You can also try the help function:

```
JXTA>man date
NAME
    date - get the current date and time

SYNOPSIS
    date


DESCRIPTION

    'date' prints the current date and time to stdout.


EXAMPLE
    JXTA>date
```

We see here that the custom command appears to be every bit as "native" as one of the built-in commands. Since they share exactly the same mechanism of construction and deployment, there is little observable difference.

Uninstalling the Custom date Command

If you are using many different sets of custom commands for different reasons (testing of new services, etc.), it is convenient to be able to load and unload them in order to keep the command namespace uncluttered (to avoid having multiple commands with the same name). This can be done by uninstalling any command JAR file that may be installed.

To uninstall a JAR file, first find out its installation ordinal number using:

JXTA>**instjar**

Then use the command uninstjar and the -i switch to remove it:

JXTA>**uninstjar -i 0**

Now the date command is no longer available.

As a final example in this chapter, we will create a significantly more involved shell command, one that will be quite useful in our daily experimentation and work with the JXTA shell.

Creating a Complex Shell Extension

One of the most frustrating things with the basic set of commands included with the JXTA shell is that we cannot just create a structured document from the command line in any simple way. In an earlier example, we needed to create a structured document using a text editor, save it into a file, and then use the importfile command to import it. This is, needless to say, very tedious.

We will now create a custom command that will enable us to:

❑ Create elements in a structured document and store them into environment variables

❑ Compile elements stored in environment variables and form new elements

❑ Create a structured document of any type consisting of one or more elements

We will call this command mkdoc.

The mkdoc command will enable us to build a complex structured document, completely using the command line. The switches available will be:

Switch	Description
-e	Create an element. The element name should immediately follow, and then any content of the element.
-c	Combine elements in environment variables to form a new element. The new element name should immediately follow, and then any environment variables that contain elements to become children of the new element.
-d	Create a structured document, of specified document type, consisting of a set of elements stored in environment variables.

For example, we can create a name element simply:

```
JXTA>name=mkdoc -e name Joe Manzini
JXTA>cat name
<name>Joe Manzini</name>
```

Or combine multiple elements into larger one:

```
JXTA>phone=mkdoc -e phone 333-3333
JXTA>cust=mkdoc -c customer name phone
JXTA>cat cust
<customer><name>Joe Manzini</name><phone>333-3333</phone></customer>
```

We can then create a structured document using:

```
JXTA>custdata=mkdoc -d CustData cust
JXTA>env
name = String (class java.lang.String)
...
custdata = StructuredDocument (class
net.jxta.impl.document.LiteXMLDocument)
...
cust = String (class java.lang.String)
phone = String (class java.lang.String)
...
```

Note that custdata is a structured document, and it contains:

```
JXTA>cat custdata
<?xml version="1.0"?>

<!DOCTYPE CustData>

<CustData>
    <customer>
        <name>
            Joe Manzini
        </name>
        <phone>
            333-3333
        </phone>
    </customer>
</CustData>
```

We can see now that we will be able to create potentially large and complex structured documents using this mkdoc command.

Coding the mkdoc Command

Now, we can follow the procedure that we have seen with the trivial `date` command to create this new command. You can, once more, find the sourcecode in the `src` directory of the code download.

Being a shell command, of course, it resides in its own package under the `bin` directory, called `net.jxta.impl.shell.bin.mkdoc`.

```
package net.jxta.impl.shell.bin.mkdoc;

import net.jxta.impl.shell.*;
import net.jxta.endpoint.*;
import net.jxta.document.*;
```

Any shell command must inherit from `net.jxta.impl.shell.ShellApp`, and mkdoc is no exception.

```
public class mkdoc extends ShellApp {
```

We will store a reference to the shell environment, which we can obtain through the inherited `getenv()` method from the `ShellApp` class, in the variable called `env`. It is through this reference that we can access all the environment variables that we will use.

```
    ShellEnv env;
```

The switches used to tell the command to define an element, combine elements, and make a document are defined next.

```
    private static final String elementDefine = "-e";
    private static final String combineElements = "-c";
    private static final String makeDoc = "-d";
```

Next, some temporary working variables for constructing our output.

```
    private String myDocType = null;

    private String elementName = null;
    private String elementContent = null;
    private String myElement = null;

    public mkdoc() {
    }
```

The core logic implementation, as with the `date` command, begins in the `startApp()` method. The `startApp()` method is equivalent to `main()` for JXTA shell commands.

```
public int startApp (String[] args) {
```

We make sure that there are at least more than three arguments, since all switch alternatives require at least this number of arguments to be meaningful. If the user has less than this, we print out a help message.

```
if ((args == null) || (args.length < 3)) {
    return reportError();
}
```

Here, we take advantage of helper methods in `ShellApp` to easily obtain the environment instance.

```
env = getEnv();
```

We check the first argument to see if it is -e, which tells us to define a new element. If it is, we lift off the second argument and store it as `elementName`. The rest of the command line is captured into the variable `elementContent`, and can contain embedded blanks.

```
if (elementDefine.equals(args[0])) { // define a new element
    elementName = args[1];
    elementContent = getRestOfArgs(args,2);
```

So now we create a new element by adding the XML angle brackets for an opening and closing tag. This resulting element will be assigned out to an environment variable later.

```
    myElement = "<" + elementName + ">" + elementContent
                + "</" + elementName + ">";
}
```

The next set of logic handles the -c switch for combining multiple elements as children of a new element.

```
if (combineElements.equals(args[0])) {
// combine elements into new element
```

The first argument after this switch is always the new element name.

```
elementName = args[1];
```

We call our own `mergeAllElements()` helper method here to do the work. The `mergeAllElements()` method will examine every subsequent argument, access them as environment variables, extract their values, and concatenate them.

```
elementContent = mergeAllElements(args,2);
```

Finally, we create a new element based on the concatenation of the content of the specified elements.

```
      myElement = "<" + elementName + ">" +elementContent +
"</"+elementName +">";


   }
```

For the third switch, -d, we need to create a new structured document instance. args[1] in this case contains the document type, which is typically the name of the root element. For example, a JXTA pipe advertisment will have a document type of Jxta:PipeAdv.

```
if (makeDoc.equals(args[0])) {// create a structured document
      myDocType = args[1];
```

Here, we use the mergeAllElements() helper method again to extract elements from each of the specified environment variables.

```
      myElement = mergeAllElements(args,2);
```

A structured document is created using the static newStructuredDocument() method of the StructuredDocumentFactory. This class takes registration of different structured document classes from the platform, and hides the construction details from the user. The version we use here simply takes a string as an argument and uses it as the content of the document.

```
StructuredDocument doc = null;
try {
   doc = StructuredDocumentFactory.newStructuredDocument (
            new MimeMediaType ("text/xml"), myDocType, myElement);
} catch (Exception ex) {
   println("mkdoc: " + ex.toString());
   return ShellApp.appMiscError;
}
```

Now, a structured document has been created, we assign it to either the left-hand side of the assignment or a new environment variable. This is taken care of us by the getReturnVariable() method courtesy of the ShellApp class. The getReturnVariable() method will fetch the environment variable referred to on the left-hand side of the assignment, if any, or create a new env? variable to hold the result if there isn't one (now you can see why so many JXTA commands create env? variables as a side effect of their work).

Note also that we can only assign objects of type ShellObject to an environment variable. Fortunately, ShellObjects are simply data structures that can contain any Java object, plus an associated name. In this case, the name is StructuredDocument. In this way, one can simply treat environment variables the same way as Java variables. Any ShellObject that we assign to an environment variable will become available to the user of the shell, and any subsequent commands that they may execute.

```
                env.add(getReturnVariable(), new
        ShellObject("StructuredDocument", doc));
                return ShellApp.appNoError;


        }
```

For the -c and -e switches, there is no need to create a
StructuredDocument ShellObject, so we store them simply as
String typed ShellObjects. This will keep them in an easy-to-
manipulate form.

```
        env.add(getReturnVariable(),new ShellObject("String",
            myElement));

    return ShellApp.appNoError;
}

public void stopApp () {
}
```

The helper getRestOfArgs() method combines all the specified
arguments into one string. It artificially inserts one blank in between
each of the detected arguments during the construction of the String.

```
public String getRestOfArgs(String [] args, int idx) {
    int arysize = args.length;
    String res = args[idx];

    for (int i=(idx + 1); i < arysize; i++) {
        res = res + " " + args[i];
    }

    return res;
}
```

The helper mergeAllElements() method works similarly to
getRestOfArgs(), but treats each of the arguments as a ShellObject
of type String. This is the way we store elements using mkdoc. The
mergeAllElements() method accesses each of the environment
variables specified in the arguments, and concatenates their contents
together. Note that unlike getRestOfArgs(), there is no need for
blank re-insertion.

```
public String mergeAllElements(  String [] args, int idx) {

    int arysize = args.length;
    String res = "";
    try {
    for (int i= idx; i <arysize; i++) {
```

3

```
                    ShellObject obj = env.get (args[i]);
                    res += (String) obj.getObject();
            }
        }
    catch (Exception ex) {
      println("mkdoc: sorry, cannot access some elements.");
      res = "";
        }
     return res;
    }
```

The reportError() method gives the user some hint on how to use the command – it is called when the command is invoked incorrectly.

```
private int reportError() {
    println ("usage: mkdoc [-e <element name> <element content>]");
    println ("                  [-c <element name> <element> .... ]");
    println ("                  [-d <doctype> <element> .... ]");
    println (" ");
    println ("'man mkdoc' to get more information.");
    return ShellApp.appParamError;
}
```

The getDescription() method gives a short description of the command, for man's summary.

```
public String getDescription() {
    return "Creates a structured document in memory.";
}
```

The help() method gives a detailed description of the command, for a 'man page' of help information.

```
public void help() {
    println("NAME");
    println("      mkdoc - create a sructured document in memory.");
    println(" ");
    println("SYNOPSIS");
    println("      mkdoc [-e <element name> <element content>]");
    println("                  [-c <element name> <element>...]");
    println("                  [-d <doctype> <element> ....]");

    println(" ");
    println("DESCRIPTION");
    println(" ");
    println("'mkdoc' provides a way to create complete structured");
    println("documents from scratch, in memory, without using
            file.");
```

```
    println(" ");
    println("First, you use -e to create environment variables
         that");
    println("contains the element you want. Then you can use -c
         to");
    println("combine them in new elements, or just create a
                structured");
    println("document using the -d option");
    println(" ");
    println("EXAMPLE");
    println("    JXTA>name=mkdoc -e name Joe Baxer");
    println("    JXTA>phone=mkdoc -e phone 223-222-3333");
    println("    JXTA>mydoc=mkdoc -d CustData name phone");
    println("Explanation");
    println("    The commands above creates a structured document
         with");
    println("      root of CustData containing the name and phone
         info.");
    println(" ");
    }
}
```

This completes the code analysis, so it's time to give this code a try.

Compiling, Archiving, and Deploying the mkdoc Command

In the src directory of the code distribution, you will find a Win32 batch file called makedoc.bat that can be used to compile the command and create the deployable JAR file. This batch file contains the following script:

```
set SHELLROOT=..
javac -classpath
%SHELLROOT%\lib\jxta.jar;%SHELLROOT%\lib\jxtashell.jar -d
%SHELLROOT%\classes net\jxta\impl\shell\bin\mkdoc\*.java
cd ..\classes
jar cvf ..\custcmds\doccmd.jar net\jxta\impl\shell\bin\mkdoc\*.class
cd ..\src
```

The resulting JAR file is called doccmd.jar and placed in the custcmds directory waiting for deployment.

Change directory to custcmds, and start the shell using the runshell.bat file.

Now, you can install the shell extension:

Finally, you can test out the `mkdoc` command. You might want to use the `custdoc` usage scenario presented earlier as your initial attempt.

We have seen yet again that extending the JXTA shell with custom command is actually quite easy once we get the hang of it. In fact, one can create one's own collection of frequently used custom commands relatively easily. The `instjar` and `uninstjar` mechanism makes using these extensions a joy.

The Versatile JXTA Shell

In this chapter, we have become intimately familiar with a the JXTA Shell. What initially appeared to be an innocent sample application has turned out to be a hardcore workhorse for JXTA developers.

Using a familiar UNIX/DOS-like interface, the JXTA shell enables developers to interact with the components view of the JXTA platform directly, without writing or compiling any programs.

The large and diverse set of commands already included with the shell enables a developer to work with advertisements, pipes, groups, and messages. One can control the caching, publishing, and propagation of advertisements and messages through these commands.

Since each shell instance is a proper JXTA peer, the shell also enables us to experiment with peer configuration and to observe the network virtualization layer of JXTA at work.

As a learning tool, the JXTA shell can be used productively in the prototyping of new JXTA services and applications – enabling the developer to quickly try out an idea without creating complex user interface frameworks. During the product testing phase, the JXTA shell can be invaluable for creating test scripts for new JXTA services and applications. Applications may also embed the shell functionality within themselves, for quick diagnostics or configuration testing.

The easy extensibility of the JXTA shell is really what makes it shine. We saw first-hand how the `instjar` and `uninstjar` commands enable us to quickly and painlessly add new custom commands to the JXTA shell during run time. We saw how to create our own custom commands, including the implementation of a relatively complex command to enable us to create structured documents in memory, supplementing the file-based `importfile` command for creating custom structured documents.

Essentially, the JXTA shell provides an "open-box" peer on the JXTA network, allowing free and unhindered experimentation with the platform and the P2P network. While we'll be coming back here again in the later chapters, we'll be concentrating on how we can go about building our own closed-box peers on the same network, using the knowledge we've gained through experimentation here.

early adopter

JXTA 4

JXTA Applications and Services

The first three chapters have given us a basic appreciation for P2P systems in general and JXTA systems in particular. We have an understanding of the composition of the JXTA infrastructure, including the embedded layering of APIs and the abstract component view that is provided to application developers.

In this chapter, our focus will be sharply tuned to creating JXTA services and client applications that use these services. More specifically, we will seek to:

1. Understand what a JXTA application is

2. Appreciate the architecture of a typical JXTA service, and its relationship to a client application(s)

3. Examine the application pattern that lends itself to JXTA/P2P implementations

4. Understand the common and unique properties of JXTA (and P2P) systems

5. Learn how to design a JXTA application, more specifically how to partition our application functionality

6. Realize that all our client-server system programming skills can immediately be leveraged in JXTA application programming

7. Discover the easiest way possible to create a variety of JXTA services, squashing the usually steep JXTA learning curve

8. Use the shell extension programming skills that we picked up in the last chapter to create test clients for our new JXTA services

In other words, all our energy in this chapter will be devoted to make JXTA work for us, NOW!

We will end the chapter by creating several of our very own JXTA services and experimenting with them. Although these services are trivial in nature, they can easily form the basis upon which more sophisticated services can be built. This is intentional since each example service and client application pair illustrates an interaction pattern that is pervasive in JXTA-based system design.

Working with these services and client applications will give us practical and immediate hands-on experience with building JXTA-based systems.

All of this may sounds like a lot of work within a chapter. However, thanks to a new JXTA programming library, called the JXTA EZ Entry Library (EZEL for short), we will accomplish all of this and more within this single chapter. EZEL greatly simplifies the learning curve of programming JXTA systems, and enables classically trained client-server developers to leverage their programming skills and expertise immediately in the distributed, non-centralized, P2P world of JXTA. We will simply be users of the EZEL library within this chapter, and will examine the design and inner workings of the library in the next.

Anatomy of a JXTA-based P2P System

This section will cover aspects of a JXTA system that is identifiable as similar to conventional systems that we know and love. A JXTA-based P2P system consists of one or more interacting JXTA applications. Let us take a look inside the typical JXTA application.

What is a JXTA Application?

A JXTA application is an application that makes use of the JXTA platform as (one of) its mean(s) of communication. Since JXTA is designed to live in a "juxtaposed" world where elements of traditional client-server computing co-exist, it is unwise to restrict the definition of a JXTA application to the JXTA platform and network transports exclusively.

> *A JXTA application will typically be simultaneously using some aspects of conventional client-server networking juxtaposed with JXTA-based P2P functionality.*

In this book, however, we will focus only on the elements of the application that are related to the use of the JXTA platform and transports. The following figure illustrates the interaction of a JXTA application with the platform.

Figure 1

In this figure, we see that a JXTA application makes use of the JXTA platform, leveraging its component view, to communicate between peers that are (potentially) dispersed among heterogeneous transports.

Typically, the application programming models of the conventional networking stack and the JXTA-based stack are quite dissimilar – since their operation models are different. However, with the EZEL library that we will be using this difference can be minimized. The figure below shows how the EZEL library eases the conceptual hurdle faced by JXTA developers coming from a client-server world.

Figure 2

This figure shows that EZEL abstracts the component view provided by the JXTA platform further, allowing the developer to look at JXTA in terms of services and clients. P2P simply implies that each and every node in the network (a potential peer) has some aspect of client and optionally some service functionality. This dichotomy is illustrated overleaf:

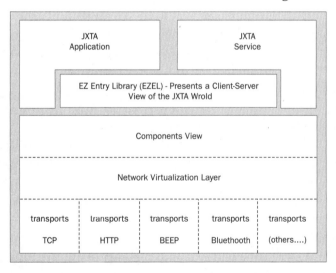

4

Figure 3

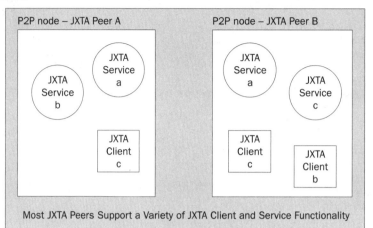

Being able to abstract P2P on a client-service level, as EZEL enable us to do, makes programming JXTA easy.

Designing JXTA Applications

However, using EZEL does not relieve us of the question: **What sort of P2P application or systems can we write?**

This, of course, is the multi-million dollar question. It is not possible, at this juncture, to exhaustively enumerate the application areas for P2P-style applications. Much of what is possible with P2P systems remains unexplored and what we know today is only the tip of the iceberg. JXTA stands to enable thinkers, designers, and developers to experiment and make discoveries of their very own.

As of today, industry experience has revealed that there are at least a few classes of application that really lend themselves to P2P network architectures. We will examine these classes in terms of application patterns – the abstract interaction and functional patterns that all applications within the same class share. The pattern that we discuss below is not or may not have to be implemented in a specific application. But the analysis provides a useful "think framework" for us to map application patterns to significant design problems in our own domain.

The Known P2P "Application Patterns"

There are at least two proven, and very well known, application patterns for P2P computing.

1. Content sharing networks

2. Ad hoc messaging networks

3. Distributed computing "server farms"

These are therefore valid application patterns for the design of JXTA applications. They are modeled after the "killer apps" that have given legitimacy to the new and exciting genre of non-centralized systems.

We will describe each of these patterns, and explain how JXTA can be used to implement applications that are modeled after these patterns.

The Content Sharing Network Pattern

This is the familiar model that is shared by Napster, Gnutella, and Morpheus. The idea here is that any number of users on the P2P network may desire to share a number of files (whose content we will not restrict in any way) with all other members of the group.

Obviously, this can be accomplished in a number of ways; many of them are centralized in nature. We can immediately think of huge clusters of FTP servers, or a web server and content disk farms, etc. All of these solutions require the collection of content in a centralized and globally (or group-wide) accessible location. The following figure illustrates this centralized implementation of a content sharing network.

Figure 4

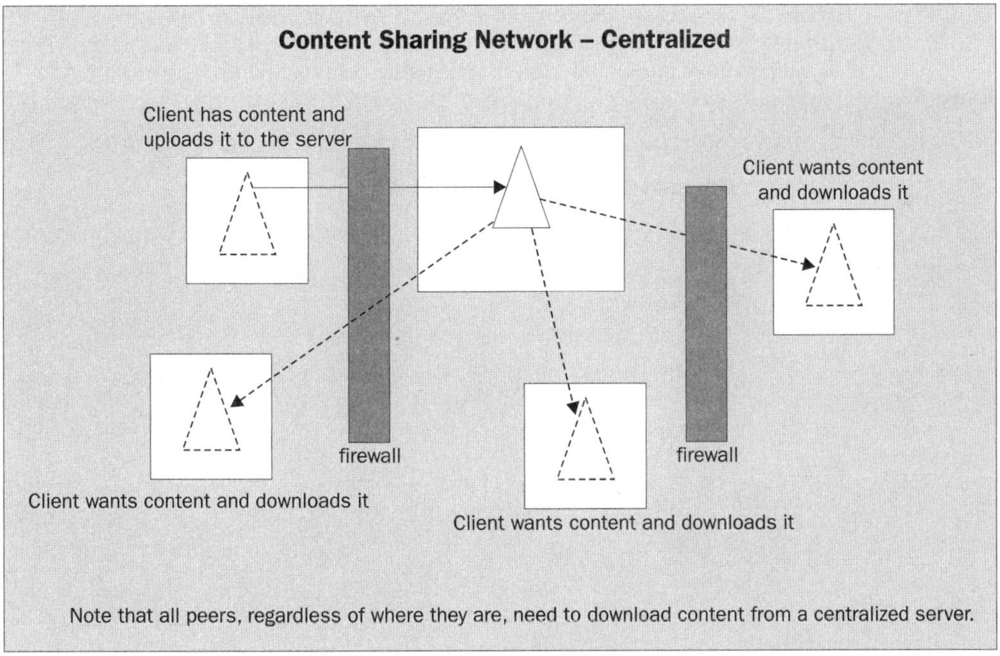

Content Sharing Network – Centralized

Client has content and uploads it to the server

Client wants content and downloads it

firewall

firewall

Client wants content and downloads it

Client wants content and downloads it

Note that all peers, regardless of where they are, need to download content from a centralized server.

In our P2P-centric view, of course, the sharing should not depend on the existence of any centralized server/services. Although many commercial implementations thus far may juxtapose conventional design onto the P2P portion for optimization, we will restrict our discussion here to the pure P2P case.

Within this application pattern, the content is shared in place. That is, the content holder does not have to explicitly "upload" the content at any time to anyone. Given that this is the case, there are only two alternatives by which content can be retrieved by a consumer peer:

1. The consumer peer directly downloads the content from the publishing peer

2. The consumer peer causes an intermediate peer to download and cache the content from the publishing peer on its behalf

The first proposition is actually a special case and we assume in this case that the publishing peer is:

1. Online at the same time as the publishing peer, and running some sort of file sharing server (such as FTP)

2. Capable of connecting directly to the consumer peer

We learned quite early in Chapter 2 that it is possible in a P2P network for the transport to be heterogeneous, and for the peers connected to such a network to change their physical addresses non-deterministically and continuously with time. Therefore, both the above assumptions may be false in a P2P network – together or independently! This means that Proposition 1 can only be applicable to problems where the topology of the network is known and deterministic. Proposition 2, however, is a very interesting and is how JXTA can be used to implement a content sharing network application pattern. The figure below illustrates how this works.

Figure 5

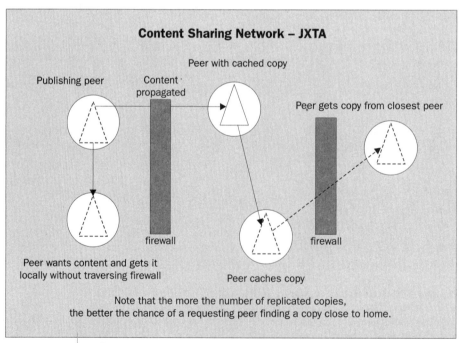

In this case, we have a network of JXTA nodes that cache content. Here is what is happening:

1. A consumer peer performs a distributed query on the JXTA network for the content that it desires

2. The query is propagated throughout the rendezvous network, assuming every peer that is currently active receives the query

3. Every peer receiving the query examines its own cache for the content

4. The peer(s) with the available content reply to the consumer peer

5. The consumer peer arranges to transfer the content from the peer(s) with the content

Step 5 deserves some careful examination. The consumer peer can transfer the content using an out-of-band means, such as HTTP or FTP, directly from the peer with the content. However, this assumes that a direct connection can be made between the two on a compatible transport. Many current commercial P2P implementations make this assumption, and it is a workable assumption over the current day Internet.

To be able to cope with the more general case, however, JXTA peers need not rely on a direct out-of-band means of connection such as FTP or HTTP to get the work done.

In a JXTA network, it is possible to perform any or a combination of the following to retrieve the content:

1. Have peers that are closest create a direct connection to the publishing peer (physically at the time of query) to download the content and cache it, and publish the content themselves as publishing peers

2. Use the JXTA network virtualization layer to make a virtual connection between the consumer peer and the peer(s) with the content and then transfer the content

3. Use a scheme where different sub-blocks of the content are transferred between different peers with the requested contents

The first point above is suggests a mechanism that is frequently used in a JXTA network to cause content to statistically replicate from a publisher toward to the population of consumers that may require it. Using this technique, the original publishing peer need not be alive and running when the consumer peer requests the content. In addition, the consumer peer also need not have a direct connection to the original publishing peer. Over time, this scheme will distribute many copies of the same content throughout the P2P network, facilitating the sharing and availability of this content. Combining the content propagate-and-cache scheme with a mechanism to count cache hits will enable a designer to put in place a cache expiry scheme that aims to keep alive the most demanded content over time.

Clearly, the pure P2P content sharing network scheme possible with JXTA can function effectively without any centralized server or addressing schemes. Because of this, the system is able to scale massively in size, and in fact the performance of the system may improve as the size of the system increases.

The Ad-Hoc Messaging Network Pattern

Instant messaging applications are not new. Some form of instant messaging system has existed from the days of the earliest timesharing mainframe systems. For example, many of us are familiar with the 'talk' command made popular by the UNIX operating system. Some of us use the AOL Instant Messenger, Yahoo Messenger, or the MSN Messenger on a daily basis. Some of us may even be IRC night owls. Most of these systems deploy many P2P features in order to enable the system to scale to very large groups of users, however, almost all of them are still based on a centralized in design in order to:

1. Guarantee a minimal level of service

2. Control and monitor the use of the system

Again, the present day popular instant messaging networks illustrate the hybrid approach in system design, leveraging P2P principles where necessarily while relying on robust and proven centralized technology where it is vital. The juxtaposed world is already with us. The following figure illustrates how a system of this type may work.

Figure 6

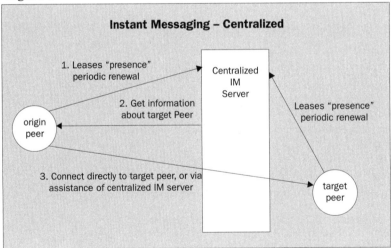

Here, users of the instant messaging network must first sign in to a centralized service to indicate their presence. Their presence is leased to the service, and the user must again approach this centralized service to renew their lease before it expires. This enforces a "regular polling period" policy that the user must adhere to. Users wishing to connect to another user must first contact the centralized server. After obtaining the information required to make a connection, the user can either connect directly to the destination user (P2P-like in this sense) and start communicating, or communicate thorough a centralized service (for example in order for users behind different firewalls to communicate with each other). The popularity of the commercial implementation mentioned above proves that this juxtaposed design works and works very well over today's Internet infrastructure.

Obviously, there also exists a pure P2P solution to the instant messaging problem, and JXTA enables a simple implementation of this solution. Let us take a look at this approach:

1. Each peer establishes its presence by publishing an "available" advertisement (which is always time-expired, and equivalent to a reverse or "pushed" lease) regularly as long as it is up and alive

2. The peer presence advertisements are cached by rendezvous that work together to implement the resolver service for the group

3. A peer wishing to connect to another (called the originating peer) starts a resolver query, looking for the "available" advertisement of the target peer

4. The originating peer receives one or more copies of the "available" advertisement of the target peer

5. The originating peer binds to the pipe of the target peer to communicate with it, sending it its own response pipe advertisement

6. The two peers start messaging each other through their respective pipes

The figure below illustrates this operation.

Figure 7

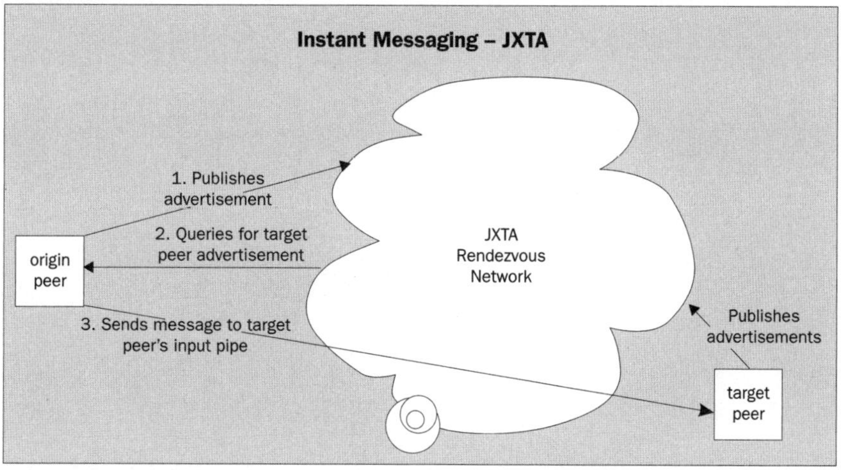

Instant Messaging – JXTA

Note that there is absolutely no centralized registry of users, or centrally maintained addressing scheme (membership database) involved in this design.

In addition, since JXTA pipes are virtualized onto peers, which are in turn virtualized onto heterogeneous transport endpoints, the communications between the peers can be conducted even though no physical connection may exist between directly between the peers involved.

Auto-roaming will certainly be an important application for wireless devices in the near future with the help of JXTA. Imagine a business person communicating with another using JXTA instant messaging over a highly reliable WiFi wireless LAN within the office on their souped up PDA. While chatting, they had to go out of the office and grab lunch. As they fades away from the coverage of the WiFi LAN, the CSMA data support on the wider area cellular network kicks in, the JXTA peer virtualization layer re-establishes the endpoint and the chat continues without skipping a beat. Throughout the day, they can travel in and out of different bidirectional or unidirectional wireless network coverage and all their JXTA-based applications will continue to work as if they had always been connected.

The Distributed Computing "Server Farms" Pattern

Unlike the previous two application patterns, the utility of applications following this pattern has not yet been proven in the P2P world. This may be due to the fact that in this case the P2P network is typically juxtaposed with a centralized work distributor/coordinator. However, a P2P computing substrate such as JXTA does facilitate this sort of application – and potentially some new and attractive solutions can come from this pattern.

The idea is to distribute work among the peers in a peer group, and have the computing resources available within the group shared through the P2P network. In this case, the set of computing peers are viewed as an interconnected farms of "servers", ready and willing to perform work on behalf of a centralized "work generator". Admittedly, having a centralized work generator to create work and collect/correlate the results centrally is not quite a pure P2P architecture. However, one can foresee a P2P variation of this pattern where every peer is potentially a work generator and a result correlator/consolidator. The following figure illustrates these patterns.

Figure 8

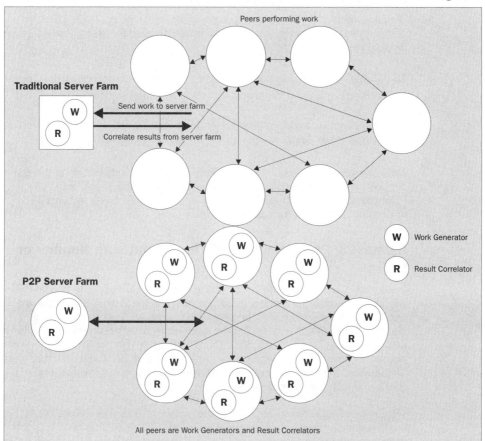

Only certain classes of problems can benefit from this sort of distributed computing. They typically involve the analysis of a massive dataset, involving operations that can be partitioned and be performed in parallel. SETI@home and United Devices have used similar techniques to analyze large and complex datasets for scientific purposes. Other applications for this "brute-force" technique could be weather prediction, cracking sophisticated encryption schemes, and solving high-order complexity problems in theoretical computer science.

Abstracting on Yet Another Level – Meta-Patterns

Understanding the above application patterns may enable us to find problems that map to these patterns, and therefore apply JXTA to solve these problems (or to provide new functionality in certain problem domains). In order to come up with new application patterns, however, we are required to abstract on yet another (higher) level. We may call this level the "meta-pattern" level. More simply put, we should be able to identify certain common properties or patterns that are shared by all P2P applications.

Some Common Properties of these Application Patterns

Well documented by the current community leader of Project JXTA, J.C. Soto, most of the application patterns that JXTA is particularly good for (today) have a couple of common properties:

1. Unlike traditional systems, as the number of users increases the "logical performance" and "statistical throughput" of the system increases

2. Spontaneous and dynamic networking is a major feature that provides added value to the business logic of the application/system

These are very profound observations indeed, and will likely be two of the many differentiators that eventually characterize new "killer applications" for JXTA (and P2P networks in general). Let us spend a little time on each one to better understand these fundamental characteristics.

Increasing Performance and Throughput with Number of Users

In conventional systems with centralized access points, these points become critically stressed as the number of users increase in the system. Eventually, the hardware and bandwidth must be upgraded to accommodate the increasing number of users. JXTA systems, on the other hand, benefit from an increased number of users because their operation is completely decentralized. They do not necessarily have any stress points that can break with an increasing number of users (the only exception with the current design of JXTA is possibly with statically configured relay service nodes).

What is more important is the fact that the normal operation of today's JXTA implementation relies heavily on the propagation and replication of messages/queries and redundancy of cached messages/advertisements. Since the number of available and redundant copies of advertisements, messages, and content will increase as the number of users increase, this means that any individual peer's ability to discover advertisements, messages, content, etc. will be improved. Ultimately this results in improved overall system performance and throughput.

For example, in JXTA-based file sharing systems, the probability of being able to find or retrieve a specific file is increased as the number of users increases. This is largely due to the increased number of cached copies of the files available. Furthermore, since the probability of finding a copy relatively close to you is also increased with the number of users, the observed performance (speed of query response and speed of download) is also improved.

Spontaneous and Dynamic Networking as Added-Value

Unlike conventional applications, spontaneous and dynamic networking – where the topology of the network is intrinsically non-deterministic – is a major plus to JXTA applications. This is uniquely different from the conventional network applications where the static topology of a network is typically exploited to optimize its operation (which is the whole essence of client-server or multi-tiered servers networking).

Even in those cases where the network constituency and topology may change over time, conventional design methodology dictates that the changes should be enumerated and dealt with in a methodical and deterministic manner in order to yield a manageable and realistically implementable design. With the design of JXTA applications or systems, this sort of assumption is no longer applicable.

Non-deterministic network constituency and topology is the norm in JXTA. For most of the application patterns, however, we can see that this adds to the value of the application, rather than detracts from it.

In an instant messaging system, the non-deterministic network constituency and topology is one of the major attractions. The ability to instantly communicate with any member of a very large group, such as worldwide ISPs (AOL, MSN for example) – is a major motivator for users. The promise of continually changing content, colorful discussion, and a constantly changing list of users is the precise allure of a group-chat type application. In all these cases, the spontaneous and dynamic networking that occurs in a non-deterministic manner adds to the perceived value of the system/product.

Identifying the Next Killer Application

While it is anybody's call what the next "killer application" for JXTA may be, one can be quite confident that it will exhibit one or both of the above characteristics to some degree.

Along the same line of thought, we now need to clear up a popular myth – that P2P means PC-to-PC. In fact, this is not the case, and the single most powerful concept in JXTA is peer abstraction. Realizing this will alleviate a "hard" restriction otherwise imposed on our search for new P2P application patterns.

P2P is not PC-to-PC

One misconception that often plagues early P2P practitioners is that P2P means PC-to-PC. While, certainly, at this early stage of development, most early adopters and experimenters of the technology are interacting with the JXTA network through their own PCs, JXTA is specifically designed to operate outside of this restriction.

Recall that binding of a peer to a network endpoint occurs as late as possible. This means that in a JXTA network, a peer has no physical manifestation until the last possible moment! This is most unintuitive, having being bred and groomed in a conventional world of centralized systems.

In absolute static networking terms, P2P is not PC-to-PC, but ether-to-ether.

Before you are tempted to dismiss the above assertion, consider this:

1. Roaming in today's device-rich environment is a very difficult problem to solve using conventional design methodology, but maps nicely to JXTA's late binding

2. Delaying the binding process, and having a lower-layer "platform" perform the tedious work, enables higher-level applications to be created on the peer-to-peer level (or "ether with an identity" to "ether with an identity") level – allowing a simplistic solution to a conventionally complex programming/design problem

Appreciating the above points will enable us to see beyond the restrictions imposed by today's implementation of non-interoperable P2P systems. It may also shed some light on potential new design methodologies and disciplines that may surface for dealing with the new paradigm.

Design Partitioning Considerations

Unlike in the conventional client-server design, the partitioning of a system's functionality into client-side work versus server-side work is not so intuitive and clear-cut in a JXTA system (or P2P systems in general). Yet, the spectrum of partitioning concepts from ultra-thin client/ultra-fat server to ultra-fat client/ultra-thin server is still applicable for the client and server components that are within every peer.

There is a lot of symmetry in a P2P system. That is, the peers in a P2P system are often cookie-cutter images of one another. A thin-client on one peer is therefore likely to be communicating with a fat-service on another peer. However, due to the inherent symmetry, both the thin-client and the fat-service are implemented on the very same peer. In this way, there appears to be a conservation of where work is performed that renders (in the case of perfect symmetry throughout the system) thin/fat architectural discussions totally irrelevant. The figure below illustrates how symmetry in JXTA peers alleviates thin/fat architectural dilemmas.

Figure 9

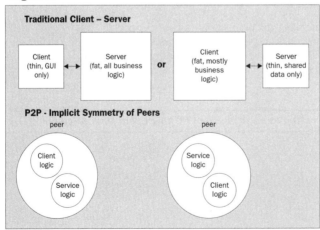

Of course, in real-world implementations, not all peers (if they correlate to machines) have the same capabilities, configurations, connectivity, and computing resources. In most implementation scenarios, there may still need to be some consideration for what should be located on each peer and how resources are apportioned to the client or server functionality provided by that peer. Since we live and work in a P2P juxtaposed world, these practical design decisions can be relegated to the client-server side of the discussion and we will refrain from forming any generalized conclusions.

> *The P2P-pure portion of a JXTA system typically is insensitive to the client or service functionality partitioning that is inherent in the design.*

Therefore, in all of the following discussions, when we speak of "service" and "client" functionality, we must remove the traditional client-server shaded glasses through which we currently see the world. Instead, we should think of them collectively (both client and service functionality) as "peer functionality" – since it is likely that they will live together on the same peer somewhere in the P2P network.

New Partitioning Criteria

The design criteria for the partitioning of client-server functionality are dramatically different from the traditional. Some metrics that are meaningful in a P2P network are meaningless in traditional networks. In P2P systems we will care more about "statistical average peer loading" than empirical "client loading" or "server loading". We may also be partitioning to even out the utilization of bandwidth (statistically) over the various portions of the physical network. These are samples of new criteria in design partitioning that one may need to think about before embarking on the creation of a JXTA application.

Guidelines for Partitioning

If anything, we can deduce some general workable guidelines for partitioning an application into client and service portions, which together form the peer functionality, by examining the two documented application patterns. The following is a brief synopsis of this analysis.

Partition to Leverage Replicated Redundant Storage

We see this in the case of the ad hoc messaging application pattern. Instead of having a centralized server (or clusters of centralized servers) that maintains "presence" information, the equivalent information is replicated and stored redundantly in the JXTA rendezvous network. Partitioning the "presence" portion of the system at this boundary allows us to leverage JXTA, enabling massive scalability without complicated design or coding. This is clearly a far superior solution to this problem than the traditional centralized approach.

In the case of the content sharing network, the partitioning to leverage replicated redundant storage is even more evident. Content itself is being replicated and propagated in this case.

4

Partition to Leverage the Virtualized Network

This is almost an acid test for the P2P suitability of your specific application. If your application can benefit from P2P, it will have a natural partitioning according to these criteria. The idea here is that the concept of "as late as possible" binding will work for your design. In other words, it will actually be beneficial for you not to know until the latest possible moment who you will be talking to and how you will be doing the talking.

The wireless roaming case that we discussed before falls into this category, and is well addressed by JXTA. This specific case leverages the virtualization of peers to physical transport endpoints.

Another example is the implementation of a fault-tolerant facility over a restricted fixed topology network. Utilizing the virtualization of pipes to peers, a network can have redundantly implemented services available to it, and failover will therefore be completely transparent to the client using a virtualized pipe.

By partitioning based on these virtualized network criteria, some subtle variations of conventional applications may become new and potentially "killer apps" in the near future. Observe, for example, how the mundane and unexciting protocol known as FTP can be transformed into the legendary beast formerly known as Napster.

Much more research is due in this fascinating new area of P2P systems and application design. The community-centric approach and the open source availability of JXTA technology will facilitate further exploration from individuals interested in sharing and furthering the art.

Creating Our Very First JXTA Service

Enough design theory and concepts, we are now ready to create our very first bona-fide JXTA service. As mentioned before, we will be using the JXTA EZEL (EZ Entry Library). This will greatly simplify our coding task, and enable us to focus our attention on what is possible with JXTA.

A Simple Service

The first JXTA service we create is a very simple one, conceptually it:

1. Creates a JXTA pipe

2. Listens to the JXTA pipe for incoming requests

The figure below illustrates the operation of this service.

Figure 10

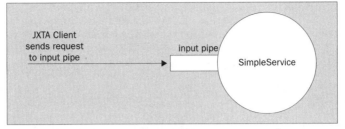

At a conceptual level, this service is indistinguishable from a service that may be listening to a TCP/IP socket for commands. It can provide the same functionality as a socket-based client-server system. The unique thing, of course, is that this is a genuine JXTA P2P service. This means that the service can enjoy the benefit of the virtualized network. Peers can roam between different endpoints while the service is still in operation, clients of the service can be on a completely different transport and may not have direct routes to the service on any particular transport, and clients of the service can survive a reboot or restart of a machine that hosts the service without causing any disruption to the operation of the service.

We find the code to this service, in the `SimpleService.java` file of the sourcecode distribution – part of the `com.wrox.ea.jxtasrvice` package. It is presented below for analysis.

The only strange package in the import list (presented below) is `net.jxta.endpoint.MessageElement`. It basically holds one single element of a structured document in a message. Picture it as one element in an XML document, and that it can also contain sub-elements. Anything that can be placed into an XML element can be sent as a request between the client and the service.

```
package com.wrox.ea.jxtaservice;
import net.jxta.endpoint.MessageElement;
import java.io.*;
```

`ServiceBase`, an abstract class in the EZEL library, does a lot of the work for us and `SimpleService` inherits from this abstract class to gain its functionality. All we need to do is to parameterize the JXTA service in the class constructor. We will explain this parameterization immediately after the listing of the following code:

```
public class SimpleService extends ServiceBase
{
  public SimpleService()
  {
    super(new JXTAServiceInfo("SimpleService",
      "Simple JXTA Service - a Wrox EA Example",
      "1.0", "wrox.com", "http://www.wrox.com/ea/jxta/SimpleService",
      "simpleservice.pipe"
    ));
  }
```

When an incoming message arrives in the JXTA pipe of the service, the serviceLogic() method will be called. This is an abstract method of the ServiceBase class and therefore every subclass must implement its own service logic using this method. The serviceLogic() method is handed an instance of an net.jxta.endpoint.MessageElement, which contains the element of the message (itself a structured document) containing the request from the client. In our implementation, we obtain an input stream from the element, and print it out. Essentially, SimpleService simply prints out the client request.

```java
public void serviceLogic(MessageElement elem)
{
  ByteArrayOutputStream bs = new ByteArrayOutputStream();
  InputStream ip = elem.getStream();

  try
  {
    while (ip.available() > 0)
      bs.write(ip.read());

    bs.flush();

    String cmd = bs.toString();

    System.out.println(cmd);
    bs.close();
  }
  catch (Exception ex) {}
}
```

The main method of the SimpleService class simply creates an instance of the service and calls the init() method. In the current implementation, the init() method will block waiting for incoming pipe messages.

```java
public static void main(String args[])
{
  SimpleService myapp = new SimpleService();
  System.out.println ("Simple service starting...");
  myapp.init();
  System.exit(0);
}
```

And that is all the code that we need to write for creating a JXTA service using EZEL. In fact, the only thing we need to code in detail is the service logic method. Here, we merely print out the incoming request. In production, the service will likely perform some work based on the request.

Therefore, when using EZEL, the only programmatic thing we have to do is to code the service logic, similar to a conventional socket server library. The rest of the JXTA application, we can control declaratively or via parameterization of the constructor. We will look at the constructor parameterization now.

The JxtaServiceInfo Class

A specific class is created, com.wrox.ea.jxta.jxtaservice.JxtaServiceInfo, to encapsulate all the service parameters that are supplied to the EZEL's versatile ServiceBase class. Here is the constructor of the JxtaServiceInfo class.

```
public JXTAServiceInfo(String name, String desc, String ver, String
                       creat, String uri, String pipe);
```

The following is an explanation of each of the arguments in the constructor. They each control a specific aspect of the resulting JXTA service. We have also supplied the parameterization used in the SimpleService coding.

Argument	Description	Parameterization in SimpleService
Name	The name of the service, which will be used in the published service advertisement (actually in the ModuleClass and ModuleSpec advertisement, see below).	"SimpleService"
desc	Description of the service, which will be used in the published service advertisement (actually in the ModuleClass advertisement, see below).	"Simple JXTA Service – a Wrox EA Example"
ver	Version of the service, which will be used in the published service advertisement (actually in the ModuleSpec advertisement, see below)	"1.0"
creat	Creator of the service, it will be used in the published service advertisement (actually in the ModuleSpec advertisement, see below).	"wrox.com"
uri	The URI that uniquely identifies the service, which will be used in the published service advertisement (actually in the ModuleSpec advertisement, see below).	"http://www.wrox.com/ea/jxta/SimpleService"
pipe	The filename of a pipe advertisement that may be used to bind to the output request pipe for the service. It is part of the service advertisement (actually in the free-formed Parm section of the ModuleSpec advertisement). In order to properly survive reboot, we really shouldn't create a new pipe (a pipe with a new Pipe ID) each time the service starts. Therefore, we persist our pipe advertisement to the disk and reuse it each time the service starts. This argument specifies the file name to use for persisting the pipe advertisement. If the pipe advertisement cannot be found, a new one is created and persisted.	"simpleservice.pipe"

The Components of a Service Advertisement

Conceptually, a JXTA service publishes a service advertisement. Initially, in the very first release of JXTA, both service and group advertisements were designed to incorporate all of the information in a service within a single service advertisement. The designers quickly realized, after implementation, that such advertisements are unwieldy in size, and for the usage pattern that applies need not be in an all-in-one form. To reduce the size, and thus enhance typical discovery performance, the conceptual service advertisement is divided up into multiple related advertisements.

Formerly, elements of this advertisement were combined into a large "service advertisement", and a `PeerGroup` advertisement consisted of a series of embedded service advertisements. This had the effect of making most `PeerGroup` advertisements extremely large.

In the current JXTA implementation, a former service advertisement is divided up into a group of three smaller advertisements. These smaller advertisements are:

1. `ModuleClass` advertisement

2. `ModuleSpec` advertisement

3. `ModuleImpl` advertisement

The figure below illustrates the relationship between the different advertisements.

Figure 11

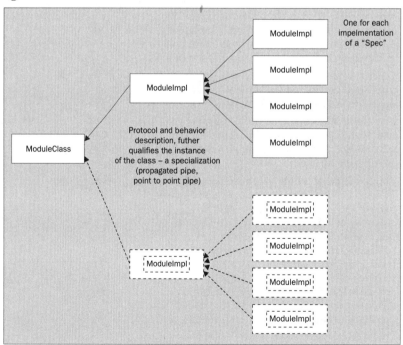

`ModuleClass` advertisements define functionality that exists per platform and is generic within its class. Each instance of this functionality is represented by a `ModuleSpec`, which is a realization of the class in the form of protocols, often referred to as a specialization. Both `ModuleClass` and `ModuleSpec` have a unique ID associated with them. `ModuleImpls` are realizations of a `ModuleSpec` (an implementation). The core idea here is that a client of the service will only need to discover the advertisement that it needs, which will eventually be almost all `ModuleImpls`.

The new design above greatly reduces the bandwidth usage.

The JXTA Work Performed by SimpleService

Coding the `SimpleService` class is simple as child's play. The interaction pattern between service and client is even consistent with the client-server case that we are used to. Hiding the involved operations underneath is exactly what EZEL is built for.

The EZEL libraries encapsulate a lot of complexity. Using the component view offered by the JXTA platform, the EZEL library has actually performed the following for `SimpleService`:

1. Create a `ModuleClass` advertisement

2. Publish the `ModuleClass` advertisement in the group

3. Create a `ModuleSpec` advertisement

4. Create a pipe advertisement for the request pipe

5. Set the `Parm` field of the `ModuleSpec` advertisement with the request pipe advertisement

6. Publish the `ModuleSpec` advertisement in the group

7. Create an input pipe associated with the request pipe

8. Listen for messages from the input pipe

9. Process the request received from the input pipe

Certainly, performing all of the above steps will require many JXTA platform API calls. Thanks to EZEL, extensive coding to perform the above is not required.

Coding a Test Harness for SimpleService

We need a client to test out the `SimpleService` class. Recall in the last chapter that we said the JXTA shell is extremely good for creating quick test clients for new services. We make good on our promise now, and will write a simple shell extension that can be used to test the simple service.

You can find the code to this shell extension in the
`net.jxta.impl.shell.bin.sstest` package, in a new shell command called
`sstest`. To make coding of this client extremely simple, we again make use of an
EZEL class to simplify things. This time a class is used for creating simple clients,
and is called `com.wrox.ea.jxtaservice.ClientBase`. Unlike `ServiceBase`,
`ClientBase` is not an abstract class. This is mainly done by design since client
classes typically need to derive from an alternative hierarchy in order to provide
inherent user interface or application functionality.

The source code for the `sstest` command is in `sstest.java`, and here is the
content of this file:

```
package net.jxta.impl.shell.bin.sstest;

import com.wrox.ea.jxtaservice.ClientBase;
import net.jxta.peergroup.PeerGroup;
import net.jxta.impl.shell.ShellApp;
import net.jxta.impl.shell.ShellEnv;
import net.jxta.impl.shell.ShellObject;

public class sstest extends ShellApp
{
```

Note that we maintain an instance of `ClientBase`, a concrete class in EZEL, to do
all our tough work.

```
ShellEnv env;

private ClientBase myClient = null;

public sstest() {
}

public void stopApp() {
}

public int startApp(String[] args)
{
   env = getEnv();

   // get the std group
   ShellObject obj = env.get("stdgroup");
   PeerGroup group = (PeerGroup)obj.getObject();
```

Once we have obtained our default group, we immediately create an instance of
`ClientBase`, using the name of the service that we want to contact,
`"SimpleService"`, and a `false` flag indicating that we do not want to use the
response pipe in the client (the service does not send a response).

```
    myClient = new ClientBase("SimpleService", false);
```

The client needs to be initialized with our current group, as this will delimit the discovery boundary when looking for services.

```
    myClient.init(group);
```

Once initialized, we can use the client to send a request to the server. In this case, it is a straight text string that contains "This is a request from the sstest client".

```
    myClient.sendRequest("This is a request from the sstest client");

    return ShellApp.appNoError;
}
```

That completes the (very simple) coding of the client, the help() method provides simple usage help with the man command in the shell.

```
  public void help()
  {
    println( "NAME" );
    println( "     sstest  - simple service test" );
    println( " " );
    println( "SYNOPSIS" );
    println( "        sstest");
  }
}
```

Before trying out SimpleService, we must compile the client and service code, and configure the JXTA environment that they will each run on.

Compiling and Testing SimpleService

A Microsoft Win32 batch file, makess.bat, has been provided in the src directory for compilation of the required class, and creation of the JAR file. The resulting jxtaservice.jar file is placed in the lib directory (together with jxta.jar) for easy location.

The makess.bat file contains the following commands:

```
javac -classpath ..\lib\jxta.jar;..\lib\jxtashell.jar -d ..\classes
com\wrox\ea\jxtaservice\*.java
javac -classpath ..\classes;..\lib\jxta.jar;..\lib\jxtashell.jar -d
..\classes net\jxta\impl\shell\bin\sstest\*.java
cd ..\classes
jar cvf ..\lib\jxtaservice.jar .
cd ..\src
```

Now, we can test out the simple service. The simplesrv directory of the source distribution contains a runit.bat Win32 batch file that can be used to start the service. It contains:

```
java -classpath
..\lib\jxta.jar;..\lib\log4j.jar;..\lib\beepcore.jar;..\lib\jxtasecurit
y.jar;..\lib\cryptix-asn1.jar;..\lib\cryptix32.jar;
..\lib\minimalBC.jar;..\lib\jxtaptls.jar;..\lib\jxtaservice.jar
com.wrox.ea.jxtaservice.SimpleService
```

The JXTA platform configuration GUI will come up the first time you start this service (if not, remove the cm and pse directory, and also any PlatformConfig file in the same directory). Configure this peer with the following:

Item to Configure	Value
Peer Name	node1
Transport	Disable: HTTP
	Enable: TCP, manual, localhost, port 9701
Rendezvous Router	Not using rendezvous, not using router
Security	Configure with your own ID and password

This will start simple service, which will create the input pipe and advertise it in the default NetPeerGroup (stdgroup). Your command screen should be similar to the screenshot below.

At the time of writing, certain binary distributions of the JXTA platform contain a bug where the built-in dependency on a Jetty servlet library causes a PeerGroup Exception when the third-party libraries are not found in the classpath during module loading. It has no detrimental effect to our experimentation, and you can safely ignore this exception. This bug may be fixed by the time you try the examples.

The simple service is now ready for commands from the client.

To open another command window go to the `test2` directory of the source distribution – we will start a shell from here and install the `sstest` command for the test. Use the runshell.bat batch file that we are familiar with to start this shell instance.

Set the JXTA configuration of this shell instance to be as follows (delete the `cm`, and `pse` directories, and `PlatformConfig` file if necessary):

Item to Configure	Value
Peer Name	node2
Transport	Disable: HTTP
	Enable: TCP, manual, localhost, port 9703
Rendezvous/Router	Not using rendezvous, not using router
Security	Configure with your own ID and password

Note that the two peers, `node1` and `node2`, are set to use TCP transport only and loop back on the local host to simulate the JXTA network. This is similar to our early shell testing.

After configuration, we should see an instance of the shell running. Next, we need to install our custom command, `sstest`. It is part of the shell extension in the resulting `jxtaservice.jar` file. From the shell, use the following to install the shell command.

```
JXTA> instjar ..\lib\jxtaservice.jar
```

You can verify that the JAR file is installed using:

```
JXTA> instjar
0 ..\lib\jxtaservice.jar
```

Now, watch the running simple service screen carefully, and issue the `sstest` command from the shell:

```
JXTA> sstest
```

In the `SimpleService` window we can see that indeed a request has made its way through the virtualized network from the client peer to the service peer. The following screenshot should be similar to what you see.

```
C:\WINNT\System32\cmd.exe                                              _□×
Security initialization in progress.
This will take 10 or more seconds ...

Getting DiscoveryService
Getting PipeService
Start the Server daemon
Trying to read simpleservice.pipe
jxta:MSA :
        MSID : urn:jxta:uuid-03B331CE63A34C52857AA5C2E0595F2BDF9FAED955B54DBDBC5
5BB7B57D28F7A06
        Name : JXTASPEC:SimpleService
        Crtr : wrox.com
        SURI : http://www.wrox.com/ea/jxta/SimpleService
        Vers : 1.0
        Parm :
                jxta:PipeAdvertisement :
                        Id : urn:jxta:uuid-5961626164616261 4E504720503250337CC19
0C2A7CB461BAE9B92874B2531FC04
                        Type : JxtaUnicast
                        Name : JXTASPEC:SimpleService

Waiting for client messages to arrive....
ServiceBase: A request has been received!
This is request for the client
```

If you look back at the command window that you started the shell instance from, you will also see a debug trace that shows us what is happening underneath. The output should be similar to:

```
C:\WINNT\System32\cmd.exe                                              _□×
ClientBase: found the advertisement
jxta:MSA :
        MSID : urn:jxta:uuid-03B331CE63A34C52857AA5C2E0595F2BDF9FAED955B54DBDBC5
5BB7B57D28F7A06
        Name : JXTASPEC:SimpleService
        Crtr : wrox.com
        SURI : http://www.wrox.com/ea/jxta/SimpleService
        Vers : 1.0
        Parm : null
                jxta:PipeAdvertisement :
                        Id : urn:jxta:uuid-5961626164616261 4E504720503250337CC19
0C2A7CB461BAE9B92874B2531FC04
                        Type : JxtaUnicast
                        Name : JXTASPEC:SimpleService

parsing <jxta:PipeAdvertisement>
parsing <Id>
parsing <Type>
parsing <Name>
Pipe ID is urn:jxta:uuid-5961626164616261 4E504720503250337CC190C2A7CB461BAE9B928
74B2531FC04
ClientBase: Output Pipe Created...
ClientBase: Output Pipe Ready - creating a response input pipe now!
ClientBase: message "This is request for the client" sent to the Server
```

Thanks to the EZEL library `ClientBase` class, the client located the service and communicated with it. Here is what happened underneath, illustrating the JXTA platform APIs that EZEL must call:

1. The client uses the JXTA resolver service to perform a distributed query for a `ModuleSpec` advertisement that is named `"SimpleService"`

2. The resulting response, the `ModuleSpec` advertisement of `"SimpleService"`, contains the pipe advertisement of the service's request pipe embedded in the `Parm` element

3. Extract this pipe advertisement

4. Bind the `"SimpleService"` pipe advertisement to an output pipe

5. Create a pipe message

6. Add a document element called `"tagdata"` and insert a simple request

7. Send the pipe message to the server

Of course, the request sent can be as complex as the application demands, and we use a simple string here to illustrate the basic concept.

Creating a More Complex JXTA Service

The simple request we have created is, well, quite simple. It only receives requests from clients, and does not provide any response (not via the JXTA network anyway – it may indeed be using more traditional, non-P2P means of accomplishing further communication).

The next example that we will look at creates a more complex JXTA service, a respond service. The interaction pattern of this service is illustrated below.

Figure 12

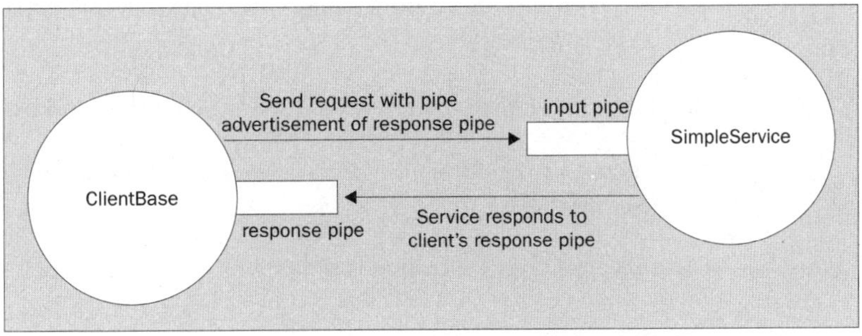

In the figure above, we can see that the client now creates its own input pipe and listens to it for responses from the server. Since JXTA pipes are intrinsically unidirectional (and the transport underneath can indeed be unidirectional), the creation of two pipes is necessary for receiving responses from the service.

Be aware that the path that the client-to-service request travels can be completely different from the path that the service-to-client response goes through. Completely different transports may be used in each case; this is the nature of JXTA.

The respond service's sourcecode is found in the `com.wrox.ea.jxtaservice` package, and is called `RespondService.java`. Here it is reproduced for analysis:

```
package com.wrox.ea.jxtaservice;
package com.wrox.ea.jxtaservice;
import net.jxta.endpoint.MessageElement;
import java.io.InputStream;
```

Note that `RespondService` class inherits from the same versatile EZEL `SerivceBase` abstract class. Note, however, that the constructor we use has one extra argument – a Boolean variable at the end that we set to `true`. This alternative constructor notifies the `ServiceBase` abstract class that this service will generate a response. The rest of the arguments are similar to those of `SimpleService`, with the changes corresponding to the change of the service name.

```
public class RespondService extends ServiceBase
{
  public RespondService()
  {
    super(new JXTAServiceInfo("RespondService",
        "JXTA Service with Respond Pipe - a Wrox EA Example",
        "1.0", "wrox.com",
"http://www.wrox.com/ea/jxta/RespondService",
        "respondservice.pipe",
        true));
  }
```

By notifying the `ServiceBase` class that this service will send a response, the underlying EZEL implementation will perform several additional tasks after receiving a request from the client:

1. Extract the client response pipe advertisement that is part of the request message

2. Bind an output pipe associated with the client response pipe

3. Upon command from the service, send a response to the client via the response pipe

The `serviceLogic()` method is similar to `SimpleService`; it simply prints out the message element (request) that is received from the client.

```
public void serviceLogic(MessageElement elem)
{
  InputStream ip = elem.getStream();
```

```
    try
    {
      while (ip.available() > 0)
        System.out.write(ip.read());
    }
    catch (Exception ex) {}

    System.out.flush();
  }
```

In this service, we override a virtual method called `respondLogic()`. This is called after the `serviceLogic()` method has been completed, and the pipe binding to the client is successful. The returned string form this `respondLogic()` method is stored in the response message destined for the client.

```
public String respondLogic()
{
  System.out.println("RESP SERV: respond logic called");

  return ("my final answer");
}
```

Like the simple service, the main method of `RespondService` simply starts an instance of the service, initializes it, then waits for incoming client requests.

```
public static void main(String args[])
{

  RespondService myapp = new RespondService();
  System.out.println ("Service with Response pipes starting...");
  myapp.init();
  System.exit(0);

}
}
```

Again, the EZEL `ServiceBase` class has made implementation very simple. We can now turn our attention in the creation of the test client, another shell extension.

Creating the RespondService Test Client

The test client for the respond service can be found in the `net.jxta.impl.shell.bin.rptest` package. It is called `rptest.java`. As with the `sstest` command before, it makes use of the EZEL `ClientBase` concrete class to simplify the code.

The `rptest.java` file is reproduced below for analysis. If you compare this to the `sstest` command earlier, the highlighted lines are the only differences you will find.

4

```
package net.jxta.impl.shell.bin.rptest;
import net.jxta.impl.shell.ShellApp;
import net.jxta.impl.shell.ShellEnv;
import net.jxta.impl.shell.ShellObject;
import com.wrox.ea.jxtaservice.ClientBase;
import net.jxta.peergroup.PeerGroup;
import net.jxta.endpoint.MessageElement;
import java.io.InputStream;

public class rptest extends ShellApp
{
  ShellEnv env;

  private ClientBase myClient = null;

  public rptest() {
  }

  public void stopApp() {
  }

  public int startApp (String[] args)
  {
    env = getEnv();

    // get the std group
    ShellObject obj = env.get("stdgroup");

    PeerGroup group = (PeerGroup)obj.getObject();
```

While the initial changes are all due to changing the command name from `sstest` to `rptest`, the following change when instantiating the `ClientBase` instance is important. Here, we set the second argument to `true`, indicating that the `ClientBase` class should handle the response from the server. In addition, we use an anonymous class definition to override the `ClientBase processResponse()` method. This method is called when the response from the server is received in the client's response pipe. In our case, we simply print out the response received. Real-world applications may need to process this response appropriately.

```
    myClient =  new ClientBase("RespondService", true)
    {
      protected void processResponse(MessageElement payload)
      {
        System.out.println("Response received...");

        try
```

```
          {
            InputStream  is = payload.getStream();

            while (is.available() > 0)
            {
              System.out.write(is.read());
            }
              System.out.flush();
              is.close();
            }
            catch (Exception ex) {}
        }
      };
```

```
  myClient.init(group);
  myClient.sendRequestToService("Request from client");
  return ShellApp.appNoError;
}

public void help()
{
  println( "NAME" );
  println( "    rptest - respondService test" );
  println( " " );
  println( "SYNOPSIS" );
  println( "        rptest");
}
}
```

The rest of this test client is very similar to sstest presented before.

Compiling and Testing RespondService

Use the makerp.bat Win32 batch file in the src directory of the source
distribution to compile the RespondService class and the rptest test client, and
create the required jxtaservice.jar file. After successful compilation, start up
the JXTA shell in the test2 directory that was used in earlier testing. Verify its
current configuration with the following details:

Item to Configure	Value
Peer Name	node2
Transport	Disable: HTTP
	Enable: TCP, manual, localhost, port 9703
Rendezvous/Router	Not using rendezvous, not using router
Security	Configure with your own ID and password

Now, install the client shell extension using the `instjar` command:

JXTA> **instjar ..\lib\jxtaservice.jar**

Next, to start another command window change into the `respsvr` directory of the source distribution. Use the `runit.bat` batch file to start the respond service. The batch file contains:

```
java -classpath
..\lib\jxta.jar;..\lib\log4j.jar;..\lib\beepcore.jar;..\lib\jxtasecurit
y.jar;..\lib\cryptix-
asn1.jar;..\lib\cryptix32.jar;..\lib\minimalBC.jar;..\lib\jxtaptls.jar;
..\lib\jxtaservice.jar com.wrox.ea.jxtaservice.RespondService
```

Configure the JXTA platform on this `RespondService` as follows:

Item to Configure	Value
Peer Name	node1
Transport	Disable: HTTP
	Enable: TCP, manual, localhost, port 9701
Rendezvous/Router	Not using rendezvous, not using router
Security	Configure with your own ID and password

Again, we have two peers using TCP transport only, looping back on the local host for testing.

At this point, the respond service should be started up, waiting for a request from the client. Your output should be similar to:

Move over to the shell that is currently running on `node2` and load the shell extension with the `rptest` command:

JXTA> **instjar ..\lib\jxtaservice.jar**

Next, enter the `RespondService` testing command.

JXTA> **rptest**

Back in the `RespondService` command window, you should see output as below:

```
C:\WINNT\System32\cmd.exe                                                  _ □ x
Getting DiscoveryService
Getting PipeService
Start the Server daemon
Trying to read respondservice.pipe
jxta:MSA :
        MSID : urn:jxta:uuid-B4F08D9D80254DFA850481A31508C7F79109A7ED047E4E60ADA
F9800404F0F0806
        Name : JXTASPEC:RespondService
        Crtr : wrox.com
        SURI : http://www.wrox.com/ea/jxta/RespondService
        Vers : 1.0
        Parm :
                jxta:PipeAdvertisement :
                        Id : urn:jxta:uuid-5961626164616261 4E5047205032503360940
097144B4C329BB29C2DD9F96EEE04
                        Type : JxtaUnicast
                        Name : JXTASPEC:RespondService

Waiting for client messages to arrive....
ServiceBase: A request has been received!
Request from clientFOUND A REPLY PIPE
ServiceBase: Output Pipe Ready - sending a message to the pipe now!
RESP SERV: respond logic called
ServiceBase: response message "my final answer" sent back to the client
```

Here, we can see that the respond service has received the request from the client, bound to the client's response pipe, and sent a response back to the client.

In the command console where you have started the shell, you should also see debug traces similar to:

```
C:\WINNT\System32\cmd.exe                                                  _ □ x
        MSID : urn:jxta:uuid-B4F08D9D80254DFA850481A31508C7F79109A7ED047E4E60ADA
F9800404F0F0806
        Name : JXTASPEC:RespondService
        Crtr : wrox.com
        SURI : http://www.wrox.com/ea/jxta/RespondService
        Vers : 1.0
        Parm : null
                jxta:PipeAdvertisement :
                        Id : urn:jxta:uuid-5961626164616261 4E5047205032503360940
097144B4C329BB29C2DD9F96EEE04
                        Type : JxtaUnicast
                        Name : JXTASPEC:RespondService

parsing <jxta:PipeAdvertisement>
parsing <Id>
parsing <Type>
parsing <Name>
Pipe ID is urn:jxta:uuid-5961626164616261 4E5047205032503360940097144B4C329BB29C2
DD9F96EEE04
ClientBase: Output Pipe Created...
ClientBase: Output Pipe Ready - creating a response input pipe now!
ClientBase: message "Request from client" sent to the Server
Clientbase: A response has been received!
Response received...
my final answer_
```

Here, we can see clearly that the client has received the response across the JXTA network.

Creating Indomitable Peer-Group Services

Recall earlier in our conceptual discussion that a JXTA service can either be a peer service, or a peer-group service. A peer service is what we have been creating so far; it is associated with a peer, and if that peers dies or goes away the peer service becomes unavailable.

A JXTA peer-group service, on the other hand, is associated with the group. This enables multiple instances of the service to be started on the group, and the service will be available as long as at least one instance of the service is still running. The JXTA Resolver service is an example of a JXTA peer group service.

We can also create our own peer group services. Using the JXTA platform to create peer-group services is not for the faint hearted. This is due to the fact that a very low-level API must be used (at the time of writing) to implement peer-group services. The JXTA peer-group picture is also rather vague, and it is reflected in the API, adding the possibility of rapid change to an already complex issue. EZEL, of course, was designed specifically to eliminate these concerns. In fact, creating a peer-group service using EZEL is simpler than creating a peer service.

The example peer-group service that we will create is called "simple group service" and consists of the SimpleGroupService class. You can find SimpleGroupService.java in the com.wrox.ea.jxtaservice package.

The sourcecode of SimpleGroupService.java is:

```java
import net.jxta.endpoint.Message;
import net.jxta.protocol.ResolverResponseMsg;
import java.io.*;

public class SimpleGroupService extends PGServiceBase
{
  public SimpleGroupService(String svcName)
  {
    super(svcName);
  }

  protected void serviceLogic(Message msg)
  {
    System.out.println("... gotta request...");
    String myCommand = msg.getString(clientDataTag);
    System.out.println(myCommand);
  }
}
```

Is this it? The answer is YES!

Simply inherit from a magical `PGServiceBase` abstract class, and implement the `serviceLogic()` method with your own service logic. There is all there is to it!

The main reason for this simplicity is the level of abstraction that EZEL attempts to provide. It is expected that the JXTA group management mechanism will be responsible for creating and publishing the advertisement of a peer-group service, and ensuring that an instance of the peer-group service is started on each peer that joins the group. Unfortunately, this mechanism is not quite yet in place within the JXTA platform (and will not be until the role of a group is completely understood). In the meantime, EZEL provides a helper class, called the `PGServiceHost`. We derive a class called `SimpleGroupServiceHost` from `PGServiceHost`. Here is the code from our `SimpleGroupServiceHost.java` file:

```
package com.wrox.ea.jxtaservice;
import net.jxta.peergroup.PeerGroup;
import net.jxta.exception.PeerGroupException;

public class SimpleGroupServiceHost extends PGServiceHost {

  public SimpleGroupServiceHost() {
  }
```

The crux of the host implementation is the static `getInstance()` method. This ensures that only one instance of the service is executed on the peer (actually, if the peer can join other groups, this should be modified to maintain one instance of the service per group). Note that the method will:

1. Create a new instance of the `SimpleGroupService` if it does not exist already

2. Call its `init()` method with the appropriate group

3. Call its `StartApp()` method

This simulates the function of a JXTA group, which will be the actions that the group takes to ensure that an instance of the peer-group service is started on every peer.

```
private static SimpleGroupService serviceInstance = null;

public static SimpleGroupService getInstance(PeerGroup group)
{
  if (serviceInstance == null)
  {
    serviceInstance = new SimpleGroupService("SimpleGroupService");

    try
    {
      serviceInstance.init(group, null, null);
```

```
        }
     catch (PeerGroupException e)
     {
        e.printStackTrace();
     }

     serviceInstance.startApp(null) ;
   }

   return serviceInstance;
}
```

The main method uses the getInstance() method to find the SimpleGroupService. It uses the PGServiceHost waitForRequest() method to wait for client requests.

```
public static void main(String args[])
{
   SimpleGroupServiceHost myHost = new SimpleGroupServiceHost();
   myHost.init();
   SimpleGroupService myapp = myHost.getInstance(myHost.getGroup());
   System.out.println ("Simple GROUP service starting...");
   myHost.waitForRequests();
   System.exit(0);
   }
}
```

Creating the Peer-Group Service Test Client

The test client for the simple group service can be found in the net.jxta.impl.shell.bin.pgtest package. It is located in the pgtest.java file. Again, we use a concrete class from EZEL, called PGClientBase, to simplify our implementation of the peer-group service client:

```
package net.jxta.impl.shell.bin.pgtest;
import com.wrox.ea.jxtaservice.PGClientBase;
import net.jxta.impl.shell.ShellApp;
import net.jxta.impl.shell.ShellEnv;
import net.jxta.impl.shell.ShellObject;
import net.jxta.peergroup.PeerGroup;
```

The variable myClient will hold the instance of PGClientBase that will do all the work for us.

```
public class pgtest extends ShellApp
{
   ShellEnv env;
   private PGClientBase myClient;
```

```
public pgtest() {
}

public void stopApp () {
}

public int startApp (String[] args)
{
  env = getEnv();

  // get the std group
  ShellObject obj = env.get("stdgroup");
```

We create an instance of PGClientBase, passing it the name of
"SimpleGroupService" that it should communicate with. We then initialize the
instance with our default NetPeerGroup.

```
PeerGroup group = (PeerGroup)obj.getObject();
myClient = new PGClientBase("SimpleGroupService");
myClient.init(group);
```

Finally, we send a message to the peer-group service using the
sendMessageToService() method. Here, we simply send a string, but it can
easily be an XML structured document if we wished.

```
myClient.sendMessageToService("Client and service in an
  unbreakable link!");

  return ShellApp.appNoError;
}

public void help()
{
  println( "NAME" );
  println( "    pgtest - peergroup service test" );
  println( " " );
  println( "SYNOPSIS" );
  println( "        pgtest");
}
}
```

Understanding the Operation of Peer-Group Services

Use the `makepg.bat` file to compile the peer-group service, the test client, and create the `jxtaservice.jar` file that is required for testing.

To test the operation of the peer-group service, we need to create:

1. One instance of the shell at `node2` as before

2. One instance of the peer-group service at `node1`

3. One instance of the peer-group service at `node3`

The idea here is to use `node2` as the client, and observe that the `SimpleGroupService` instance at either `node1` or `node3` will be used during normal operation. If we then simply shut down one of the nodes, say `node3`, then the `SimpleGroupService` instance at `node1` will be used exclusively. If we now shut down `node1` and restart `node3`, the `SimpleGroupService` instance at `node3` will be used again. This illustrates conclusively that a peer-group service will be available as long as one single instance still exists within the group – providing very high availability for all the peers in the group. The screenshot below illustrates this testing scenario.

Now, let us configure the three nodes according to the following settings:

To start the shell, go to the `test2` directory, and execute `runshell.bat`. Verify the configuration as:

Item to Configure	Value
Peer Name	node2
Transport	Disable: HTTP
	Enable: TCP, manual, localhost, port 9703
Rendezvous/Router	Not using rendezvous, not using router
Security	Configure with your own ID and password

Now, use the following to load the shell extension that contains the `pgtest` command:

```
JXTA> instjar ..\lib\jxtaservice.jar
```

Next, go to the `pgserv1` directory and execute the `runit.bat` file there to start an instance of the `SimpleGroupServiceHost`. Configure this node as:

Item to Configure	Value
Peer Name	node1
Transport	Disable: HTTP
	Enable: TCP, manual, localhost, port 9701
Rendezvous/Router	Not using rendezvous, not using router
Security	Configure with your own ID and password.

The instance of `SimpleGroupService` should be waiting for client requests. Your output should be similar to:

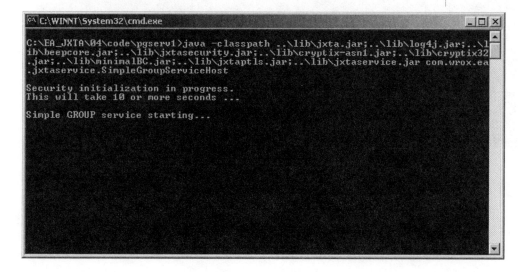

To start another peer with a redundant `SimpleGroupService` instance, go to the `pgserv2` directory and execute the `runit.bat` file to start another instance. Configure this peer as:

Item to Configure	Value
Peer Name	node3
Transport	Disable: HTTP
	Enable: TCP, manual, localhost, port 9705
Rendezvous/Router	Not using rendezvous, not using router
Security	Configure with your own ID and password

Now we are ready to test out action of the peer group service. Go to the shell and enter the test command:

`JXTA> ` **`pgtest`**

On either `node1` or `node3`, the `SimpleGroupService` will have reported a request arrival. Note that, because of the non-deterministic nature of JXTA networks, we cannot predict which one of the redundant instances will be contacted. Keep trying it yourself and see that sometimes the request reaches one instance, and sometimes the other (or always one instance). A message arrival at `node3` is illustrated in below:

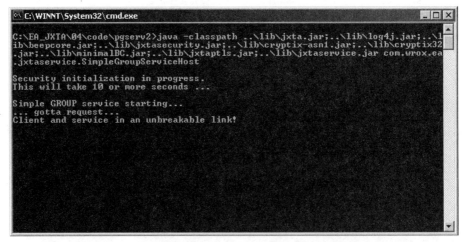

Now, hit *Control-c* or break out of the `SimpleGroupService` running on `node3`. The only remaining `SimpleGroupService` is now on `node1`. Try the test command in the shell again. Note that now the client reaches only the instance running on `node1`.

Once you're convinced that all requests now go to `node1`, break out of the `node1` instance, and restart the `node3` instance of the `SimpleGroupService`. Try the test command in the shell again.

Lo and behold, the client has located the only remaining instance of the service on the resurrected `node3` and started using it.

One can easily imagine the application that this sort of redundant instance with automatic reconnect would be good for. Peer-group services are another aspect of JXTA that can be readily exploited.

Due to the complexity of the underlying work performed by EZEL, we will postpone the discussion of what is actually happening underneath at the JXTA platform until the next chapter.

Summary

In this chapter, we have examined the architecture of a JXTA system and contrasted it with the conventional client-server systems that we are familiar with.

We have examined a couple of applications patterns that P2P systems have proven to be effective in, and surmise that any applications that follow these patterns will benefit from a JXTA implementation.

Abstracting common properties from the application patterns, we are able to deduce some meta-patterns that all future P2P applications should have in common. The inverted response of better performance with higher loading is one such property, as is the ability to add value through formation of dynamic and spontaneous networks.

When designing P2P applications, we have discovered that partitioning of client and server-side work is a rather artificial exercise – due to the inherent symmetry of P2P networks. We concluded that a new and non-conventional set of partitioning goals and criteria must be used, and provided a few possible example criteria.

In the second part of the chapter, we created many JXTA services. The `SimpleService` class is a JXTA service that takes a request from a client through its own response pipe. The `RespondService` class is a JXTA service that is identical to `SimpleService`, but also sends a response back from the service to the client's response pipe. The `SimpleGroupService` class is a peer-group service that can be redundantly implemented across a peer group.

Using the versatile EZEL library we created each of these JXTA services, as well as corresponding test clients that are implemented in the form of JXTA shell extensions. We configured multiple peers on a loop-back via a TCP transport and performed the test of our JXTA services on a single machine.

Without the EZEL, we will not have been able to cover so much ground and create three different JXTA services with three different clients in the space of one single chapter. In the next chapter, however, we will get under the hood and reveal how EZEL performs its job.

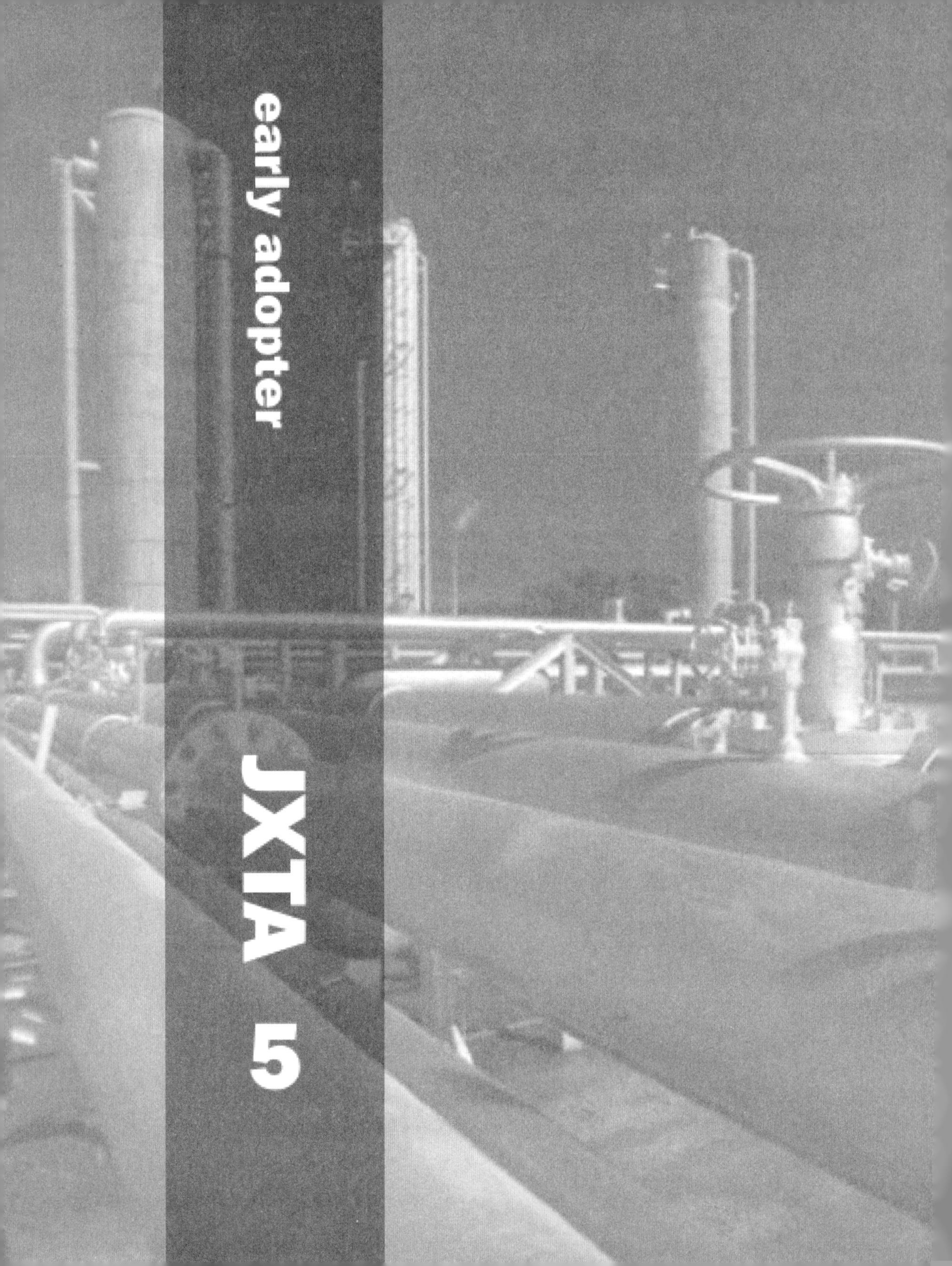
early adopter
JXTA 5

Programming the JXTA Platfrom

The purpose of this chapter is two-fold. First, we continue our coverage of the EZEL library for JXTA, a programming library that assisted us in our exploration of JXTA service and client creation in the last chapter. Secondly, we will learn how to program the JXTA platform using the APIs supporting the component view.

Our coverage of the EZEL library will include:

❏   The rationale for its design

❏   The goals of the library

❏   The anticipated usage patterns of the library

❏   The code modules that make up the library

❏   Future expansion possibilities for the library

❏   How the library will change in the future

In the second part of the chapter, we will actually present the sourcecode of the EZEL, library, one module at a time. Looking through the EZEL code, we will discover how to:

❏   Create JXTA services using the Platform API

❏   Create JXTA group services using the Platform API

❏   Create JXTA clients for the various styles of services

❏   Work with JXTA pipes on a low level

❏   Work with the JXTA Resolver service

❑   Code with the JXTA Endpoint service

❑   Create our own fault-resilient peer-group service using the Platform API

By understanding how EZEL works under the hood, we will be able to better utilize it during our day-to-day JXTA programming. This knowledge will allow us to supplement EZEL with direct Platform API programming if necessary. Furthermore, it opens up the possibility of modifying EZEL for our own needs or tastes.

The JXTA EZ Entry Library

The main rationale behind the creation EZEL is this:

> *Learning how to program in JXTA, via the raw Platform API, requires a steep learning curve!*

It is difficult because of a major conceptual hurdle, transitioning from client-server to P2P, as well as a vast and interrelated Platform API with a profusion of specific terminology. The fact that JXTA is still in a very early stage of development, with certain functionality drifting in and out of stable operation, further increases the learning curve required to master the technology.

EZEL is designed to make the transition to JXTA programming as painless as possible. It does so by catering to the traditional client-server programming principals that most developers are already familiar with. EZEL provides a programming model that centers around:

1.   Services

2.   Clients

Services receive requests from clients and process them, optionally generating responses. Clients send requests to services, in order to have some work performed on their behalf. This interaction pattern is completely identical in JXTA to that in the conventional client-server world. The major difference, of course, is that a typical JXTA peer takes on a balance of both client and service functionality – as described in previous chapters.

EZEL itself is a layer of APIs written directly on top of the JXTA core Platform API, shielding its complexity from developers using it. When using EZEL, the component view provided by the JXTA platform needs not be directly visible to the EZEL user unless they desire access at that level.

Design Goals of EZEL

Visiting the design goals of EZEL will enable us to appreciate how best to utilize the library, and give some insight on where and how it will grow in the near future.

To recap, the main design goal of EZEL is to:

❑ Create a library that will make programming JXTA easy for developers already familiar with standard client-server style programming

Alongside this goal we have a couple of secondary design goals of EZEL that add value to the library. They also guide the evolution of the library as it grows and matures. These secondary goals include:

1. Buffer and isolate changes in the underlying API

2. Enable easy JXTA target integration into popular IDEs

The following is a brief description of each of these sub-goals and a description of some of the measures that EZEL takes in order to try and meet these goals.

Isolation of Change

JXTA, being still in its very early stage of development, is subject to constant changes. In fact, changes may come both at the programming API level, and occasionally even at the protocol/specification level. Any application that is written directly to the API, or generates protocol messages directly, will need to closely track these changes as they take place. The larger body of code, the more difficult this tracking will be.

At the time of writing, many aspects of the JXTA platform (including the underlying protocols) are still being defined and refined. Without EZEL, every single developer, including new developers experimenting with JXTA, will constantly have to modify their code to match the changing platform API.

EZEL provides a higher-level, client-service-based view and interface to the applications whenever possible. Where this is not possible – for example, when working directly with components in the components view of JXTA (such as pipes, advertisements) – the most common operations performed are extracted, and the API code that actually performs the most common operations with these components is bundled together and assembled into readily callable APIs.

This means that in most cases, user of EZEL will not have to change the code that they have developed even if the underlying JXTA platform API changes. Instead, one only needs to update the older version of EZEL to a newer one that matches the JXTA platform you wish to use.

EZEL buffers change of the underlying platform from the application programmer, enabling developers to better focus on their application domains. Complexity is greatly reduced when this goal is reached, and a larger population of developers will find experimentation with JXTA both enjoyable and rewarding.

Ease of Integration into IDE Tools

While it may sounds like a goal of a tool vendor to increase sales, this is in fact one of the best ways (and least known) to capture the imagination of the largest possible pool of developers. In other words, "let them try it and they will come".

5

Incorporating JXTA client-service target designer functionality into IDE tools can be a key accelerator for the adoption of JXTA by mainstream developers. More developers may experiment with JXTA technology if their favorite IDE tool can generate the code skeletons required for JXTA-based applications with one button click. EZEL is designed with facilitating IDE tool integration from day one. Eventually, it is hoped that additional project members will realize this goal of creating target plug-ins for some of the most popular Java IDEs available, such as JBuilder, Webgain, Forte, and VisualAge.

To make EZEL friendly to the large variety of IDEs available, it is vital to ensure that the class design within EZEL enables programming that is:

1. Regular and easy to generate

2. Lends itself to "data-driven" or "declarative" configurations (similar to the deployment/run time configuration in J2EE servlet engines)

In general, following the first point above will lead to rapid and easy-to-program coding, and therefore it is a win-win situation for EZEL. The second point is more interesting, and is an attribute that JXTA is already beginning to take on that is likely to be even more pronounced as the Platform evolves.

Here is the model that EZEL follows, which mirrors what is happening within the design of JXTA as well. More classic systems such as the Tomcat reference engine have also adopted a similar scheme. The figure below illustrates this model.

Figure 1

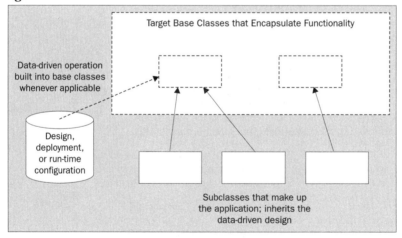

In this model, code structure is provided to incorporate application logic wherever necessary (and these locations will become obvious as the technology matures and the application pattern stabilizes), while the crux of customization occurs in terms of declarative programming (also called deployment/run-time configuration). Take an example in JXTA: since the number of transports is finite and the coupling between the transport and higher level is (or will be somewhat) fixed, we can relegate the composition of the transport used in a JXTA peer to a run-time configuration (an example is the GUI configurator in JXTA that appears the first time when you start the JXTA platform)

In EZEL, a JXTA service that is created using the `ServiceBase` abstract class may or may not send responses back to a client. The same physical code base is used to implement both a responding service and a non-responding service, the difference, as we discovered in the last chapter, is the use of a Boolean flag variable (data-driven) to indicate the type of the server.

Another example in EZEL is that whenever one creates a JXTA service, there is a mundane set of "must do" procedures that includes creating advertisements, creating pipes, registering listeners for pipe messages, etc. However, in EZEL this is all part of the library code. The interface we adopt to configure this part of the process is completely data-driven through an additional data encapsulation class called `JxtaServiceInfo`.

Following this design philosophy will ensure that EZEL (and therefore JXTA services and clients) can be integrated relatively easily into most modern IDE tools. EZEL's ability to isolate the JXTA API and lower-level changes will further benefit the IDE "plug-ins" that can be created – they will be buffered from the low-level changes at the Platform API and protocol level that may occur from time to time.

EZEL as a Work in Progress

EZEL is not complete at this time. In fact, it will remain a living project, likely to be hosted at the JXTA community site **www.jxta.org**. It cannot be completed at this time because:

1. The JXTA project itself is not yet completed

2. Many aspects of the JXTA model of operation still need to be worked out (security, membership policies, etc.)

3. The depth of programming experience with JXTA is still very shallow

The last point deserves some additional mention. As JXTA matures, a set of "best practices" will be discovered – typically through blood and sweat, and trial-and-error in the field – for implementation of JXTA systems or coding of JXTA applications. Over time, it is the intention that EZEL will capture this pool of knowledge and make it part of EZEL itself. For now, EZEL rests as a library that can get people using JXTA immediately, without hesitation, without days and days of roaming through cryptic code or weeding through outdated documentation or tutorials.

> *Due to lead-time required in book publishing, by the time you read this, the actual EZEL implementation will have evolved significantly. Please note that all samples using EZEL and the EZEL code within this chapter assume that the service and clients all work over the default* `NetPeerGroup` *that is associated with the default application created by the Platform. This is essentially a peer group consisting of "everyone on the reachable JXTA network". A very large classification of JXTA applications can work over this simplistic assumption (most applications that are using the content sharing application pattern, or the instant messaging application pattern fall into this category). Some readers, however, may need more flexibility in creating more restrictive groups in their applications. EZEL is being evolved to accommodate services that can start in a particular group other than the default. Please consult the latest EZEL library sourcecode to see how this is accomplished.*

5

The Architecture of EZEL

The architecture of the EZEL library is extremely simple to follow. It consists of several base classes, one corresponding to each type of service or client target – as well as a collection of "Mechanix" classes that encapsulate commonly used JXTA components.

Base Target Classes

Developers will select the base class to inherit from depending on the target service that they want to create. More specifically, the following are the available EZEL base classes:

Class Name	Target Service	Description
ServiceBase	General JXTA peer service	This is an abstract class. The target service receives client requests via a JXTA pipe. The service's advertisement is published, and the service has an option to send a reply to the client. Services deriving from `ServiceBase` will be associated with an individual peer and must be specifically located by the client.
PGServiceBase	General JXTA peer-group service	This is an abstract class. The target service receives client requests via a JXTA pipe. The EZEL code will be transitioned in real-time (still on the work-to-do list) to the JXTA peer-group service handling mechanism. Currently, the service is started by custom code that the client must supply. Eventually, the group management mechanism should start these types of peer-group services. There can be multiple instances of this service running on the JXTA network – and the JXTA platform will ensure that the most appropriate instance responds to the request.

Class Name	Target Service	Description
ClientBase	General JXTA client	Instances of this class can be used to contact JXTA services. The implementation will perform the necessary query for advertisements, and resolving pipes. Optionally, the client can also be configured to receive and process responses from the service.
PGClientBase	General JXTA peer-group service client	Instances of this class can be used to contact JXTA peer-group services. This currently means that the Resolver service must be used to find the instance of the peer-group service to use, and then the EndpointService service be used to send messages to the service instance directly. As the JXTA platform provides higher-level interface abstraction around this behavior, it will be integrated into the EZEL code.
PGServiceHost	Class used to bootstrap a PGService	This class can be used to create hosts for starting up peer-group services in a default peer-group without using the current 'hooks' into service restriction and startup within the peer-group mechanism in JXTA. The content of this class is subject to rapid change as the peer-group operations model of JXTA is refined in practice. For now, the simple skeleton class is sufficient for peer-group services derived from PGServiceBase.

5

An Assortment of Mechanix Classes

Other than these base classes, any JXTA service and client may need to work with a variety of JXTA components. For example, a client may need to create a structured document in the form of a message that must be sent to a service. A service may want to manage the EZEL-created pipes itself, or add them to a collection that it already manages. The exact style of interaction with these fundamental JXTA components is still not clear at this early stage of development. To buffer changes in this area, EZEL has a collection of Mechanix classes. Each Mechanix class gathers together common operations that clients and services may want to perform frequently. At the time of writing, the following Mechanix classes are defined in EZEL:

Class Name	Description
GroupMechanix	Anticipated to handle create, join, and leave operations on peer groups.
PipeMechanix	To create new pipes or to obtain access to the pipes that are maintained by EZEL. Can potentially become a unifying pipe-in-use manager.
MessageMechanix	Collects common operation on messages.
DocMechanix	Collects common operations on structured documents.
PeerMechanix	Obtains information on all peers known to EZEL, all rendezvous known to EZEL, and also obtains specific peer information (via the Peer Information Protocol).
PersistenceMechanix	Collects common operations that involve persistence of application information to disk.

Admittedly, the collection of Mechanix classes is a hodgepodge of operations that JXTA clients and JXTA services typically perform – other than handling requests and sending responses. These Mechanix classes will be the bins in which such operations are collected. Through time, and evolution, some of these Mechanix classes may evolve into more complex hierarchies of classes. However, a design decision has been made not to enforce this sort of factoring at the beginning, but allow these Mechanix classes to transform as they mature. One great benefit of this approach is that it does not force the beginning JXTA developer to learn any new complex object or operational model, other than those associated with the target base classes. Essentially, the Mechanix classes are groupings of frequently used, flat, non-object-oriented APIs – reminiscent of subroutine libraries or operating system APIs.

How It All Fits Together

The figure below illustrates the hierarchy of classes currently in the EZEL library.

Figure 2

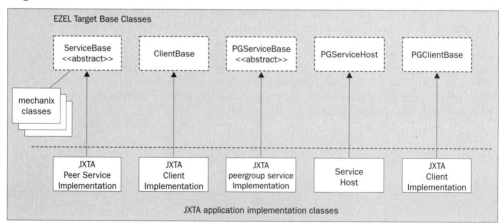

We can see in the figure above that each of the base classes has its own instances of the Mechanix class. This approach is taken for two reasons:

1. The base classes themselves make use of a Mechanix class to ease thier own programming

2. Some Mechanix classes have a "current group" context that the base class can provide

An example of the second category is the `PeerMechanix` class. The set of peers that are visible at any time is certainly sensitive to the context of the "current group". Whenever the current group changes, the set of peers maintained will have to be switched. This is the main reason that applications written using EZEL will typically use instances of the Mechanix classes from the base class rather than creating their own instances.

Creating JXTA Services Using the Platform API

The `ServiceBase` class completely encapsulates the work required to create and maintain a JXTA peer service. We discovered in the last chapter how the user of the `ServiceBase` class simply inherits from this base class and parameterizes the constructor to start the service.

JxtaServiceInfo Class for Service Parameterization

The parameterization of the constructor is via an instance of the `JxtaServiceInfo` class. It is a straightforward class that holds the information required to customize a JXTA service all in one place. It also provides accessors to this information. Here is the sourcecode for the simple `JxtaServiceInfo` class:

```
package com.wrox.ea.jxtaservice;

public class JXTAServiceInfo {
   private String Name            = null;
   private String Description     = null;
   private String Version         = null;
   private String Creator         = null;
   private String URI             = null;
   private String PersistedPipeAdv = null;
   private boolean hasResponsePipe = false;
```

Note that it currently tracks the name, description, version, creator, URI, file name of the service pipe's advertisement, and whether the service will send a response back to the client. We have already examined these arguments in the previous chapter. This set of information may expand in the future if the underlying JXTA platform changes.

5

```
public JXTAServiceInfo(String name, String desc, String ver, String
   creat, String uri, String pipe) {
   setVars(name, desc, ver, creat, uri, pipe);
}
```

For convenience, this class has two constructors. One constructor is used for the service(s) that do not send a response, such as the version above, and the other constructor for services that will send a response, such as the version below.

```
public JXTAServiceInfo(String name,String desc, String ver,
   String creat, String uri, String pipe,  boolean hasResp) {
   hasResponsePipe = hasResp;
   setVars(name, desc,ver,creat,uri,pipe);
}

private void setVars(String name,String desc, String ver,
   String creat, String uri, String pipe) {
   Name        = name;
   Description = desc;
   Version     = ver;
   Creator     = creat;
   URI         = uri;
   PersistedPipeAdv = pipe;
}
```

The accessor methods below provide the ServiceBase class with a uniform way of obtaining this configuration information – and also enable tool integrator programmatic access to the same information.

```
public String getName() { return Name; }
public String getDescription() { return Description; }
public String getVersion() { return Version; }
public String getCreator() { return Creator; }
public String getURI() { return URI; }
public String getPersistedPipeAdv() { return PersistedPipeAdv; }
public boolean hasResponse() { return hasResponsePipe; }
}
```

ServiceBase Implementation

The sourcecode to `ServiceBase` is reproduced below. The import list for the `ServiceBase` class is quite exhaustive, and this is because getting a JXTA service up and running is quite an involved process. Let us take a look at a few of the packages in the import list where we use many classes, and explain their significance.

Package Imported from	Reason
`net.jxta.document.*`	The manipulation of advertisements frequently requires structured document manipulation, and the classes in the package provide this functionality.
`net.jxta.endpoint.*`	For working with messages and message elements. The message mechanism is how requests and responses are sent between the client and service.
`net.jxta.protocol.*`	Interfaces for working with the various advertisement types – pipe advertisement, `ModuleClass` advertisement, `ModuleSpec` advertisement.

Here is the list of import statements used by the `ServiceBase` class:

```
package com.wrox.ea.jxtaservice;

import java.io.ByteArrayInputStream;

import net.jxta.document.StructuredDocumentFactory;
import net.jxta.document.StructuredTextDocument;
import net.jxta.document.StructuredDocument;
import net.jxta.document.MimeMediaType;
import net.jxta.document.Element;
import net.jxta.document.StructuredDocumentUtils;

import net.jxta.platform.Application;

import net.jxta.document.Advertisement;
import net.jxta.document.AdvertisementFactory;

import net.jxta.endpoint.Message;
import net.jxta.endpoint.MessageElement;

import net.jxta.pipe.InputPipe;
import net.jxta.pipe.PipeService;
import net.jxta.pipe.PipeMsgListener;
import net.jxta.pipe.PipeMsgEvent;
import net.jxta.pipe.OutputPipeListener;
```

```
import net.jxta.pipe.OutputPipeEvent;
import net.jxta.pipe.OutputPipe;

import net.jxta.id.IDFactory;
import net.jxta.id.ID;

import net.jxta.peergroup.PeerGroup;
import net.jxta.peergroup.PeerGroupID;
import net.jxta.peergroup.PeerGroupFactory;

import net.jxta.impl.peergroup.Platform;
import net.jxta.impl.peergroup.GenericPeerGroup;

import net.jxta.protocol.PeerGroupAdvertisement;
import net.jxta.protocol.PipeAdvertisement;

import net.jxta.impl.endpoint.MessageElementImpl;

import net.jxta.discovery.DiscoveryService;

import net.jxta.exception.PeerGroupException;

import net.jxta.protocol.ModuleSpecAdvertisement;
import net.jxta.protocol.ModuleClassAdvertisement;

import net.jxta.platform.ModuleClassID;
```

Note that `ServiceBase` is an abstract class; every child of this class must implement the abstract `serviceLogic()` method – since each and every service has its own way of handling requests. We can see here that `ServiceBase` also implements two interfaces:

Interface	Description
net.jxta.pipe. PipeMsgListener	This can be used to listen for incoming messages on a bound JXTA input pipe instance. It implies the implementation of a `pipeMsgEvent()` method. This method is called whenever a message is received via the input pipe instance.
net.jxta.pipe. OutputPipeListener	This is used to notify the service of the successful binding of an output pipe. It requires the implementation of a `outputPipeEvent()` method. This method is called by the Platform immediately following the successful binding of the pipe advertisement and on the availability of output.

```
public abstract class ServiceBase implements
  PipeMsgListener, OutputPipeListener {
```

Next, we see the set of Mechanix class instances.

```
private DocMechanix instanceDocm           = null;
private GroupMechanix instanceGroupm       = null;
private MessageMechanix instanceMessagem = null;
private PipeMechanix instancePipem         = null;
private PersistenceMechanix instancePersistencem = null;
private PeerMechanix instancePeerm         = null;

static  PeerGroup group = null;
static  PeerGroupAdvertisement groupAdvertisement = null;

private DiscoveryService disco;
private PipeService pipes;
private InputPipe myPipe;            // Input pipe for the service
private Message msg;                 // Pipe message received
private ID gid;                      // Group ID
```

The class `instanceInfo` is the parameterization class that comes in via the constructor.

```
private JXTAServiceInfo instanceInfo;
```

Some constants are defined up front here. Note the structured (XML) document tag name used to carry request and response pipe information is defined here with constants. These constants are accessed directly from the `ClientBase` class whenever necessary, and this ensures that the expectations at both ends are consistent.

```
public static final String MODULE_CLASS_PREFIX = "JXTAMOD:";
public static final String MODULE_SPEC_PREFIX  = "JXTASPEC:";

public static final MimeMediaType textPlainType =
  new MimeMediaType("text/plain");
public static final MimeMediaType textXmlType   =
  new MimeMediaType("text/xml");
public static String requestDataTag  = "WroxCall";
public static String responsePipeTag = "WroxResponse";

private String advertisedServiceName = null;
private String advertisedPipeName    = null;
```

The constructor of `ServiceBase` takes an instance of the `JxtaServiceInfo` class as discussed previously. We will be creating two different advertisements. The name used in the `ModuleClass` advertisement is stored in the `advertisedServiceName` variable, while `advertisedPipeName` is the name used in the `ModuleSpec` advertisement.

```
public ServiceBase(JXTAServiceInfo  inServ) {
  instanceInfo = inServ;
  advertisedServiceName = MODULE_CLASS_PREFIX +
    instanceInfo.getName();
  advertisedPipeName = MODULE_SPEC_PREFIX + instanceInfo.getName();
}
```

At the current stage of development, EZEL only supports the starting of an application in the default NetPeerGroup (see earlier highlighted note in this chapter). The startJxta() helper method is used to start this default group. We can see here that a static method of the PeerGroupFactory class is used for this purpose.

The startJxta() code here is very plain, it simply starts the Platform with the default NetPeerGroup.

```
private void startJxta() {
  try {
    // Create, and start the default jxta NetPeerGroup
    group = PeerGroupFactory.newNetPeerGroup();
  } catch (PeerGroupException e) {
    // Could not instantiate the group, print the stack and exit
    System.out.println("ServiceBase : group creation failure");
    e.printStackTrace();
    System.exit(1);
  }
}
```

The init() method here is used to start the JXTA platform with the default group (via the startJxta() method). Once the group instance is available, we obtain references to the peer-group services for discovery and pipe binding. We also create instances of our Mechanix classes, parameterizing them with the current group wherever applicable. Most of these Mechanix classes are not used in the current version of ServiceBase. However, it is foreseeable that their functionality will be fortified within the near future, and the ServiceBase class will make more extensive use of them.

```
public void init(){
  startJxta();

  groupAdvertisement = group.getPeerGroupAdvertisement();
  System.out.println("Getting DiscoveryService");

  disco = group.getDiscoveryService();
```

```
      System.out.println("Getting PipeService");

      pipes = group.getPipeService();

      instanceGroupm       = new GroupMechanix(group);
      instancePipem        = new PipeMechanix(group);
      instanceMessagem     = new MessageMechanix();
      instanceDocm         = new DocMechanix();
      instancePeerm        = new PeerMechanix(group);
      instancePersistencem = new PersistenceMechanix( group);
      startService();
}
```

The `StartService()` method is called after the `ServiceBase` class has
completed construction. Here, we need to create three advertisements:

1. A `ModuleClass` advertisement

2. A `ModuleSpec` advertisement

3. A pipe advertisement for our request pipe, if not already stored on disk

The `Parm` section of the `ModuleSpec` advertisement is where we will stash the
pipe advertisement for now. This means that the client will only have to discover
this `ModuleSpec` advertisement to reach our request pipe. Note the use of our
`JxtaServiceInfo` instance, called `instanceInfo`, to obtain the various
information fields required when creating an advertisement.

```
private void startService() {
  System.out.println("Start the Server daemon");

  try {
```

The `static newAdvertisement()` method of the
`net.jxta.document.AdvertisementFactory` class is always used to make
advertisements. The JXTA platform will register the various factory methods
associated with the different advertisements with this single
`AdvertisementFactory` class.

```
    // Create the service advertisement
    ModuleClassAdvertisement classAdv = (ModuleClassAdvertisement)
      AdvertisementFactory.newAdvertisement(
        ModuleClassAdvertisement.getAdvertisementType());
    classAdv.setName(advertisedServiceName);
    classAdv.setDescription(instanceInfo.getDescription());
```

```
ModuleClassID classID = IDFactory.newModuleClassID();
classAdv.setModuleClassID(classID);
```

Once created, we use the discovery service instance to publish the advertisement. First it is published locally (cached), and then remotely (throughout the peer group).

```
disco.publish(classAdv, DiscoveryService.ADV);
disco.remotePublish(classAdv, DiscoveryService.ADV);
```

The `ModuleSpec` advertisement is next, and we need to include our request input pipe advertisement.

```
ModuleSpecAdvertisement specAdv = (ModuleSpecAdvertisement)
  AdvertisementFactory.newAdvertisement(
    ModuleSpecAdvertisement.getAdvertisementType());

specAdv.setName(MODULE_SPEC_PREFIX + instanceInfo.getName());
specAdv.setVersion(instanceInfo.getVersion());
specAdv.setCreator(instanceInfo.getCreator());
specAdv.setModuleSpecID(IDFactory.newModuleSpecID(classID));
specAdv.setSpecURI(instanceInfo.getURI());
```

Here, we make use of our instance of the `PersistenceMechanix` class to create a new pipe advertisement and persist it to disk if an existing pipe advertisement cannot be found. In any case, `pipeadv` will contain our input pipe advertisement after this call.

```
PipeAdvertisement pipeadv =
 instancePersistencem.CreatePipeAdvIfNotExist(advertisedPipeName,
   instanceInfo.getPersistedPipeAdv());

StructuredTextDocument paramDoc = (StructuredTextDocument)
StructuredDocumentFactory.newStructuredDocument(
  textXmlType,"Parm");
```

The following statement creates a structured document that contains the single param element. The content of this element will be the pipe advertisement.

```
StructuredDocumentUtils.copyElements(paramDoc, paramDoc,
  (Element)pipeadv.getDocument(textXmlType));
specAdv.setParam((StructuredDocument) paramDoc);
```

After the complete creation of our `ModuleSpec` advertisement, we again publish it using the discovery service – both locally and remotely throughout the group.

```
disco.publish(specAdv, DiscoveryService.ADV);
disco.remotePublish(specAdv, DiscoveryService.ADV);
```

We use the `dumpDoc()` method of our own instance of the `DocMechanix` class to print out the content of the published `ModuleSpec` advertisement. This will enable us to verify the (embedded) pipe advertisement being published.

```
instanceDocm.dumpDoc(specAdv.getDocument(textPlainType),
    System.out);
```

Finally, we create the request pipe (by binding to the advertisement for an input pipe) and register ourselves as a listener for incoming messages. Recall that the `pipeMsgEvent()` method will be called later when messages arrives at the pipe.

```
    // Create a pipe and subscribe to incoming messages
    myPipe = pipes.createInputPipe(pipeadv, (PipeMsgListener)this);
} catch (Exception ex) {
    ex.printStackTrace();
    System.out.println("ServerBase: advertisement creation
        failure");
}

System.out.println("Waiting for client messages to arrive....");
```

Meanwhile, we just hang around without terminating, awaiting requests from the client.

```
synchronized(this) {
    try {
        wait();
    } catch (Exception ex) {}
}
}
```

Whenever a message arrives in the input pipe (the service's request pipe), the following method will be called. The `getMessage()` method of the `PipeMsgEvent` class that is passed in as a argument can be used to obtain the incoming message.

```
public void pipeMsgEvent( PipeMsgEvent ev) {
    System.out.println("ServiceBase: A request has been received!");

    PipeAdvertisement pipeAdv = null;
    Message inReq = ev.getMessage();
```

The element associated with the `requestDataTag` contains the actual request data. We extract it into the `coreMsg` element. This is what we will pass to the service's own implementation of the `serviceLogic()` method.

```
      MessageElement coreMsg = inReq.getElement(requestDataTag);

   try {
      if (coreMsg != null)
         serviceLogic(coreMsg);
```

If this service will send a response to the client, we look for another element tag in the message. This is the responsePipeTag. Once we have located this tag, we know that it contains a pipe advertisement (since it is part of our protocol) that refers to the client's response pipe. In this case, we extract the advertisement and we bind an output pipe to it, registering ourselves to be notified when the output pipe is bound.

```
      if (instanceInfo.hasResponse()) {
         System.out.println("FOUND A REPLY PIPE");
         MessageElement respPipe = inReq.getElement(responsePipeTag);

         if (respPipe != null) {
            //response pipe included
            pipeAdv = (PipeAdvertisement)
               AdvertisementFactory.newAdvertisement(
                  textXmlType, respPipe.getStream());
            pipes.createOutputPipe(pipeAdv, this);
         }
      }
   } catch (Exception ex) {}
}
```

The serviceLogic() method is abstract, forcing subclasses to implement it, and also making the ServiceBase class abstract itself.

```
   protected abstract void serviceLogic(MessageElement el);
```

The respondLogic() method is equivalent in function to serviceLogic(), but is provided for the service to customize the construction of the response that will be sent back to the client. The content should be the return value. This method is useful only for those subclasses that will send a response back to the client. Because of this, we use a method to be overridden by subclasses, rather than making it abstract.

```
protected String respondLogic() {
   return "";
}
```

The `outputPipeEvent()` method is called when the binding to the output pipe completes. We can use the `getOutputPipe()` method of the `OutputPipeEvent` instance passed in to find the output pipe. Here, we simply call the `respondLogic()` method – allowing the service to create its own response – and then create a message and send it back through the output pipe. This will send the response directly to the client's response pipe.

```java
public void outputPipeEvent(OutputPipeEvent evt) {
  // Create the data string to send to the server
  System.out.println("ServiceBase: Output Pipe Ready - sending a
    message to the pipe now!");
  OutputPipe myPipe = evt.getOutputPipe();
  String data       = respondLogic();

  // Create the pipe message
  msg = pipes.createMessage();

  try {
  // Store the client data into the message with the requestDataTag
    ByteArrayInputStream ip = new
      ByteArrayInputStream(data.getBytes());
    MessageElement myElem = new
      MessageElementImpl(ServiceBase.requestDataTag,textXmlType,ip);
    ip.close();
    msg.addElement(myElem);
    myPipe.send(msg);
  } catch (Exception ex) {
    System.out.println("ServiceBase: message creation failed");
    ex.printStackTrace();
  }

  System.out.println("ServiceBase: response message \"" + data
    + "\" sent back to the client");
}
```

The remaining methods are accessor methods for subclasses to obtain the various Mechanix instances that were created by the `ServiceBase` class.

5

```
public DocMechanix getDocMechanix() {
  return instanceDocm;
}

public GroupMechanix getGroupMechanix() {
  return instanceGroupm;
}

public MessageMechanix getMessageMechanix() {
  return instanceMessagem;
}

public PeerMechanix getPeerMechanix() {
  return instancePeerm;
}

public PersistenceMechanix getPersistenceMechanix() {
  return instancePersistencem;
}

public PipeMechanix getPipeMechanix() {
  return instancePipem;
}
}
```

This completes our examination of the `ServiceBase` class. We can appreciate the complex API programming that underlies the simple usage of this EZEL class. Next, we look to the client side.

ClientBase Implementation

As with the `ServiceBase` class, the `ClientBase` implementation also requires quite a comprehensive import list. This is not surprising since the client will need to:

1. Create a pipe advertisement for the respond pipe

2. Bind an input pipe to the respond pipe

3. Discover the service by querying for its `ModuleSpec` advertisement

4. Extract the service's request pipe advertisement from the `Parm` section of the `ModuleSpec` advertisement

5. Bind an output pipe to the server

6. Create a message representing the request (optionally embedding our response pipe advertisement) and send it to the server

This comprehensive list of tasks encompasses the various areas of the class's functionality, resulting in a very large import list.

```java
package com.wrox.ea.jxtaservice;

import java.io.ByteArrayInputStream;
import java.io.IOException;
import java.io.InputStream;

import java.util.Enumeration;

import java.net.URL;

import net.jxta.pipe.PipeService;
import net.jxta.pipe.OutputPipeListener;
import net.jxta.pipe.PipeMsgListener;
import net.jxta.pipe.PipeMsgEvent;
import net.jxta.pipe.OutputPipeEvent;
import net.jxta.pipe.OutputPipe;
import net.jxta.pipe.PipeID;

import net.jxta.document.StructuredTextDocument;
import net.jxta.document.TextElement;
import net.jxta.document.Document;
import net.jxta.document.AdvertisementFactory;
import net.jxta.document.MimeMediaType;

import net.jxta.peergroup.PeerGroup;
import net.jxta.protocol.PipeAdvertisement;

import net.jxta.discovery.DiscoveryService;
import net.jxta.discovery.DiscoveryListener;
import net.jxta.discovery.DiscoveryEvent;

import net.jxta.impl.shell.ShellApp;
import net.jxta.impl.shell.ShellEnv;
import net.jxta.impl.shell.ShellObject;
```

5

```
import net.jxta.protocol.DiscoveryResponseMsg;
import net.jxta.protocol.ModuleSpecAdvertisement;

import net.jxta.endpoint.Message;
import net.jxta.endpoint.MessageElement;

import net.jxta.impl.endpoint.MessageElementImpl;

import net.jxta.id.IDFactory;
```

Since the client creates an input pipe and an output pipe, like the ServiceBase class does, we need to implement the PipeMsgListener and OutputPipeListener listener interfaces. In addition, since the client must also discover the service, we also implement net.jxta.discovery.DiscoveryListener.

Implementing DiscoveryListener means that the class must implement the discoveryEvent() method. The client has access to the newly discovered advertisement within this method.

```
public class ClientBase implements DiscoveryListener,
OutputPipeListener, PipeMsgListener {
  static final String NAME_ATTRIBUTE = "Name";
  static final String PIPE_ADV_TAG   = "jxta:PipeAdvertisement";
  static final String ID_TAG         = "Id";
  static final String TYPE_TAG       = "Type";
```

Notice how we ensure that the client and service both agree on the message tag that is used to embed the request, and the respond pipe information.

```
  static final String RESP_PIPE_TAG = ServiceBase.responsePipeTag;
  static final String CALL_TAG = ServiceBase.requestDataTag;

  private String ServiceName            = null;
  private PeerGroup gp                   = null;
  private DiscoveryService disco         = null;
  private PipeService pipes              = null;
  private boolean hasResp                = false;
  private OutputPipe myPipe              = null;
  private Document respondInputPipeDoc   = null;
```

The ClientBase class constructor parameterization is considerably simpler than that of ServiceBase. We simply need to know the name of the service that we want to connect to, and whether we should process responses from the server.

```
public ClientBase(String srvName, boolean resp) {
  ServiceName = ServiceBase.MODULE_SPEC_PREFIX + srvName;
  hasResp    = resp;
}
```

The init() method is where we set up properties that depend on the current group. As we have mentioned earlier, the client requires a "client host" class to start up the Platform with the default NetPeerGroup. We will see this host class shortly, as it is the host class that is responsible for calling this init() method. Here, we store the discovery service and the pipe binding service.

```
public void init(PeerGroup group) {
  gp    = group;
  disco = gp.getDiscoveryService();
  pipes = gp.getPipeService();
  System.out.println("ClientBase: init...");
  System.out.println("ClientBase: Searching for the service
    advertisement");
```

Next, we perform discovery using the discovery service. We search locally for the advertisement first, then remotely throughout the peer group.

```
Enumeration enum = null;

try {
  enum = disco.getLocalAdvertisements(DiscoveryService.ADV,
    NAME_ATTRIBUTE, ServiceName);

  if ((enum != null) && enum.hasMoreElements()) {
    processAdv(enum);
    return;
  }
```

Note that remote discovery is asynchronous, and therefore we register ourselves as a listener (the last argument). We need to delay a little (5 seconds in this case) before returning – because the client may try to send a message immediately and the pipe may not yet be ready.

```
  disco.getRemoteAdvertisements(null, DiscoveryService.ADV,
    NAME_ATTRIBUTE, ServiceName, 1, this);

  Thread.sleep(5000);    // Delay for discovery
} catch (Exception e) {
```

```
    // Found nothing!  Move on
  }
}
```

The following method is called whenever an advertisement is discovered by the discovery service. It is called after local discovery (from the peer's own cache) within the `init()` method, and also called directly from the `discoveryEvent()` method when performing remote discovery.

```
public void processAdv(Enumeration enum) {
  System.out.println("ClientBase: found the advertisement");
```

Note that we are accessing the found advertisement, the very first element of the enumeration passed in as an argument, directly and assuming it is the `ModuleSpec` advertisement we want. This is not completely safe, since other advertisements (including the `ModuleClass` advertisement) may have the same name. Later EZEL versions will improve on this. For the purpose of demonstration, this approach is sufficient since we are creating both the client and the service side of the application.

```
ModuleSpecAdvertisementspecAdv = (ModuleSpecAdvertisement)
  enum.nextElement();
```

First, we use the `static dumpDoc()` method of the `DocMechanix` class to print out the entire ModuleSpec advertisement.

```
try {
  DocMechanix.dumpDoc(specAdv.getDocument(
    ServiceBase.textPlainType), System.out);
} catch(Exception ex) {}
```

Next, we extract the pipe advertisement that is in the `Parm` section of the `ModuleSpec` advertisement. More specifically, we obtain the pipe ID and pipe type.

```
// We can extract the pipe information to connect to the service
// From the advertisement as part of the Param section of the
// advertisement
StructuredTextDocument paramDoc = (StructuredTextDocument)
  specAdv.getParam();

// extract both the Pipe ID and the Pipe Type
String pID   = null;
String pType = null;
Enumeration docElements = paramDoc.getChildren();
TextElement pipeAdvElem = null;
```

```
while(docElements.hasMoreElements()) {
  pipeAdvElem = (TextElement)docElements.nextElement();
  String nm   = pipeAdvElem.getName();
  System.out.println("parsing <"+ nm + ">");

  if (nm.equals(PIPE_ADV_TAG))
    break;
}

Enumeration elements = pipeAdvElem.getChildren();

while(elements.hasMoreElements()) {
  TextElement elem = (TextElement)elements.nextElement();
  String nm = elem.getName();

  System.out.println("parsing <"+ nm + ">");

  if(nm.equals(ID_TAG)) {
    pID = elem.getTextValue();
    continue;
  }

  if(nm.equals(TYPE_TAG)) {
    pType = elem.getTextValue();
    continue;
  }
}
```

5

With the pipe ID and type available, we can create a new pipe advertisement.

```
System.out.println("Pipe ID is " + pID);
PipeAdvertisement pipeadv = (PipeAdvertisement)
  AdvertisementFactory.newAdvertisement(
    PipeAdvertisement.getAdvertisementType());

try {
  URL pipeID = new URL(pID);
  pipeadv.setPipeID((PipeID)IDFactory.fromURL(pipeID));
  pipeadv.setType(pType);
}
```

```
catch (Exception badID){
  badID.printStackTrace();
  throw new IllegalArgumentException( "Bad pipe ID in
    advertisement" );
}
```

Now, we bind an output pipe to the service's request pipe, and register ourselves to be notified when binding succeeds.

```
try {
  pipes.createOutputPipe(pipeadv, this);
} catch (Exception ex) {
  ex.printStackTrace();
  System.out.println("Client: Error sending message to the
    service");
}
}
```

This implements the `DiscoveryListener` interface, and is called whenever a remote discovery is successful. Here, we obtain the discovered advertisement(s) and call the `processAdv()` method (seen earlier) with it.

```
public void discoveryEvent(DiscoveryEvent evt) {
  System.out.println("Remote discovery succeeds!");
  DiscoveryResponseMsg dmsg = evt.getResponse();

  if (dmsg.getResponseCount() > 0) {
    Enumeration enum = dmsg.getResponses();
    processAdv(enum);
  }
}
```

Since `ClientBase` is not an abstract class, customization of client behavior is done via override. This is the method that a subclass should override if it needs to process the response from the server.

```
protected void processResponse(MessageElement payload) {
  // Override only if client has response pipe
}
```

The `pipeMsgEvent()` method is called whenever the client's response pipe has an incoming message (from the service). Here, we basically call the `processResponse()` method that a subclass can override for custom processing.

```
public void pipeMsgEvent( PipeMsgEvent ev) {
  Message inReq = ev.getMessage();
  MessageElement coreMsg = inReq.getElement(
    ServiceBase.requestDataTag);

  if (coreMsg != null) {
    System.out.println("Clientbase: A response has been received!");
    processResponse(coreMsg);
  }
}
```

The `outputPipeEvent()` method is called when the output pipe binding (to the service's request pipe) is completed. Here, we store a reference to the output pipe in the `myPipe` variable. This is also the best time to create the input response pipe, registering ourselves as a listener for messages coming in to this response pipe. Note that currently, EZEL will create the response pipe and not use it if the client set the `hasResp` Boolean flag to `false`. A future version of EZEL will remove this unnecessary operation.

```
public void outputPipeEvent(OutputPipeEvent evt) {

  PipeAdvertisement respPipeAdv = null;
  System.out.println("ClientBase: Output Pipe Created...");

  System.out.println("ClientBase: Output Pipe Ready - creating a
    response input pipe now!");
  respPipeAdv = (PipeAdvertisement)
    AdvertisementFactory.newAdvertisement(
      PipeAdvertisement.getAdvertisementType());

  try {
    respPipeAdv.setPipeID(IDFactory.newPipeID(gp.getPeerGroupID()));
    respPipeAdv.setType("JxtaUnicast");
    pipes.createInputPipe(respPipeAdv, (PipeMsgListener) this);
    respondInputPipeDoc = respPipeAdv.getDocument(
      ServiceBase.textXmlType);
  }
  catch (Exception badID)
```

```
{
  badID.printStackTrace();
}

myPipe = evt.getOutputPipe();
}
```

The method sendRequestToService() is used by a client to send a request to a service. We take as input a string (which can be a partial XML document), and then create a message with it (tagging it with the CALL_TAG element). On the same message, we also bundle in the RESP_PIPE_TAG and supply our response pipe advertisement as part of the message.

```
public void sendRequestToService(String inReq) {
  if (null != myPipe) {
    // Create the pipe message
    Message msg = pipes.createMessage();
    ByteArrayInputStream dataIs =
      new ByteArrayInputStream (inReq.getBytes());

    try {
      InputStream ip = respondInputPipeDoc.getStream();
      msg.addElement( new MessageElementImpl(
        RESP_PIPE_TAG,ServiceBase.textXmlType,ip));
      msg.addElement( new MessageElementImpl(
        CALL_TAG, ServiceBase.textXmlType, dataIs));

      // Send the message to the service pipe
      myPipe.send (msg);
    } catch (Exception ex) {}

    System.out.println("ClientBase: message \"" + inReq +
      "\" sent to the Server");
  }
}
}
```

Again, we witness that creating a JXTA client is non-trivial and requires an understanding of a substantial cross section of the JXTA platform APIs.

A Sample Mechanix Class

As we have noted before, the Mechanix classes are groups of "flat" functional APIs that can often be useful for implementing JXTA client and services. Many of the Mechanix classes in EZEL are still not fully defined.

PersistenceMechanix Implementation

Here, we will examine one partially defined Mechanix class – the PersistenceMechanix class. In fact, the ServiceBase class uses this class.

```
package com.wrox.ea.jxtaservice;
import net.jxta.document.*;
import net.jxta.protocol.*;
import net.jxta.pipe.*;
import java.io.*;
import net.jxta.id.IDFactory;
import net.jxta.peergroup.*;

public class PersistenceMechanix {
```

Since PersistenceMechanix is sensitive to the notion of the "current group", we have a constructor with a PeerGroup parameter as the argument, as well as a changeGroup() method.

```
protected PeerGroup currentGroup = null;

public PersistenceMechanix(PeerGroup group) {
  currentGroup = group;
}

public void changeGroup(PeerGroup group) {
  currentGroup = group;
}

public void PersistDoc(StructuredDocument doc) {
}

public void PersistAdv(Advertisement ad) {
}
```

The `CreatePipeAdvIfNotExist()` method is useful for JXTA services. This method will check a specified file name; if it exists, the pipe advertisement within the file will be returned and used. If it does not exist, a new pipe advertisement will be created and persisted. This is particularly useful since services should reuse the same pipe ID for its request pipe between restarts. Doing so will ensure that previously propagated advertisements that contain the pipe advertisement, potentially being cached throughout the network, will continue to be valid. This mechanism therefore avoids the proliferation of advertisements.

```
public PipeAdvertisement CreatePipeAdvIfNotExist(String pipeName,
  String fileName) {
  System.out.println("Trying to read " + fileName);
  PipeAdvertisement pipeAdv = null;
  FileInputStream is        = null;
  FileOutputStream os       = null;
  Document myDoc            = null;

  try {
    is = new FileInputStream(fileName);
    pipeAdv = (PipeAdvertisement)
    AdvertisementFactory.newAdvertisement(
      new MimeMediaType("text/xml"), is);
    is.close();
  } catch (Exception e) {
    System.out.println("cannot read " + fileName + ",
      now creating new one.");

    try {
      pipeAdv = (PipeAdvertisement)
        AdvertisementFactory.newAdvertisement(
          PipeAdvertisement.getAdvertisementType());
      PipeID pipeID = IDFactory.newPipeID((PeerGroupID)
        currentGroup.getPeerGroupID());
      pipeAdv.setPipeID(pipeID);
      pipeAdv.setName(pipeName);
```

Note that the type of pipe that we create is limited to Unicast (unidirectional, non-propagated) for now. Future versions of EZEL will make this an application-supplied parameter.

```
    pipeAdv.setType(PipeService.UnicastType);
    System.out.println("... created new pipe Advertisment....");
    myDoc = pipeAdv.getDocument(new MimeMediaType("text/xml"));
```

If we do not find the advertisement already persisted on the local disk, we create a
new one and store it there.

```
      os = new FileOutputStream(fileName);
      myDoc.sendToStream(os);
      os.flush();
      os.close();
      System.out.println("new pipe advertisement peristed!");
    } catch (Exception ex) {
      System.out.println("PersistenceMechanix: problem while
        persisting");
      ex.printStackTrace();
    }
  }

  return pipeAdv;
  }
}
```

Underneath a Peer-Group Service

In the last chapter, we experimented with PGServiceBase class and discovered
that services based on it can have multiple instances running within the same
group. The PGServiceBase class, in conjunction with the PGClientBase class,
will ensure that somehow an instance of the service will be located and used as
long as at least one instance is running. We promised that we would look under the
hood and see how this works in the last chapter. Now we will fulfill this promise.

PGServiceBase and PGClientBase collaborate to create the illusion of seamless
communication – something that is not possible without JXTA's distributed query and
virtualized network support. In fact, both classes use the following JXTA core services:

1. Resolver service – works with network of rendezvous to form
   JXTA's support for distributed queries

2. Endpoint service – works with routers and relays to virtualize the
   network of interconnected peers

Here's precisely what happens. We will first describe the process conceptually, them
look at the code, and even experiment with the code later.

5

On the service end, the `PGServiceBase` class is registered as both a query handler and an endpoint handler. What this means is that it will be receiving the distributed queries that are being propagated by the rendezvous network, and it will also be listening at a virtual peer endpoint (not a physical transport endpoint) for messages. This virtual peer endpoint is called an "endpoint address" in JXTA lingo. This JXTA address, when made available to any member of the peer group, can be used to locate the specific registered handler again with the help of the endpoint service.

The following figure shows what a `PGServiceBase` service looks like inside.

Figure 3

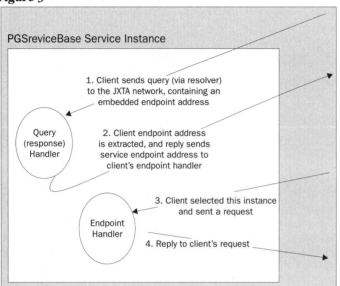

On the client end, the implementation is supplied by the `PGClientBase` class. It too is an endpoint handler, and has a virtual endpoint address. When it needs to make a request to a service, it will first create a simple `QueryResolver` client that will send out a distributed query looking for all the services (in the group) registered with the handler name (service name `SimpleGroupService` in last chapter's scenario). This query, incidentally, also contains the `PGClientBase` registered handler's virtual endpoint address.

Since the query will be propagated throughout the peer group by the network of rendezvous, any service on a peer that has a registered handler satisfying the query (for example `name=SimpleGroupService`) will respond. Instead of responding in-band to the resolver using the resolver response mechanism, however, the service instance(s) will reply directly to the endpoint handler that is registered back in the client. The response contains the endpoint address of the service itself.

In this way, the endpoint handler on the client can hear back from many different service instances. It can use some arbitrary means of deciding which service instance to use (the first one that comes back is typically a reasonable choice – assuming the first one back is closest, and therefore the roundtrip request/response is reduced). With a service instance's endpoint address, the client can send requests directly to the handler of the service. The figure opposite shows this interaction.

Figure 4

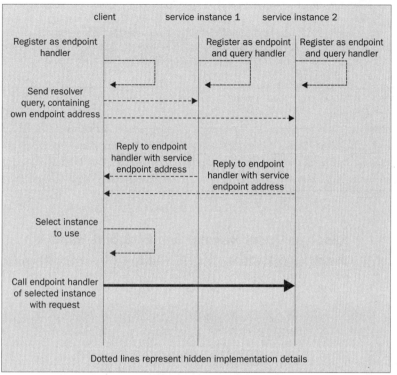

In summary, on the client side:

1. Client registers as an endpoint handler

2. Sends a distributed query (containing client's own endpoint address) to all peers in the group

3. Collects returned information from services that replied, and determines the one to use for the actual request

4. Uses the returned service endpoint address to locate the service and send messages to it

On the service side:

1. Service registers as an endpoint handler

2. Service registers to receive distributed queries

3. Upon receiving a distributed query, service strips client's endpoint address and sends a reply – containing its own endpoint address – to the client's handler

This is repeated on every single request sent from client to service. The net effect is that the client determines and learns about all the reachable instances of a service before deciding to make a call to one of them. This fully implements the peer-group service semantics, and therefore failover between service instances can be made completely transparent. If the client loses communication with a service instance, it simply repeats the above procedure to connect to another instance.

> *We must reiterate here, to avoid misunderstanding, none of what we illustrate here – no matter how neat and elegant – is "the way JXTA does things". The JXTA specification simply specifies the semantics of a peer-group service (that it can have redundant instances and will work as long as one instance is still alive), but does not say how it should or must be done. What we are covering here, really, is a specific design approach that EZEL has taken – using the Java reference implementation of JXTA – to achieve peer-group service semantics.*

A Resolver Query Handler and Endpoint Handler

Let us now take a look at the JXTA Platform APIs that are actually used to accomplish this. The code can be found in the `PGServiceBase` class (the `src\PGServiceBase.java` file).

`PGServiceBase` is abstract, like `ServiceBase`, and subclasses must implement the `serviceLogic()` method.

Package	Purpose
`net.jxta.resolver.*`	The service will register a query handler to process incoming distributed queries. The resolver core service handles distributed queries.
`net.jxta.endpoint.*`	The service will register an endpoint listener to handle incoming messages directly to the endpoint address. The endpoint core service provides resolution to an endpoint address.

The import list reflects something new and different from `ServiceBase`:

```
package com.wrox.ea.jxtaservice;

import java.lang.reflect.InvocationTargetException;
import java.io.ByteArrayInputStream;
import java.io.File;
import java.io.FileInputStream;
import java.io.FileOutputStream;
import java.io.InputStream;
import java.io.IOException;

import net.jxta.discovery.DiscoveryService;
```

```
import net.jxta.document.Advertisement;
import net.jxta.document.AdvertisementFactory;
import net.jxta.document.Document;
import net.jxta.document.MimeMediaType;
import net.jxta.endpoint.EndpointService;
import net.jxta.endpoint.EndpointAddress;
import net.jxta.endpoint.EndpointListener;
import net.jxta.endpoint.EndpointMessenger;
import net.jxta.endpoint.Message;

import net.jxta.exception.PeerGroupException;
import net.jxta.exception.NoResponseException;
import net.jxta.exception.ResendQueryException;
import net.jxta.exception.DiscardQueryException;

import net.jxta.id.ID;
import net.jxta.id.IDFactory;

import net.jxta.peergroup.PeerGroup;
import net.jxta.peergroup.PeerGroupID;

import net.jxta.platform.Module;

import net.jxta.protocol.ResolverQueryMsg;
import net.jxta.protocol.ResolverResponseMsg;

import net.jxta.resolver.QueryHandler;

import net.jxta.impl.protocol.ResolverResponse;
```

PGServiceBase handles incoming queries by implementing the `QueryHandler` interface, and responds to direct endpoint messages by implementing the `EndpointListener` interface.

```
public abstract class PGServiceBase
  implements Module, EndpointListener, QueryHandler {
```

Note that the `clientDataTag` in this class is synchronized with the `clientDataTag` in the `ClientBase` class.

```
  public static final String serviceAddressTag = "address";
  public static final String clientDataTag =
    PGClientBase.clientDataTag;
  private static String serviceName = null;
```

The constructor simply stores the service name for the client to contact.

```
private PeerGroup group = null;

public PGServiceBase(String inName){
  serviceName = inName;
}
```

In the init() method, we simply store away the group information. Ultimately, the group start mechanism in JXTA will call this init() method, passing the newly created group as the first argument.

```
public void init(PeerGroup group, ID assignedID,Advertisement impl)
  throws PeerGroupException {
  this.group = group;
}
```

With the startApp() method, we register our QueryHandler and the EndpointListener using group information in combination with the service name.

```
public int startApp(String[] arg) {
  // register the message listener

  group.getEndpointService().addListener(serviceName +
    getGroupId(group), this);

  group.getResolverService().registerHandler(serviceName +
    getGroupId (group), this);

  return 1;
}
```

The next two helper methods create text-based unique IDs (for use in JXTA's XML-based messages) that correspond to a group or a peer.

```
public static String getGroupId(PeerGroup group) {
  return group.getPeerGroupID().getUniqueValue().toString();
}

public static String getPeerId(PeerGroup group) {
  return group.getPeerID().getUniqueValue().toString();
}
```

```
public void stopApp(){
}

public EndpointService getEndpointService() {
  return group.getEndpointService();
}
```

The endpoint address for the handler that we registered can be obtained from the getEndpointAddress() method below. The address is a URI that combines the specific peer ID, the group, and the service name. This is the address that can be used to uniquely locate the endpoint handler.

```
public String getEndpointAddress() {
  return "jxta://" + getPeerId(group) +
    "/" + serviceName +
    "/" + getGroupId(group);
}
```

The serviceLogic() method is identical to that in the ServiceBase class.

```
protected abstract void serviceLogic(Message msg);

public void processIncomingMessage(Message message,
  EndpointAddress srcAddr, EndpointAddress dstAddr) {
  serviceLogic(message);
}
```

resolverQueryLogic() is a method that a subclass can override to intercept the query. It is called by the processQuery() method that is called by the Platform anytime a distributed query has been received. In practice, however, there are few situations where overriding the resolverQueryLogic() method will be necessary, as the query was actually used to propagate the client's endpoint address.

```
protected void resolverQueryLogic(String str) {
}
```

The processQuery() method is the implementation of QueryHandler interface. The getQuery() method of the incoming ResolverQueryMsg instance can be used to obtain the entire query. Recall that the query is actually a combination of the client's endpoint address and an actual query string – separated by a ";" character. Here, upon retrieval of this query string, we break it up into an addressStr (client's endpoint address in URI form) and the actual query substring.

```
public ResolverResponseMsg processQuery(ResolverQueryMsg query)
  throws NoResponseException, ResendQueryException,
    DiscardQueryException, IOException {
  String queryStr = query.getQuery();

  int index = queryStr.indexOf(';');
  String addressStr = queryStr.substring(0, index);
  String subString = queryStr.substring(index+1);
```

Using the `EndpointService`, we obtain a messenger for the client's endpoint address and send our message to the client. This is the response to the query, but it is delivered out-of-band to the endpoint handler. Note that the message that we send is associated with the `serviceAddressTag` XML element and contains our own endpoint address in URI form. This will provide the client with the location of our service in virtual endpoint address form.

```
  Message message = group.getEndpointService().newMessage();

  message.setBytes(serviceAddressTag,
    getEndpointAddress().getBytes());
  EndpointAddress myAddr =
    group.getEndpointService().newEndpointAddress(addressStr);
  EndpointMessenger myMess =
    group.getEndpointService().getMessenger(myAddr);
  myMess.sendMessage(message);
  myMess.close();
  resolverQueryLogic(subString);

  throw new NoResponseException();
}
```

The method `resolverRespondLogic()` can be overridden by a subclass that may want to handle custom query responses. In our case, this is never necessary, because we throw a `NoResponseException` at the end of query processing – indicating that we do not need a response, since we have sent one out-of-band already.

```
protected  void resolverResponseLogic(ResolverResponseMsg resp) {
}
```

The `processResponse()` method is a required method, and is part of the `QueryHandler` interface implementation. As explained above, it is never called in our case.

```
public void processResponse(ResolverResponseMsg response) {
  resolverResponseLogic(response);
}
```

```
  public void finalize () {
    stopApp();
  }
}
```

We can see that there is quite a bit of query propagation and message passing that goes on underneath even before the very first real request is sent from the client to the service. The peer-group service functionality is not accomplished by magic, but by a rather brute-force implementation on top of the flexible JXTA platform.

Working with the JXTA Core Resolver Service

The PGClientBase class is a concrete class that is typically instantiated by a client wishing to work with PGServiceBase implementations. It works collaboratively with PGServiceBase, implementing the peer-group service semantics.

Since the client must also be an endpoint handler, in order to receive a response from the query, the import list is a subset of that we have seen used with the PGServiceBase class.

```
package com.wrox.ea.jxtaservice;
import net.jxta.impl.shell.ShellApp;
import net.jxta.impl.shell.ShellEnv;
import net.jxta.impl.shell.ShellObject;
import net.jxta.peergroup.PeerGroup;
import net.jxta.impl.protocol.ResolverQuery;
import net.jxta.endpoint.Message;
import net.jxta.endpoint.EndpointListener;
import net.jxta.endpoint.EndpointAddress;
import net.jxta.endpoint.EndpointMessenger;
import net.jxta.endpoint.EndpointService;
```

Here, we see that PGClientBase is indeed an endpoint handler. Note the synchronization between our serviceAddressTag (used as part of the query string) and the equivalent string in PGServiceBase.

```
public class PGClientBase implements EndpointListener {
  public static final String serviceAddressTag =
    PGServiceBase.serviceAddressTag;
  public static final String clientDataTag = "dataTag";
  private String serviceAddress          = null;
  private String serviceName             = null;
  private EndpointService myEPS          = null;
  private String PeerID                  = null;
  private String GroupID                 = null;
  private EndpointAddress myAddress      = null;
  private String myAddressStr            = null;
```

The constructor simply sets the service name, and this is used to create the name of the handler when used in conjunction with the peer-group ID.

```
public PGClientBase(String svName) {
    serviceName = svName;
}
```

In the `init()` method, the current group is available. We store away a unique `PeerID` and `GroupID` string value, used later to create URIs. We also locate the `EndpointService` of the group, which is useful for resolving endpoint addresses later on. Note that storing away `EndpointService` references (as with any peer-group service) is a theoretically questionable practice because the reference may become invalid at any time (the referenced endpoint machine becomes unavailable). Theoretically, a new query should be performed each and every time the service is used, via the `getEndpointService()` method of the group. In practice, however, what we are doing is typically sufficient.

```
public void init(PeerGroup group) {
    PeerID = group.getPeerID().getUniqueValue().toString();
    GroupID = group.getPeerGroupID().getUniqueValue().toString();
    myEPS = group.getEndpointService();
```

Our endpoint address is constructed here in the recommended URI form. We then create a native form representation using the `EndpointService` `newEndpointAddress()` method. Note that the name "Resolved" is used here, but any name would work since this is simply a "callback point" for the service to respond to.

```
    myAddressStr = "jxta://" + PeerID + "/Resolved" + "/"+ GroupID;

    myAddress = myEPS.newEndpointAddress(myAddressStr);
```

Next, we register an endpoint handler with the endpoint address.

```
    myEPS.addListener(myAddress.getServiceName()
      + myAddress.getServiceParameter(), this);
```

With the endpoint handler in place, we check to see if we already have the endpoint address of the service. If not, we create the query string by combining our URI-form endpoint address with an arbitrary query substring ("Just Some Data" in this case).

```
    if (null == serviceAddress) {
      try {
        String tpmsg = myAddressStr + ";Just Some Data";
```

Now we create a resolver query, and send it to the query propagation network (network of rendezvous) to find peers who will answer our query. Note that the service-side handler name is re-created by combining the service name with the group ID. This is how the match-up is done by the resolver service on the service side, and the reason why our query string is not actually used. Note that we have hard-coded the query ID last parameter to 100. This ID is used to correlate responses from a service to a client should there be multiple outstanding queries pending. In our case, we will only have one outstanding query, and using the fixed ID will be sufficient.

```
ResolverQuery query = new ResolverQuery(serviceName +
    group.getPeerGroupID().getUniqueValue().toString(),
    null,
    group.getPeerID().toString(),
    tpmsg,
    100);

group.getResolverService().sendQuery(null, query);
```

Again, we wait a short while for the query to propagate, and our client node to select the desired service to communicate with.

```
    Thread.sleep(5000);
  } catch (Exception ex) {
    ex.printStackTrace();
  }
 }
}
```

The sendMessageToService() method is used by the client to send the actual request to the service. Its implementation is straightforward. We assume that the underlying client logic has already selected an available service instance, specified in the serviceAddress URI that we should use to send the message. This method simply uses the EndpointService to create a messenger that in turn is used to send our message.

```
public void sendMessageToService(String inMsg) {
  try {
   if (null != serviceAddress) {
      System.out.println("TRYING TO SEND MESSAGE TO SERVICE
        now...");
      EndpointAddress liveAddr =
        myEPS.newEndpointAddress(serviceAddress);
      EndpointMessenger myMsgr = myEPS.getMessenger(liveAddr);
```

```
        Message message = myEPS.newMessage();
        message.setBytes(clientDataTag, inMsg.getBytes());
        myMsgr.sendMessage(message);
        myMsgr.close();
    }
} catch ( Exception ex ) {
    ex.printStackTrace();
}
}
```

The `processIncomingMessage()` method is implemented by every endpoint handler, and the `PGClientBase` is no exception. In our case, these are responses from our propagated query, and any peer with eligible service instances running will respond with a message. Here, we simply store the value of the `serviceAddressTag` to the `serviceAddress` variable. This is the URI form of the service's endpoint address. Note that when there are multiple services responding to our distributed resolver query, this has the effect of taking only the first one that replies.

The `tapIncomingMessage()` method can be overridden in a subclass to gain access to the message as it comes into the handler. This is method seldom used, however, except for demonstration purposes.

```
public void tapIncomingMessage(Message msg) {
}

public void processIncomingMessage(Message message,
    EndpointAddress srcAddr, EndpointAddress dstAddr) {

    if (null == serviceAddress) {
        serviceAddress = message.getString(serviceAddressTag);
        tapIncomingMessage(message);
    }
}
}
```

This completes our discussion of the `PGClientBase` class. We should now fully understand how the peer-group service semantics can be implemented with a combination of:

1. JXTA's propagated resolver queries

2. JXTA's virtualized endpoint address peer-to-peer network

It should also be a little clearer why the resolver service, and the endpoint service on JXTA, must both be made "core" services.

Creating a Single Instance Peer-Group Service per Peer

The last important class in EZEL that we have used is the PGServiceHost class. As mentioned previously, this class is necessary to perform a function that is not yet well defined in the JXTA platform. This situation may change, however, and if so the implementation of this class will need to change with it.

In particular, this class provides a base for subclasses to host the peer-group service by locating an instance (there should only be one per peer associated with the current group) of the service.

```
package com.wrox.ea.jxtaservice;
import net.jxta.peergroup.PeerGroup;
import net.jxta.peergroup.PeerGroupFactory;
import net.jxta.exception.PeerGroupException;

public class PGServiceHost {
  protected PeerGroup group = null;

  public PGServiceHost() {
  }

  public PeerGroup getGroup() {
    return group;
  }
```

The waitForRequest() method suspends the thread waiting for incoming client requests.

```
public void waitForRequests() {
  synchronized(this) {
    try {
      wait();
    } catch (Exception ex) {}
  }
}
```

The init() method simply starts the Platform with the default NetPeerGroup in this implementation.

```
public void init() {
  startJxta();
```

```
    }

  private void startJxta() {
    try {
      group = PeerGroupFactory.newNetPeerGroup();
    } catch (PeerGroupException e) {
      System.out.println("PGServiceHost: group creation failure");
      e.printStackTrace();
      System.exit(1);
    }
  }
}
```

Note that the instantiation (or location) of the actual service instance is not part of the base class. This is because it requires parameterization based on class, and not instance. Instead, each subclass is expected to implement its own `static` `getInstance()` method.

The implementation of the peer-group service semantics is one of the most interesting areas of JXTA, and it is significantly different from the conventional client-server style of interaction. Let us examine this further by actually conducting some experiments.

Revealing the Implementation of High Availability

To see beneath the veil of the peer-group service implementation, we have created a transparent custom service that we can run. You can find the service in the `com.wrox.ea.jxtaservice` package. The service class is called `PeerGroupRevealed`. Here is the sourcecode of `PeerGroupRevealed.java` file.

```
package com.wrox.ea.jxtaservice;
import net.jxta.endpoint.Message;
import net.jxta.protocol.ResolverResponseMsg;
```

This class is a peer-group service that derives from the `PGServiceBase` class.

```
public class SimpleGroupRevealed extends PGServiceBase {
  public SimpleGroupRevealed(String svcName) {
    super(svcName);
  }
```

```
protected void serviceLogic(Message msg) {
    System.out.println("... gotta request...");
    String myCommand = msg.getString(PGServiceBase.clientDataTag);
    System.out.println(myCommand);
}
```

Here we have hooked the resolver query intercept method
resolverQueryLogic(), revealing the hidden message that is passed between
the client and the service – before the request is actually sent.

```
protected void resolverQueryLogic(String str){
    System.out.println(".. gotta RESOLVER REQUEST...");
    System.out.println("Query = " + str);
}
```

We even hook the resolver query response. However, it will not be used in this case.

```
protected void resolverResponseLogic(ResolverResponseMsg resp){
    System.out.println("!!!!Got a Response!!!!!");
}
}
```

As with the other PGServiceBase subclass, this one will also need a host; we find
the host in the PGServiceRevealedHost class:

```
package com.wrox.ea.jxtaservice;
import net.jxta.peergroup.PeerGroup;
import net.jxta.exception.PeerGroupException;

public class SimpleGroupRevealedHost extends PGServiceHost {
    public SimpleGroupRevealedHost() {
    }

    private static SimpleGroupRevealed serviceInstance = null;

    public static SimpleGroupRevealed getInstance( PeerGroup group) {
        if ( null == serviceInstance ) {
            serviceInstance =
                new SimpleGroupRevealed("SimpleGroupRevealed");

            try
```

5

```
      {
        serviceInstance.init( group, null, null );
      } catch ( PeerGroupException e ) {
        e.printStackTrace();
      }

      serviceInstance.startApp( null) ;
    }

    return serviceInstance;
  }

  public static void main(String args[]) {
    SimpleGroupRevealedHost myHost = new SimpleGroupRevealedHost();
    myHost.init();
    SimpleGroupRevealed myapp = myHost.getInstance(myHost.getGroup());
    System.out.println ("Simple GROUP service REVEALED starting...");
    myHost.waitForRequests();

    System.exit(0);
  }
}
```

The SimpleGroupRevealedHost code is identical to that of the SimpleGroupServiceHost class, the only difference is in the type (or name) of the class. However, this is a perfect candidate for forming a template in future.

A Shell Extension for Transparent Peer-Group Service Clients

For the client side, we will create two test clients. They are, of course, created as shell extensions. The first one simply illustrates the resolver query mechanism, and is contained in the net.jxta.impl.shell.bin.qrytest package. The command is called qrytest.

```
package net.jxta.impl.shell.bin.qrytest;

import net.jxta.peergroup.PeerGroup;
import net.jxta.impl.shell.ShellApp;
import net.jxta.impl.shell.ShellEnv;
import net.jxta.impl.shell.ShellObject;
import net.jxta.resolver.QueryHandler;
import net.jxta.impl.protocol.ResolverQuery;
import net.jxta.impl.protocol.ResolverResponse;
```

This is a very simple command, and does not use any of the EZEL classes. Instead, it simply creates a resovler query and propagates it through the peer group.

```java
public class qrytest extends ShellApp {
ShellEnv env;

  public qrytest() {
  }

  public void stopApp () {
  }

  public int startApp (String[] args) {
    env = getEnv();

    // get the std group
    ShellObject obj = env.get("stdgroup");

    PeerGroup group = (PeerGroup)obj.getObject();

    try {
      ResolverQuery query = new ResolverQuery("SimpleGroupRevealed" +
        group.getPeerGroupID().getUniqueValue().toString(),
        null,
        group.getPeerID().toString(),
        "just a query string",
        100);
      group.getResolverService().sendQuery(null, query);
    } catch ( Exception ex ) {
      ex.printStackTrace();
    }

    return ShellApp.appNoError;
  }

  public void help() {
    println( "NAME" );
    println( "      qrytest - test of query propagation" );
    println( " " );
```

5

```
      println( "SYNOPSIS" );
      println( "        qrytest" );
  }
}
```

We will use this qrytest command later to observe the effect of query propagation within the peer group.

The other command we create is contained in the net.jxta.impl.shell.bin.pgrvtest package. It is the pgrvtest command and this command does use an EZEL PGClientBase instance.

```
package net.jxta.impl.shell.bin.pgrvtest;
import com.wrox.ea.jxtaservice.PGClientBase;
import net.jxta.impl.shell.ShellApp;
import net.jxta.impl.shell.ShellEnv;
import net.jxta.impl.shell.ShellObject;
import net.jxta.peergroup.PeerGroup;
import net.jxta.endpoint.Message;

public class pgrvtest extends ShellApp {
  ShellEnv env;
```

The myClient object will hold our PGClientBase instance.

```
  private PGClientBase myClient;

  public pgrvtest() {
  }

  public void stopApp() {
  }
```

The startApp() method logic is identical to that of the pgtest command that we saw in the last chapter.

```
  public int startApp (String[] args) {
    env = getEnv();

    // get the std group
    ShellObject obj = env.get("stdgroup");

    PeerGroup group = (PeerGroup)obj.getObject();
```

5

The major difference is here, however, is that we are hooking and displaying the message that was received by the (previously hidden) endpoint service handler. This is in direct response to the resolver query that the PGClientBase sends.

```
    myClient = new PGClientBase("SimpleGroupRevealed") {
      public void tapIncomingMessage(Message msg) {
        System.out.println("GOT A REPLY MESSAGE");
        System.out.println("Message contains reply address of - " +
        msg.getString("address"));
      }
    };

    myClient.init(group);

    myClient.sendMessageToService("Now we see what's
      happening underneath!");

    return ShellApp.appNoError;
  }

  public void help() {
    println( "NAME" );
    println( "      pgrvtest - peergroup service REVEALED test" );
    println( " " );
    println( "SYNOPSIS" );
    println( "      pgrvtest" );
  }
}
```

Seeing the Transparent Peer-Group Service in Action

In the code distribution directory, in the src directory, you will find a makepgrv.bat file. Run this batch file to compile the SimpleGroupRevealed and SimpleGroupRevealedHost classes, as well as the two custom commands. This batch file will also create and update the lib\jxtaservice.jar archive file.

Now, change directory to the test2 directory, and execute the runshell.bat file there to start an instance of the shell. Check the configuration to ensure that it is set to:

5

Item to Configure	Value
Peer Name	node2
Transport	Disable: HTTP
	Enable: TCP, manual, localhost, port 9703
Rendezvous/Router	Not using rendezvous, not using router
Security	Configure with your own ID and password.

You may need to remove the cm and pse directory, as well as the PlatformConfig file to get this shell configured properly.

Next, to install the new shell commands via the extension facility use the command:

JXTA> **instjar ..\lib\jxtaservice.jar**

Now, create a new command console, change directory to the pgrv1 directory, and execute the runit.bat file to start an instance of the SimpleGroupRevealed service. Configure this peer as:

Item to Configure	Value
Peer Name	node1
Transport	Disable: HTTP
	Enable: TCP, manual, localhost, port 9701
Rendezvous/Router	Not using rendezvous, not using router
Security	Configure with your own ID and password

You should now see the instance of SimpleGroupRevealed running; the output should be similar to the figure below:

```
C:\EA_JXTA\05\code\pgrv2>java -classpath ..\lib\jxta.jar;..\lib\log4j.jar;..\lib
\beepcore.jar;..\lib\jxtasecurity.jar;..\lib\cryptix-asn1.jar;..\lib\cryptix32.j
ar;..\lib\minimalBC.jar;..\lib\jxtaptls.jar;..\lib\jxtaservice.jar com.wrox.ea.j
xtaservice.SimpleGroupRevealedHost
Simple GROUP service REVEALED starting...
```

Next, create a third command console, move to pgrv2 directory, and run the runit.bat file there to start another instance of the SimpleGroupRevealed service. Configure this third peer as:

Item to Configure	Value
Peer Name	node3
Transport	Disable: HTTP
	Enable: TCP, manual, localhost, port 9705
Rendezvous/Router	Not using rendezvous, not using router
Security	Configure with your own ID and password

Finally, we are ready to see the transparent peer group service at work. First, we will move to the shell, and enter the command:

JXTA> **qrytest**

This will send a resolver query to the group that is propagated throughout the group. Check the two instances of SimpleGroupRevealed. You will see that both of them will have claimed to have received the propagate query. The screen output should be similar to the figure below:

```
C:\WINNT\System32\cmd.exe                                              _ □ ×
C:\EA_JXTA\05\code\pgrv2>java -classpath ..\lib\jxta.jar;..\lib\log4j.jar;..\lib
\beepcore.jar;..\lib\jxtasecurity.jar;..\lib\cryptix-asn1.jar;..\lib\cryptix32.j
ar;..\lib\minimalBC.jar;..\lib\jxtaptls.jar;..\lib\jxtaservice.jar com.wrox.ea.j
xtaservice.SimpleGroupRevealedHost
Simple GROUP service REVEALED starting...
.. gotta RESOLVER REQUEST...
Query = just a query string
```

Back at the JXTA shell instance, issue the pgrvtest command, as follows:

JXTA> **pgrvtest**

This time, you should see that the service was queried first, and then a request was sent from the client only after a reply was received from the service by the client's endpoint handler. Your output on the service side should indicate the receipt of the query, as below:

```
C:\WINNT\System32\cmd.exe                                              _ □ ×
C:\EA_JXTA\05\code\pgrv1>java -classpath ..\lib\jxta.jar;..\lib\log4j.jar;..\lib
\beepcore.jar;..\lib\jxtasecurity.jar;..\lib\cryptix-asn1.jar;..\lib\cryptix32.j
ar;..\lib\minimalBC.jar;..\lib\jxtaptls.jar;..\lib\jxtaservice.jar com.wrox.ea.j
xtaservice.SimpleGroupRevealedHost
Simple GROUP service REVEALED starting...
.. gotta RESOLVER REQUEST...
Query = Just Some Data
... gotta request...
Now we see what's happening underneath!
```

If we examine the console where we've started the JXTA shell instance, we can also see that the client is sending the resolver query, and then receiving the service's response (with its endpoint address) before the actual request is sent. The output from this console should be similar to the screenshot overleaf:

5

```
C:\WINNT\System32\cmd.exe                                    _ □ ×
C:\EA_JXTA\05\code\test2>java -classpath ..\lib\jxta.jar;..\lib\jxtashell.jar;..
\lib\log4j.jar;..\lib\beepcore.jar;..\lib\jxtasecurity.jar;..\lib\cryptix-asn1.j
ar;..\lib\cryptix32.jar;..\lib\minimalBC.jar;..\lib\jxtatls.jar net.jxta.impl.p
eergroup.Boot
Jxta is now taking off. Please fasten your seat belts and extinguish all smoking
 materials.
Looking for NetPeerGroup advertisements.
  NetPeerGroup by default
GOT A REPLY MESSAGE
Message contains reply address of - jxta://uuid-5961626164616261A78746150325033
7DD0140001421AB78A48DA6369170D16703/SimpleGroupRevealed/jxta-NetGroup
GOT A REPLY MESSAGE
Message contains reply address of - jxta://uuid-5961626164616261A78746150325033
6899C6AA20CD4AF8B414AA3629D4A64A03/SimpleGroupRevealed/jxta-NetGroup
TRYING TO SEND MESSAGE TO SERVICE now...
```

Helping to Build EZEL

One of the best ways to master a new technology is to actually work with it. EZEL is a brand new project that needs new participants who wish to build more and more involved JXTA services and clients (beyond the demonstration ones that we create in this book).

Feel free to experiment with EZEL by modifying it for your own requirements. By all means, contribute your expertise and discoveries to the living EZEL project so that all users of EZEL will benefit from your findings. This is the spirit of the EZEL project, and certainly a key attraction of JXTA itself.

Painless JXTA Migration

In this chapter, we have covered EZEL completely. From its design goals, to its architecture, through to its detailed implementation. More importantly, we have looked underneath and become familiar with the JXTA platform APIs that are used to implement each and every aspect of EZEL's functionality.

Through examination of the EZEL code, we have become comfortable with:

1. Creating and working with various types of Advertisements (pipe, `ModuleClass`, `ModuleSpec`)

2. Publishing advertisement, both local and remote

3. Working with structured documents and JXTA messages

4. Working with pipes

5. Sending message to pipes and receiving them, using the listener interfaces

6. Discovering advertisements on a JXTA network, both local and remote

7. Creating endpoint handlers and resolver query handlers

8. Working with JXTA's core endpoint service and resolver service

In fact, we are more than ready to create our own JXTA client and services from scratch, without EZEL.

At the end of the chapter, we turned our attention to the peer-group semantics that are demonstrated by the `PGServiceBase` class example at the end of the last chapter. This time, we looked under the hood and saw how the class is implemented. The combination of JXTA's distributed query propagation and virtualized peer network provide the basis for this implementation.

5

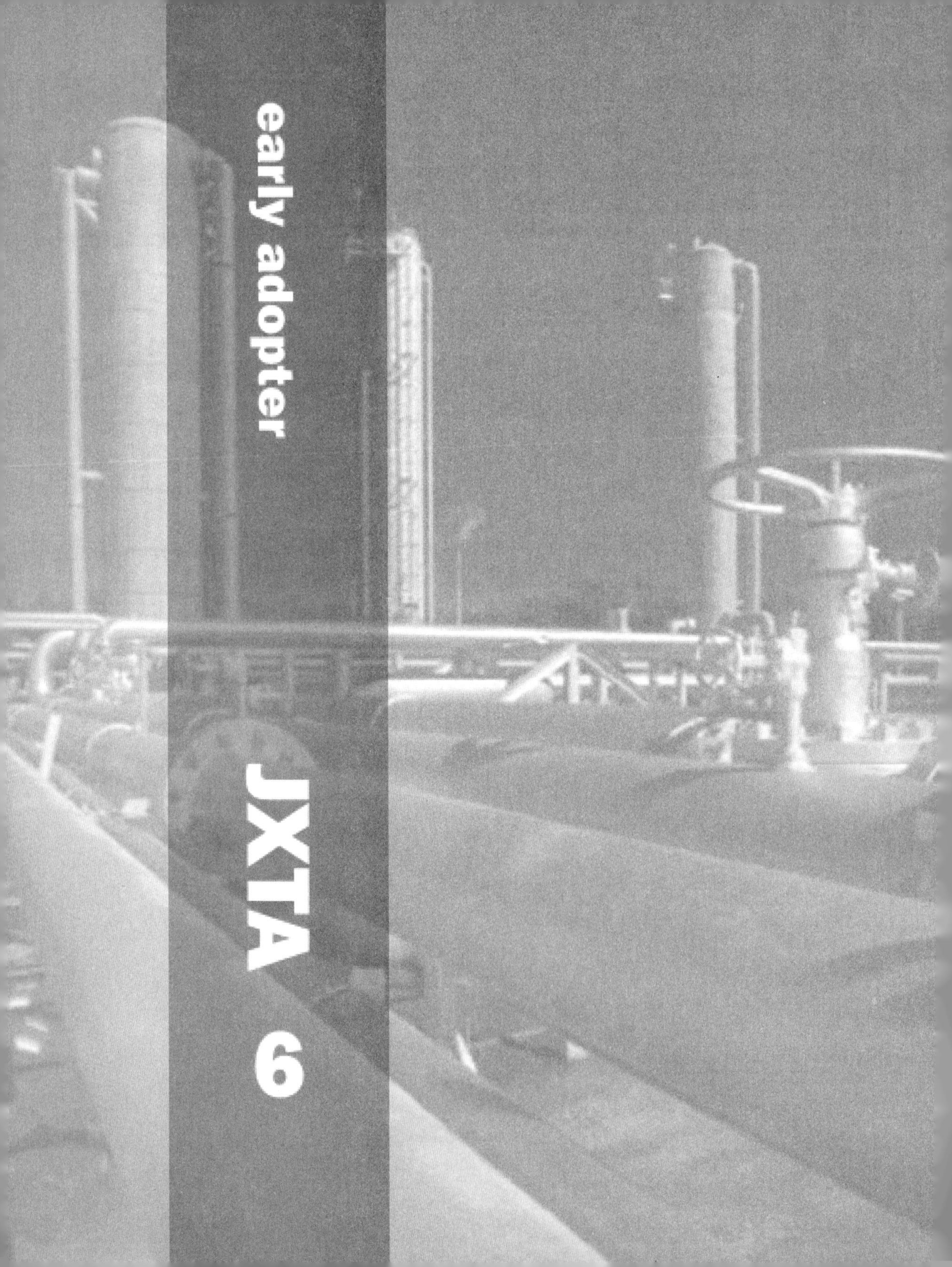
early adopter
JXTA
6

WroxShare:
A JXTA Application Case Study

The first few chapters of this book gave us a solid background on P2P technology, and more specifically, on how JXTA provides an interoperable platform for building P2P systems. In the last couple of chapters, we have gone code-intensive and created JXTA services and clients on top of EZEL. Finally, in Chapter 5, we went down a level, and examined the JXTA platform APIs that are used by EZEL to carry out its operations. Overall, we should now have an understanding of JXTA from concepts to detailed design, and we have experienced coding both on a high level (services and client), and close to the bare iron, at the platform-API level. We are now ready for a challenge in this chapter; that challenge is to write a complete JXTA application.

Now, the space available in this single chapter, or in this entire book for that matter, is not sufficient to present the design and coding of any meaningful application. Instead of attempting this futile feat, we present the skeleton (or a stripped down version) of a JXTA application. By skeleton, we do not mean something that is a sample or non-functional. Rather, we will be creating a prototype that may lack a sophisticated user interface, exception handling, and so on; but is fully complete in terms of its functionality.

As we have discussed at length before, there are only a couple of well known "application patterns" (see Chapter 4) that individual JXTA applications tend to evolve around today. The application that we will be creating is an instance of the Content Sharing Network application pattern.

We call this application "WroxShare". It enables users on a network to share files easily – via a drag-and-drop enabled GUI. This chapter will cover WroxShare, from conceptual design, through to detailed coding, and finally testing. WroxShare will give us some solid, hands-on experience of programming with the platform APIs. It will also demonstrate how we can leverage built-in (or freely available open source) services in JXTA for our own applications.

The WroxShare Project

In our coverage of the WroxShare project, we will first describe the functionality that we desire – in the form of a small functional specification. Next, we will cover the high-level design and show how to satisfy the functional requirements. This coverage will also shed light on some of the design decisions (or choices) that we have made, and provide some justifications. Many of these issues are common to most JXTA or P2P projects.

Then we cover the detailed design, and examine the protocols and classes that will be used within the project. Finally, we present the code and show how the platform API is used to realize the WroxShare utility.

WroxShare Functional Analysis

WroxShare presents a very simple GUI of two lists. The screenshot below shows how the simple GUI will look.

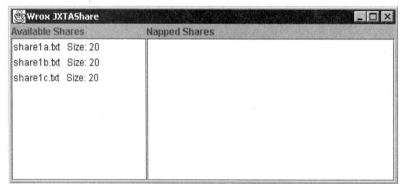

Any files that are shared by the users in this group will automatically appear on the left-hand "Available Shares" list.

A user, seeing files that they would like, can simply drag and drop the file onto the right-hand "**Napped Shares**" The term "**Napped shares**" probably derives from the word kidnap and simply refers to those shared files that the user is trying to grab. This node will not share the files in this list until the WroxShare application restarts.

Any user of WroxShare can share files on the network; they simply place files in the sharedir subdirectory of the WroxShare start up directory.

Upon restart, the peer – potentially providing another peer with a "closer" copy – will share any file that was napped in the previous session. This will enable widely requested files to be quickly replicated throughout the network, further increasing their availability and the probability of finding a desired file. Figure 1 illustrates the operation of WroxShare.

Figure 1

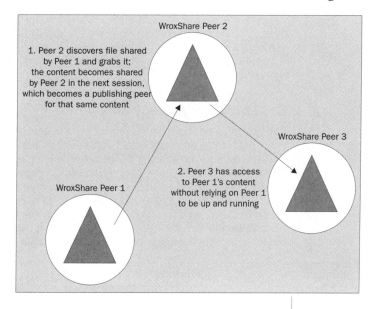

If you run `WroxShare` on a TCP/IP based LAN, everyone on the same subnet will be able to freely share files immediately – due to the JXTA default `NetPeerGroup`. If you configure the JXTA platform to use the Internet, `WroxShare` will also work over the virtualized JXTA network, on top of and across any other supported transport. It will again work within the JXTA default `NetPeerGroup` – which can be quite large in the Internet scenario.

Note that `WroxShare` exhibits some of the key properties of a P2P application:

❑ It does not require any particular individual peer to be running on the network; as long as there are two sharing peers running – sharing can take place

❑ It will work with non-deterministic network topologies where peers can disconnect at any time, and may never reconnect again

❑ The more peers there are operating on the network, the better the chance of seeing a file you want, and the better the chance of finding a copy nearby – "nearby" meaning in this case roughly the first peers to respond to a query

WroxShare High-Level Design

In order to create `WroxShare`, we will need:

❑ A service that manages shared files (or content in general) on each peer, the service should be designed as a peergroup service – like the `SimpleGroupService` that we created in Chapter 4.

❑ A client component that can query the service for what it contains.

❑ A client GUI that can display the list of files available from all instances of the service in the group (network). The client GUI should also handle drag-and-drop action and translate it to commands for fetching remote files.

❑ A client component that will request and download a file from another peer.

It sounds like a lot of work, and it is! Fortunately, we don't have to do the work for the toughest parts. Points one, three, and four all can be handled by a service that is supplied with the JXTA platform. In particular, point 1 can be handled by the Content Management Service (CMS) – note, however, that it isn't a JXTA core service, yet.

Content Management Service

CMS is a JXTA peergroup service that can be used to manage shared content on every peer, and make that content available for sharing throughout the peer group. CMS manages a local index of the content that is available for sharing on a peer. This includes file name, size, description, and a unique ID representing the content. The files being shared are left in place; the CMS does not maintain or cache these files. The CMS does not have any active client components. However, the CMS library has client APIs that CMS client applications should (must) use in communicating with the CMS service. When using these library APIs, the CMS service accepts two different types of request from clients:

Request	Description
ListContent Request	A "tell me what you are sharing" request; the CMS being queried will return a series of content advertisements. The returned advertisements are those that match the criteria specified in the `ListContentRequest`. Each content advertisement contains the indexed details of the associated piece of content available (name, description, size, etc.) for sharing.
GetContent Request	This is the "give me the file" request. Given a content advertisement, this request will start transmission of the content from the sharing peer to the requesting peer.

Figure 2 illustrates the operation of CMS.

Figure 2

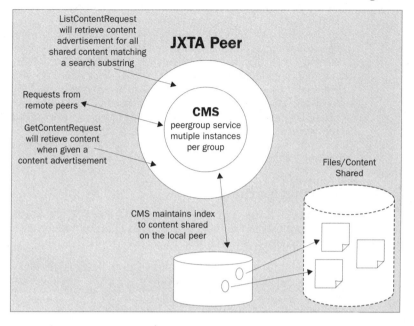

Note that each WroxShare peer contains both the client and the service functionality of CMS within it. Each WroxShare peer shares its list of files and discovers/queries for the files shared by all other WroxShare peers.

The messaging protocol for these two requests is well defined, making them potentially interoperable with other implementations of the same service. It also enables the protocol to eventually become one of the foundation protocols of JXTA.

Indeed, CMS may someday soon become part of the JXTA platform core services. A portion of a separate project, called JXTA-wire, has just (at the time of writing) been incorporated into the core of the JXTA platform. This sort of incorporation of stable new services that enhance the usability of JXTA will continue to occur, and appears to be part of the culture of the JXTA community. For one thing, the JXTA-wire propagation technology makes applications that follow the Instant Messaging Network application pattern very easy to write. Together CMS and JXTA-wire cover the universe of known and popular applications for P2P networking. In the near future, it is foreseeable that new application patterns may surface, and the platform team may come up with other internal features that will facilitate the creation of applications following these new patterns.

In this chapter, we will show you physically that the CMS will make applications that follow the Content Sharing Network application pattern very easy to write.

Uniquely Identifying Content

Anyone familiar with file sharing networks will recognize the frustration that comes with downloading huge files that may have different names, but turn out to have identical content. CMS keeps track of content, not using its filename (which users can change at any time), but via a unique ID. For text files, this unique ID is generated with a hashing algorithm that practically guarantees duplicate files are detected. For binary files, the unique ID is a generated UUID. JXTA already has the Codat concept, described in Chapter 2, – and uses a similar ID system. Eventually, these two unique content identification systems may be unified. This unique way of identifying content enables content replication to occur based on the unique content ID, rather than meaningless and unreliable user-selected file names. It promotes a more efficient use of bandwidth and storage in the JXTA network. However, a side effect of this design is that there is a chance users may give two files with different content the same name.

Swinging for the GUI

We will be using the JDK's built-in Swing GUI library to construct the `WroxShare` applications user interface. It offers us three attractive functionalities that make our development task especially easy:

❑ The list, panel, and button-based GUI can be easily created using library components

❑ Drag-and-drop handling is built into the library

❑ It supports an MVC (Model View Controller) programming model that will simplify the design of our application

With these design decisions out of the way, the rest of the design and coding exercise becomes coordinating the Swing GUI with the CMS client functionality.

EZEL not Applicable for WroxShare

EZEL cannot be used for `WroxShare` because we are actually not writing both the client and service end of what's inside `WroxShare`. The service side is pre-written and pre-tested – the CMS. In fact, even the client part is provided as a part of the CMS library – which we'll learn about later.

The WroxShare Architecture – Detailed Design

From the high-level design, it is clear that we will:

❑ Use the MVC model of Swing to co-ordinate between GUI and client functionality

❑ Use CMS as the service component

❑ Handle drag-and-drop using Swing

This means that we will need at least of two concurrent threads of execution. Here is what each thread will be doing:

Thread Number	Duties
1	Starts the application, starts the local CMS instance, sets up the GUI, sets up the GUI listeners, and then lets the Swing library handle the GUI – the original application startup thread actually dies. The Swing-managed thread will handle GUI operations including drag-and-drop operations.
2	Works in a loop, discovering newly shared content, handing new content to GUI, and checking to see if any drag-and-drop content needs to be transferred.

The classes that we will need in the WroxShare application are described below:

Class Name	Description
ShareFrame	This is the main class that starts up the entire application. As expected, it inherits from Swing's JFrame. Its main duty is to start the JXTA platform and create the GUI. Most of the components used are standard run-of-the-mill Swing components, except for the displayed lists. These are custom subclasses that we'll fabricate – ShareList, covered next.
ShareList	This is a subclass of Swing's JList, in which we enable drag-and-drop. This class represents the "View + Controller" in the MVC design pattern. Both of our list instances on the GUI are instances of this ShareList class. It collaborates with the Model (covered next) in ensuring that the data displayed is synchronized with the actual set of shares discovered. Ideally, we should have two subclasses of JList since one will always be a drag source and the other a drop target. However, we have overloaded a single subclass in order to conserve GUI code footprint and focus on JXTA application.
ShareListModel	This is where the data resides – the "Model" in the MVC design pattern. In fact, it supplies data for display on the "**Available Shares**" list. While both lists on the GUI look the same, the "**Available Shares**" list is special in that the data that it displays is the same as the collection of files that has been discovered by the CMS client.

Table continued on following page

6

Class Name	Description
FinderThread	All of the other classes we mentioned thus far live and execute largely on the GUI handling thread this FinderThread class lives on its own thread. This is the "backend" or the worker thread of the application. As discussed previously, it continuously looks for newly shared files and updates the list in the model with this information. Every so often, it will also check to see if a user has performed a drag-and-drop operation; if so, this thread is also responsible for transferring the file requested.
SearchResult	This class represents a piece of content that has been located. It has the correct semantics for equals() and toString() for the WroxShare application.
SearchListener	This is the listener interface defined for asynchronous coupling between ShareListModel and FinderThread.

Figure 3 shows how all the classes in WroxShare work together.

Figure 3

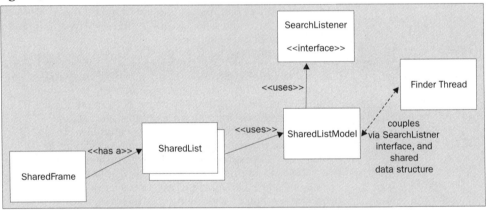

We can see that one thread of operation is responsible for starting the application and handling the GUI user interface. The other thread of operation is looping in the FinderThread() and manages dynamic lookup of new content, list updates, and transfer of any selected files. There exist two places where the front-end GUI thread is synchronized with the back-end discovery/worker thread:

❑   The data within ShareListModel

❑   The list of files that are waiting to be transferred

In the first case, the background thread is the producer (adding newly discovered files to the model), and the GUI thread is the consumer. In the second case, the GUI thread is the producer (indicating the file(s) that needs to be transferred), and the background thread is the consumer – actually transferring the file(s). Figure 4 shows this coupling.

Figure 4

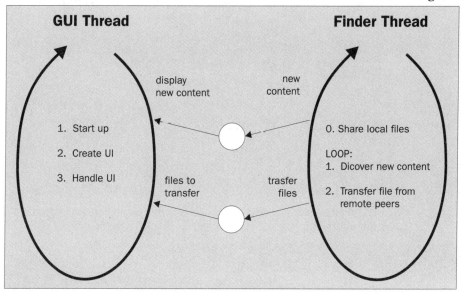

Obviously, the data structures that are used between the two threads should be protected with synchronized access. We will see that this is the case, later in the code. This sort of design partitioning between an MVC maintained front-end, and one or more background working threads that are managing the client part of a JXTA service, is a very common in JXTA. Tighter coupling between the front end and the back is usually not possible, because many of the events that occur in the P2P or JXTA world are asynchronous – and often even non-deterministic. GUI designers will have to be especially vigilant on this last point. Unlike other deterministic systems, JXTA GUI designer must be tolerant to failed or very long requests, and deal with constant topological changes.

If you understand how WroxShare works with the above two-thread design work partition, it should be easy to comprehend the code that is presented next.

Coding the WroxShare Application

Now that we have completed its detailed design, the application is practically written already. Let us verify our proposed architecture and examine the code of each class that's involved.

ShareFrame – The Main Program and GUI Assembler

This class is the main program that starts the entire application; it is also where the GUI is assembled. You can find the sourcecode in the com.wrox.ea.jxtashare package of the code download and it's presented below as well:

WroxShare

6

243

```
package com.wrox.ea.jxtashare;

import java.awt.BorderLayout;
import java.awt.event.WindowAdapter;
import java.awt.event.WindowEvent;
import javax.swing.JFrame;
import javax.swing.JList;
import javax.swing.JPanel;
import javax.swing.JLabel;
import javax.swing.ListModel;
import javax.swing.DefaultListModel;
import javax.swing.BoxLayout;
import javax.swing.JScrollPane;
```

We can detect the usual cast of characters for a Swing based application in the import list, followed by the now familiar payers of a JXTA application:

```
import net.jxta.peergroup.PeerGroup;
import net.jxta.peergroup.PeerGroupFactory;
import net.jxta.exception.PeerGroupException;
```

The ShareFrame class derives from Swing's JFrame, and the targetModel variable holds an instance of the model backing our visual "**Available Shares**" list:

```
class ShareFrame extends JFrame {

  static SharedListModel targetModel = null;
  private String pname = null;
  private PeerGroup group = null;
```

The first method is startJxta(); it is a helper method used to start an instance of the JXTA platform, and the default NetPeerGroup. Note that the successfully started group is assigned to the private group variable.

```
private void startJxta() {
  try {
    // create, and start the default jxta NetPeerGroup
    group = PeerGroupFactory.newNetPeerGroup();
  } catch (PeerGroupException e) {
    System.out.println("ShareFrame : group creation failure");
    e.printStackTrace();
    System.exit(1);
  }
}
```

Next, the constructor of the ShareFrame. The JList parent is first initialized, next, the ShareFrame instance will start the JXTA platform using the startJxta() helper method.

```
public ShareFrame() {
  super("Wrox JXTAShare");
  System.out.println("Starting jxta ....");
  startJxta();
```

Next, the GUI is assembled using standard Swing component assembly code. However, for the two listboxes in the GUI, we are using our own drag-and-drop enabled specialization of JList, called SharedList. More specifically, the list on the left, referenced by the availList variable, also has an instance of the SharedListModel as its model. The ShareListModel encapsulates the data that is presented in the list (currently discovered and available shared contents), and keeps it perfectly synchronized. Note that content discovery, as with any distributed query-based operation, occurs only within the peer-group boundary. This is the reason why SharedListModel must be instantiated with the current group.

```
System.out.println ("Starting UI....");
SharedListModel availModel = null;
ShareList availList = new ShareList();
if (null != group) {
  availModel = new SharedListModel(group);
} else {
  System.out.println("ShareFrame: group must be initialized before
    building" + " UI");
  System.exit(1);
}
JPanel availPanel = getListPanel(availList, "Available Shares",
  (ListModel)availModel);
```

The right-hand side list is more ordinary; it contains the visual response from a drop operation – in fact, as we shall see later, the actual underlying file transfer may not have succeeded). It collects the "napped shares" in the current session. The list model used here is just the plain vanilla DefaultListModel of Swing.

```
ShareList napList = new ShareList();
DefaultListModel napModel = new DefaultListModel();
JPanel napPanel = getListPanel(napList, "Napped Shares",
                               napModel);
```

The last bit of GUI assembly code creates the containing panel, sets the size, and makes sure that the exit button at the title bar will work by adding an anonymous adapter that traps the windowClosing event – vintage Swing programming.

```
JPanel mainPanel = new JPanel();
mainPanel.setLayout(new BoxLayout(mainPanel, BoxLayout.X_AXIS));
mainPanel.add( availPanel );
mainPanel.add( napPanel );
```

```
getContentPane().add( mainPanel );
setSize (500, 300);
addWindowListener (new WindowAdapter() {
   public void windowClosing(WindowEvent e) {
      exitFrame();
   }
});
setVisible (true);
}
```

getListPanel() is just a method that factors out some common operations during the GUI assembly. This method makes the GUI assembly code a little less cluttered.

```
private JPanel getListPanel(ShareList list, String labelName,
                            ListModel listModel ){
   JPanel listPanel = new JPanel();
   JScrollPane scrollPane = new JScrollPane(list);
   list.setModel(listModel);
   JLabel nameListName = new JLabel(labelName );
   listPanel.setLayout( new BorderLayout());
   listPanel.add(nameListName, BorderLayout.NORTH);
   listPanel.add( scrollPane, BorderLayout.CENTER);

   return listPanel;
}
```

The exitFrame() method is called whenever the close button is clicked on the application's title bar. This enables application termination by the user.

```
private void exitFrame () {
   this.setVisible(false);
   this.dispose();
   System.exit(0);
}
```

The main method, as we can imagine by now, simply creates an instance of the ShareFrame, then it dies and lets the GUI thread, managed by the Swing runtime, take care of the GUI handling.

```
public static void main(String args[]) {
   ShareFrame myapp = new ShareFrame();
}
}
```

By careful design, we have managed to keep this initiating class extremely simple – and hopefully easy to understand and maintain. Most of the other work has been partitioned accordingly to the other classes of the application. The visual display of shared content is next.

ShareList – The Visualization of Shares

The ShareList class provides several essential functions. First, it is the "View + Controller" class in the MVC design pattern for the JList subclass. This means it presents the data that's maintained by the underlying model, and makes sure that it is synchronized with the display. Other than this important task, it also handles the drag-and-drop action supported by the user interface.

Files that are dropped onto the "**Napped Shares**" list are all collected in a Vector that is internal to the FinderThread class (as we shall see later), and accessed indirectly through a setFileToTransfer() method of the SharedListModel.

The design of this class, ShareList, is done with minimal GUI code footprint in mind. Since we do not want to pollute the JXTA discussion with complex GUI handling code, we have opted for some design decisions (discussed shortly) that may be irritating to some GUI gurus.

The import list of this class reflects the classes required to handle the drag-and-drop operation:

```
package com.wrox.ea.jxtashare;

import java.awt.dnd.DragSourceListener;
import java.awt.dnd.DropTargetListener;
import java.awt.dnd.DragGestureListener;
import java.awt.datatransfer.*;
import java.awt.dnd.DropTarget;
import java.awt.dnd.DropTargetDragEvent;
import java.awt.dnd.DropTargetDropEvent;
import java.awt.dnd.DropTargetEvent;
import java.awt.dnd.DragGestureEvent;
import java.awt.dnd.DragSourceDropEvent;
import java.awt.dnd.DragSourceDragEvent;
import java.awt.dnd.DragSourceEvent;
import java.awt.dnd.DragSource;
import java.awt.dnd.DnDConstants;
import java.util.Iterator;
import javax.swing.JList;
import javax.swing.DefaultListModel;
```

For the simple drag-and-drop behavior that we desire, we must implement the methods that are part of the three interfaces:

❑ java.awt.dnd.DropTargetListener

❑ java.awt.dnd.DragSourceListener

❑ java.awt.dnd.DragGestureListener

These are all the methods that are contained in this class. The rest of the programming is just to hook up the content to the underlying helper methods of the model.

```
public class ShareList extends JList implements DropTargetListener,
        DragSourceListener, DragGestureListener {
  DropTarget dropTarget = null;
  DragSource dragSource = null;
```

The constructor creates a dropTarget and a dragSource, the same list taking double duty to simplify usage, since both the "**Available Shares**" (a drag source) and the "**Napped Shares**" (a drop target) will use the same base class. We also want to detect the drag gesture, in order to start file transfer as early as possible, and therefore we install a listener for the DefaultDragGestureRecognizer.

```
public ShareList() {
  dropTarget = new DropTarget (this, this);
  dragSource = new DragSource();
  dragSource.createDefaultDragGestureRecognizer(this,
    DnDConstants.ACTION_MOVE, this);
}
```

Here, the list always accepts drags:

```
public void dragEnter (DropTargetDragEvent event) {
  event.acceptDrag (DnDConstants.ACTION_MOVE);
}
```

We do nothing with the dragExit() or dragOver() hints:

```
public void dragExit (DropTargetEvent event) {}
public void dragOver (DropTargetDragEvent event) {}
```

Now, since the "**Available Shares**" list should never take a drop, we make sure that this is the case. Otherwise, we check the drop to make sure it is a String, and we accept it. An apology is due to GUI purists out there, as this overloading of functionalities makes it difficult to reuse this class. Please be reassured that it is done for a good cause, reducing GUI code footprint so we can focus on the JXTA application.

```
public void drop (DropTargetDropEvent event) {
  if (this.getModel() instanceof SharedListModel) {
    event.rejectDrop();
    return;
  }
  try {
    Transferable transferable = event.getTransferable();
    // we accept only Strings
    if (transferable.isDataFlavorSupported (DataFlavor.stringFlavor))
{
      event.acceptDrop(DnDConstants.ACTION_MOVE);
```

```
      String s = (String) transferable.getTransferData(
        DataFlavor.stringFlavor);
      addElement( s );
      event.getDropTargetContext().dropComplete(true);
    } else {
      event.rejectDrop();
    }
  } catch (Exception ex) {
    ex.printStackTrace();
    event.rejectDrop();
  }
}

public void dropActionChanged ( DropTargetDragEvent event ) {}
```

Here is where we cheat a little, upon the detection of a drag from the "Available Shares" list, we actually call the setFileToTransfer() method of the model and queued the demand to transfer the file. In other words, we assume that anyone dragging a file from the "Available Shares" list intends to drop it into the "Napped Shares" list. The GUI purist amongst the readership may baulk at this point. However, doing so avoids a fair bit of complex code that we really could not afford to highlight in the context of the already complex topic of JXTA.

```
public void dragGestureRecognized( DragGestureEvent event) {
  SharedListModel sm;
  if (!(this.getModel() instanceof SharedListModel)) {
    return;
  } else {
    sm = (SharedListModel) this.getModel();
  }

  Object selected = getSelectedValue();
  if ( selected != null ){
    StringSelection text = new StringSelection(
      selected.toString());
    sm.setFileToTransfer(selected);
    dragSource.startDrag (event, DragSource.DefaultMoveDrop, text,
      this);
  } else {}
}
```

The rest of the methods are obligatory methods to implement the required drag-and-drop interfaces.

```
public void dragDropEnd (DragSourceDropEvent event) {
  if ( event.getDropSuccess()) {}
}
```

```
public void dragEnter (DragSourceDragEvent event) {}
public void dragExit (DragSourceEvent event) {}
public void dragOver (DragSourceDragEvent event) {}
public void dropActionChanged (DragSourceDragEvent event) {}
```

The addElement() and removeElement() methods synchronize with the underlying model's methods of the same name. This is what keeps the "Available Shares" list always displaying the currently available content.

```
public void addElement( Object s ) {
    ((DefaultListModel)getModel()).addElement (s.toString());
}
public void removeElement(){
    ((DefaultListModel)getModel()).removeElement(getSelectedValue());
}
}
```

The next major class we visit will be the SharedListModel that is backing the "Available Shares" list. Before we can understand its operation, we must first examine two classes that it uses – SearchListener, and SearchResult.

SearchListener – Coupling Between Two Threads

The SharedListModel implements this interface, and then it adds itself as a listener to the FinderThread class. This is how the two independently running threads are synchronized. When the FinderThread discovers new contents, the SharedListModel is notified through the searchUpdate() method of this interface. Since the SharedListModel is always synchronized with the "View component" ShareList, the user will always see the latest list of available content to share.

```
package com.wrox.ea.jxtashare;

public interface SearchListener {
    public void searchUpdate();
}
```

SearchResult – Representing Unique Content

While we could have kept a list of content advertisements around as the search result that we've obtained, the methods of the ContentAdvertisement interface are not too friendly for our list display and maintenance purposes (namely, no equals() operator to compare two content advertisements to see if they represent the same content). Therefore, we wrap a discovered ContentAdvertisement with a friendlier SearchResult class. This class provides two very useful features around an underlying ContentAdvertisement. It overrides the toString() and equals() method from Object, and implements the correct semantics that makes our list programming dramatically easier.

```
package com.wrox.ea.jxtashare;

import net.jxta.share.ContentAdvertisement;

public class SearchResult {
```

As we can see here, the SearchResult is just a wrapper or adapter if you will, for a raw ContentAdvertisement in the WroxShare application. In order words, for each discovered ContentAdvertisement, there will be exactly one instance of the SearchResult class.

```
public ContentAdvertisement contentAdv = null;

SearchResult(
  ContentAdvertisement inContent) {
    contentAdv = inContent;
}

public ContentAdvertisement getContentAdvertisement(){
  return contentAdv;
}
```

The toString() implementation is used as an item on the SharedList (by default javax.Swing.ListCellRenderer) to display the file name and the size.

```
public String toString() {
  return (contentAdv.getName() + "   Size: " +
    contentAdv.getLength());
}
```

The equals() method is implemented such that instances of SearchResults can be compared directly. The semantic implemented is simple but extremely useful in eliminating duplicate search items: two SearchResults are equal if and only if their content ID is identical. This ability to directly compare SearchResult instances makes the list model implementation quite straightforward.

```
public boolean equals(Object inObj) {
  boolean retval = false;
  if (inObj instanceof SearchResult) {
    SearchResult tpSR = (SearchResult) inObj;
    retval = contentAdv.getContentId().equals(
              tpSR.getContentAdvertisement().getContentId());
    if (retval) {
      System.err.println("-- compared IS equal");
    } else {
      System.err.println("--- compared NOT equal");
```

```
      }
    }
    return retval;
  }
}
```

Now, we are ready to examine the SharedListModel, and see how it manages the discovered SearchResults (wrapped ContentAdvertisements) and keep them synchronized with the ShareList "View".

SharedListModel – Managing Discovered SearchResults

The SharedListModel class is where data, in this case SearchResults (or equivalently ContentAdvertisements), are managed. It implements a ListModel for the ShareList instance that has the "**Available List**" label. Much of the grunt work involved in implementing a ListModel is taken care of by the AbstractListModel base class from Swing; the SharedListModel simply overrides the methods that we are interested in implementing.

```
package com.wrox.ea.jxtashare;

import javax.swing.AbstractListModel;
import java.util.Vector;
import net.jxta.peergroup.PeerGroup;
```

Note that SharedListModel implements the SearchListener interface. This interface provides the coupling between the independent FinderThread and the SharedListModel. Anytime the FinderThread locates some new content, the SharedListModel is called back via this interface.

```
public class SharedListModel extends AbstractListModel implements
SearchListener {
  SearchResult [] foundSharedItems = null;
  FinderThread backgroundFinder = null;
  Thread bkgThread = null;
  Vector listData = null;
  Vector displayData = null;

  public SharedListModel() {
    super();
  }
```

The listData that is managed by the SharedListModel is kept in a double-buffered set of Vectors. The raw data is contained in the listData vector; occasionally a snapshot of listData is created and used in displayData. Using this double-buffered set of Vectors will enable us to present a static view to the ShareList while the listData underneath may be undergoing modification. We will see this in operation later on.

Here, we can also see that the constructor of the SharedListModel actually starts FinderThread. This is appropriate in this application, to avoid the need to have the main program looking after this easy-to-miss detail. Essentially, this design says that the SharedListModel is useless without an associated FinderThread, and vice versa. This is certainly true in the WroxShare application; the mapping between SharedListModel and FinderThread in this simple application is always one-to-one.

```
public SharedListModel(PeerGroup pg) {
  super();

  listData = new Vector();
  backgroundFinder = new FinderThread(pg);
  backgroundFinder.setListener(this);

  bkgThread = new Thread(backgroundFinder);
  bkgThread.setPriority ( Thread.MAX_PRIORITY -1  );
  bkgThread.start();
}
```

Here are the implementation methods of ListModel. The "View" class, ShareList, will call these methods to determine how to display the list content. The getSize() method below enables the ShareList to find out what the size of the displayed list should be.

```
public int getSize() {
  int retval;
  if (null == displayData) {
    retval = 1;
  } else {
    retval = displayData.size();
  }
  return retval;
}
```

We simply return the size of the displayData vector. Recall that this is the snapshot version of the dynamic listData vector. Note also, that we return a list size of at least one before the snapshot list is created because we need a placeholder, otherwise GUI packing will make the list invisible.

```
public Object getElementAt(int parm1) {
  System.out.println("****called element at with param=" + parm1);
  if (null == displayData) {
    return ("searching, please wait .......");
  } else {
    return ( displayData.get(parm1));
  }
}
```

The ShareList will call into the model to get an element for display. Here, we simply return the corresponding element in the displayData vector. Initially, before the snapshot is available, we display a "searching" message in the single placeholder element.

FinderThread calls the searchUpdate() method, asynchronously, every time there is newly discovered content (SearchResults). As this is happening on another thread, it can occur at any time.

```
// implementation of SearchListener
public void searchUpdate() {
```

Here, we set a Boolean flag indicating that nothing new is available; we will set this to true if we find new content. Next, we call the FinderThread's grabResults() method, which returns an array of SearchResults into the foundSharedItems variable. Then, we go through this foundSharedItems array an element at a time, and compare the SearchResult to the ones already in the listData vector. Thank goodness for the equals() method of SearchResult; we can use the powerful contains() method of the Vector to simplify this comparison. Essentially, the Vector's contains() method will now go through the entire listData vector and compare each SearchResult for us to see if a SearchResult (wrapped ContentAdvertisement) is already in the Vector.

```
boolean newAdditions = false;
foundSharedItems = backgroundFinder.grabResults();
int startIndex = listData.size();
for (int i=0; i<foundSharedItems.length; i++) {
  SearchResult tpRes = foundSharedItems[i];

  // add it if not already in the list
  if (!listData.contains(tpRes)) {
    listData.add(tpRes);
    newAdditions = true;
  }
}
```

Any newly found content that we do not already have would be added to the listData vector, which we know is the "backup" vector for the actual displayed data. Therefore, we next determine if any new additions have been made to the listData; if so, we place a clone into the displayData variable. We also notify the "View" (ShareList in our case) that the list content has changed. This will keep the displayed list synchronized with the actual discovered content.

```
if (newAdditions) {
  this.displayData = (Vector) this.listData.clone();
  this.fireIntervalAdded(this, startIndex, listData.size());
  System.err.println("**** called update with " + listData.size()
                     + " items");
} else {
```

```
        System.err.println("**** called update but no new updates");
    }
  } //of searchUpdate
```

The final method is used for posting a file to be transferred (via CMS's GetContent request) from a remote peer. The FinderThread will be handling these transfers whenever it has time available.

```
public void setFileToTransfer(Object inFile) {
  if (inFile instanceof SearchResult) {
    SearchResult tpRes = (SearchResult) inFile;
    backgroundFinder.fetchFile(tpRes);
  }
}
}
```

For the work that the SharedListModel does, it is quite a compact class.

Finally, we will look at its partner in crime, the background worker, and CMS master – the FinderThread class.

FinderThread – The Asynchronous Background Worker Thread

Yes, FinderThread is one of the most complex classes in the entire WroxShare project. However, it is also the easiest to understand – because everything it does is procedural and methodical.

We can see from its relatively large import list that it will be covering a lot of the JXTA platform API.

```
package com.wrox.ea.jxtashare;

import java.io.File;
import java.io.FileInputStream;
import java.util.Vector;
import java.util.Iterator;
import net.jxta.document.Advertisement;
import net.jxta.exception.PeerGroupException;
import net.jxta.peergroup.PeerGroup;
```

Of special interest, here are the helper client-side CMS classes that we import. These include CachedListContentRequest and GetContentRequest. These classes live in the net.jxta.share.client package, and any CMS client can use them. These classes alleviate the need for a client to work with the Resolver service and the Endpoint service, in the same manner as the PGClientBase class that we have seen in the last chapter.

```
import net.jxta.share.client.CachedListContentRequest;
import net.jxta.share.client.GetContentRequest;
```

The rest of the CMS package is in the net.jxta.share package. Here are all the
server-side classes that relate to CMS, including CMS itself. ContentManager is the
actual workhorse of CMS; it manages the content index on the local peer.
Therefore, we can access ContentManager directly to find out about local shares –
without working through the long-drawn loopback ListContentRequest query.

```
import net.jxta.share.CMS;
import net.jxta.share.Content;
import net.jxta.share.ContentManager;
import net.jxta.share.ContentAdvertisement;
import net.jxta.share.ContentId;
import net.jxta.share.ContentIdImpl;
```

Since FinderThread runs independently, it derives from Thread to enable the
independent execution of the logic in its run() method – the only method in a
Runnable interface.

DISC_FILTER_PATTERN is the argument string for the GetContentRequest
query. A "" empty string acts as a wild card, fetching all shared contents.
WROX_BASEDIR is where CMS will be storing its own index information.
shareDirName is where we will be placing the WroxShare files (actual files, not
indexes) to be shared.

```
public class FinderThread extends Thread {
    private static String DISC_FILTER_PATTERN = "";
    private static String PEER_PREMIERE = null;
    private static String WROX_BASEDIR = "WROX_SHARE";
    private static final String shareDirName = "sharedir";
    private static final int WAIT_TIME = 10 * 1000;  // 10 secs
    private PeerGroup group = null;
```

The doQuit flag is used to shutdown the thread for debugging; results stores a
Vector of SearchResults. The listReq variable holds the currently outstanding
ListContentRequest issued to the CMS at any time. filesToFetch stores all
the files that the front-end GUI thread has asked us to transfer from remote peers.
The listener variable is used to hold a reference to the currently registered
listener (only one, the SharedListModel instance). The inSearch Boolean will
tell us if there are uncompleted ListContentRequest.

```
    private boolean doQuit = false;
    private static Vector results = new Vector();
    private ListRequestor listReq = null;
    private static Vector filesToFetch = new Vector();
    private SearchListener listener = null;
    private static boolean inSearch = false;
    private static CMS cms = null;
```

In the constructor, we initialize the `doQuit` flag and set the `group` (query propagation boundary) that we will be searching within.

```
public FinderThread(PeerGroup grp) {
  doQuit = false;
  group = grp;
}
```

The helper `isInSearch()` method can be used to determine if there exists a pending `ListContentRequest` to the CMS.

```
public boolean isInSearch() {
  return inSearch;
}
```

For debugging purposes, the `cancel()` method can be used to stop this thread.

```
public void cancel() {
  this.doQuit = true;
}
```

The `shareLocal()` method scans the `sharedir` directory, and calls the `ContentManager` in the local CMS instance to share every one of the files (for instance creating a `ContentAdvertisement` and propagating it). Note the use of `ContentIdImpl` to create a unique ID based on the hash of the actual file content.

```
private void shareLocal() {
  System.out.println("*** SHARE LOCAL*****");
  File shareDir = new File(shareDirName);
  ContentManager cmgr = cms.getContentManager();

  if ((null != shareDir) && ( shareDir.isDirectory())) {
    File [] filesToShare = shareDir.listFiles();
    try {
      for (int i=0; i< filesToShare.length; i++) {
        System.out.println("trying " +
          filesToShare[i].getAbsolutePath());
        ContentIdImpl mycid =
          new ContentIdImpl(new FileInputStream(filesToShare[i]));

        Content [] match = cmgr.getContent(mycid);
        if (0 == match.length) {
          cmgr.share(filesToShare[i]);
          System.out.println("*** SHARED 1 FILE -- "
                               + filesToShare[i].getAbsolutePath());
        }
      }
    } catch (Exception ex) {
```

```
      ex.printStackTrace();
    }
  }
}
```

The run() method contains the logic that is executed on the independent thread. It consists of a "do once" part, and a while() loop that repeats things.

```
public void run() {
  int waitTime = WAIT_TIME;
```

In the "do once" portion, we make sure the local instance of CMS is running, and then share all the files we have in the sharedir directory via the helper shareLocal() method. This is the only place that local files are shared (where ContentAdvertisements created and published), and therefore any later napped shares will not become shared in the group until WroxShare restarts.

```
cms = getCMSinstance(this.group);  // get CMS singleton instance
shareLocal();  // share all the local files
```

Then we go into the loop (which is terminated by the debug doQuit flag). Inside the loop, we will perform a ListContentRequest search if one is not started. We then sleep for a little while, about 10 seconds with the currently set constant. Next, we check to see if there are any files to be fetched from the remote peer – and transfer them into our sharedir directory if any. This is the exact logic we have pinpointed in early detailed design.

```
while (!doQuit) {
  getLocalFiles();
  if (!inSearch) {
    checkSharedFiles();
  }
  try {
    Thread.sleep(waitTime);
  } catch (InterruptedException e) {}
  transferFiles();
  }
}
```

The getLocalFiles() method obtains the list of files that are shared locally. This can be readily done via the ContentManager within the local CMS instance. We use the getContent() method of the ContentManager to perform this task. Note that we load it up into the results vector, and then notify any registered listener of the update – meaning that we notify the SharedListModel.

```
private void getLocalFiles() {
  System.out.println("****  GET LOCAL****");
  ContentManager contentManager = cms.getContentManager();
  Content[] foundContent = contentManager.getContent();
  System.out.println("found " + foundContent.length + " files");
```

```
    ContentAdvertisement tpAdv;
    if( foundContent != null){
      synchronized(results) {
        for (int i=0; i<foundContent.length; i++) {
          tpAdv = foundContent[i].getContentAdvertisement();
          System.out.println("trying to add one");
          SearchResult searchResult = new SearchResult(tpAdv);
          if ( searchResult != null ) {
            results.addElement(searchResult);
            System.out.println("added one!");
          }
        }
      } // of synchronized

      if (null != listener) {
        listener.searchUpdate();
      }
    }
  }
```

The checkSharedFiles() method performs the remote CMS search. This is done via the helper ListRequestor class; we will see a little later that this class is a very thin wrapper based on the CachedListContentRequest class supplied by the client-side CMS library. This client-library base class takes care of calling the Resolver and Endpoint services in communicating with remote CMS instances. A ListRequestor is not active until the activateRequest() call is made. clearListReq() is a helper method to stop the running ListContentRequest, this is used only for debugging purposes.

```
private void checkSharedFiles() {
  clearListReq();
  listReq = new ListRequestor(group,DISC_FILTER_PATTERN);
  inSearch = true;
  listReq.activateRequest();
  System.out.println("*** starting search now *****");
}

public void clearListReq() {
  if (null != listReq) {
    listReq.cancel();
  }
}
```

The setListener() and resetListener() methods allow the SharedListModel class instance to "hook into" this FinderThread class instance during run time.

```
public void setListener(SearchListener l) {
  listener = l;
}


public void resetListener(SearchListener l) {
  listener = null;
}
```

Here is our thin wrapper class around the CMS client library's CachedListContentRequest class. It is called ListRequestor, and we only override the notifyMoreResults() method. The CachedListContentRequest will cache all content advertisements discovered and only notify us of more discovered results through the overridden callback method.

```
// wrapper class, handling the notification and propagate back to
listener
  class ListRequestor extends CachedListContentRequest {
    public ListRequestor( PeerGroup group, String inSubStr ) {
      super( group, inSubStr );
    }
```

In the notifyMoreResults() method, we load the results vector with an instance of a SearchResult for each of the content advertisements found (remember that the CMS client-side library only deals with content advertisements). Once the results vector is loaded, the listener (SharedListModel) is notified, and it can grab the results.

```
public void notifyMoreResults() {
  System.err.println("..*..*.. notifyMORE");
  ContentAdvertisement[] foundContent = this.getResults();
  if( foundContent != null){
    synchronized(results) {
      for (int i=0; i<foundContent.length; i++) {
        SearchResult searchResult = new
          SearchResult(foundContent[i]);
        if ( searchResult != null ) {
          results.addElement( searchResult );
        }
      }
    }
  }
  // notify the listener
  if (null != listener) {
    listener.searchUpdate();
  }
  inSearch = false;
  System.out.println("**** Search succeed");
}
```

```
    public void notifyFailure() {
      System.err.println("..*..*.. notify  FAILURE");
      inSearch = false;
      System.out.println("**** Search FAILED");
    }
  }
```

The listener class (SharedListModel) calls grabResults() when it is notified of new content discovery. It simply creates an array version of the results vector for the listener to work with locally.

```
public SearchResult[] grabResults() {
  SearchResult[] res = new SearchResult[results.size()];
  results.copyInto(res);
  return res;
}
```

Like our getInstance() method in the EZEL's PGServiceHost class, the getCMSinstance() method ensures that there is only one instance of the CMS running for the current group, on the local peer.

```
public static CMS getCMSinstance(PeerGroup group) {
  if (null == cms) {
    cms = new CMS();
    try {
      cms.init(group,null, group.getImplAdvertisement());
    } catch (PeerGroupException e) {
      e.printStackTrace();
    }
    cms.startApp(new File(getGroupDir(group), CMS.DEFAULT_DIR));
  }
  return cms;
}
```

getGroupDir() is a helper method to return the directory that CMS will use to store the content index for this particular group. It will be created under the WROX_BASEDIR master CMS directory, and will be in a subdirectory that has a unique name directly derived form the peer group ID.

```
private static File getGroupDir(PeerGroup grp) {
  File dir = null;
  // make sure the root directory exists
  File rootDir = new File(WROX_BASEDIR);
  if (!rootDir.exists()) {
    rootDir.mkdir();
  }
  // create a unique subdir per group
```

```
   dir = new File(rootDir,
      grp.getPeerGroupID().getUniqueValue().toString());
   if (!dir.exists()) {
      dir.mkdir();
   }
   return dir;
}
```

The transferFiles() method examines the filesToFetch vector to see the pending files that the GUI thread has asked the FinderThread to transfer from remote peers. It goes through them one at a time and generates a CMS GetContentRequest to get the file transferred – asynchronously. Note that it uses the client-side CMS library class GetContentRequest to get the transfer done. Once the request has started, it's considered done so the file is removed from the list of files to fetch. This can be made more robust by additional verification code.

```
public void transferFiles() {
   if (filesToFetch.size() > 0) {
      ContentManager cmgr = cms.getContentManager();
      Iterator it = filesToFetch.iterator();
      while (it.hasNext())   {
         SearchResult sr = (SearchResult) it.next();
         ContentAdvertisement tpAdv = sr.getContentAdvertisement();
         System.err.println(".....requesting content");
         GetContentRequest req = new GetContentRequest(group, tpAdv,
                     new File(shareDirName + File.separator +
                        tpAdv.getName()) );
      } // of while
      filesToFetch.removeAllElements();
   } // of if
}
```

The fetchFile() method is called by the SharedListModel to add files to the filesToFetch() list.

```
public void fetchFile(SearchResult inRes) {
   filesToFetch.add(inRes);
}
}
```

This concludes our coverage of the code involved in our case study. We will now proceed to compile and test these code modules – to see the WroxShare application in action.

Compiling and Testing WroxShare

In the `src\wroxshare` directory of the code download, we have provided a Win32 batch file for compiling and archiving the `WroxShare` application. It is called `makeshare.bat` and contains the following commands:

```
javac -classpath ..\..\lib\jxta.jar;..\..\lib\cms.jar  -d
..\..\classes com\wrox\ea\jxtashare\*.java
cd ..\..\classes
jar cvf ..\lib\wroxshare.jar .
cd ..\src\wroxshare
```

The `jar` utility, as shown above, is used to create an archive called `wroxshare.jar` that is placed into the `lib` directory of the source distribution. This is where we will locate and run the `WroxShare` application later.

To run three instances of `WroxShare`, each with its own JXTA platform configuration, and each with its own set of files to share, we can create three directories:

Directory Name	Details
test1	Set up JXTA peer named node1. sharedir contains share1a.txt, share1b.txt, and share1c.txt
test2	Set up JXTA peer named node2. sharedir contains share2a.txt, share2b.txt, and share2c.txt
test3	Set up JXTA peer named node3. sharedir contains share3a.txt, share3b.txt, and share3c.txt

Within each directory, you will find a `runit.bat` Win32 batch file for starting the `WroxShare` application. Each `runit.bat` contains:

```
java -classpath ..\lib\jxta.jar;..\lib\log4j.jar;..\lib\beepcore.jar;
    ..\lib\jxtasecurity.jar;..\lib\cryptix-asn1.jar;
    ..\lib\cryptix32.jar;
    ..\lib\minimalBC.jar;..\lib\jxtaptls.jar;..\lib\cms.jar;
    ..\lib\wroxshare.jar com.wrox.ea.jxtashare.ShareFrame
```

Now, start three command console windows on your system. Change directory to test1, test2, and test3 respectively. Then start three instances of `WroxShare` one at a time, configuring the JXTA platform according to the table overleaf.

Home Directory	Peer Name	Configuration
test1	node1	TCP enabled, HTTP disabled; manual TCP, localhost, 9701;
		no Rendezvous, no Gateway; your own security password
test2	node2	TCP enabled, HTTP disabled; manual TCP, localhost, 9703;
		no Rendezvous, no Gateway; your own security password
test3	node3	TCP enabled, HTTP disabled; manual TCP, localhost, 9705;
		no Rendezvous, no Gateway; your own security password

This will set up three instances of WroxShare, each on an independent peer over the network (simulated by loopback connection). Each peer has been set up to have different files to share.

After you start the first peer, node1, you should see its own three files to share on the GUI. The output should be similar to the screenshot below:

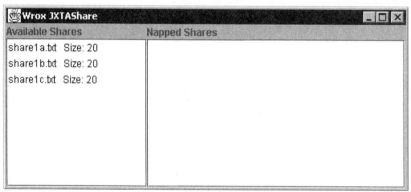

After you start the second peer, node2, you are bringing an additional three newly shared files onto the network. Both node1 and node2 should now display six shared files on the GUI. Your output from either node1 or node2 should be similar to the screenshot opposite:

Finally, when you start `node3`, now the network has nine files to share collectively. Each of `node1`, `node2`, and `node3` will show all nine files available. The screenshot bellow illustrates this network wide sharing of content.

Testing Drag-and-Drop File Transfer

Now, let us test the drag-and-drop file transfer capabilities. On the `node2` peer, which we know does not currently have a copy of the `share1a.txt` file; drag the `share1a.txt` file from the "**Available Share**" list to the "**Napped Share**" list. Wait about 15 second for `FinderThread` to get around to transferring the file. Now, shut down the `node2` peer, and check its `sharedir` directory. You will note that the `share1a.txt` file has been fetched and stored there.

Testing Content Replication

For something even more interesting, perform the following:

❑   Shut down `node1`; this disables the sharing of `share1a.txt`, `share1b.txt`, and `share1c.txt`

❑   Shut down `node3`

❑   Start up `node2`

❑   Restart node3

Now, imagine that the node3 peer wants the share1a.txt file but the publishing peer, node1, is unavailable for some reason. Does this mean that node3 can never get share1a.txt? Not in this JXTA network! node2, now started up, has published its own copy of share1a.txt. This means that node3 now has access to node1's content, even though node1 is no longer running – and may never run again. This is what we mean by "content replicating towards the users who want it" in a P2P content sharing network.

Try it out; drag and drop the share1.txt file from "**Available Shares**" to "**Napped Shares**" on node3. Shut down node3, and check the sharedir to ensure that indeed the content of node1 has survived its own demise.

Food for Thought

Now, astute readers will ask: what if we don't shut down and restart node3? This is interesting, because the attempt to transfer the share1.txt file will not immediately succeed. This illustrates a very subtle policy-based design decision that we have made when coding WroxShare.

We have decided to keep only the very first ContentAdvertisement that arrives for any specific file, uniquely identifiable by its ContentId. This is a very good policy most of the time, because the first peer to respond to a query is probably the closest peer to us that we have good connectivity with. However, a side effect of this, apparently wise, design decision is the fact that if that peer goes down, we need to wait until its content advertisement expires before we can have access to the file via another peer's advertisement. It still doesn't mean that the design policy is bad, since it's very likely in most scenarios that node1 will come back up and we will be able to retrieve the content again. This effectively buffers system restarts up to the expiry duration of an advertisement. Since all advertisements eventually expire, the network will only display content that is "most recently available" at any time over the long term. However, it is true that if we add a little more logic to perform a live query again whenever a GetContent request fails, we could overcome this problem.

This discussion gives us a taste of the very different design dilemmas that we face when working with P2P/JXTA networks that have non-deterministic topology.

Taking WroxShare Further

Obviously, one could make different enhancements to WroxShare, and some of them would make good programming exercises for the interested reader – here are some ideas:

❑   Add a custom renderer for the SharedList, showing different types of file with different graphical icons

❑   Add filtering based on the category of files for sharing over very large groups

❑   Add local SearchResult indexing to work with a very large set of available shares; more specifically, add some file classification mechanism for cases when hundreds or thousands of files may be shared

- Add group selection and changing

- Add a status display for file transfer, giving the option of notifying the user when a file transfer is completed

- Add content re-sharing/re-publishing capability without requiring application restart

- Modify the `SearchResult` caching policy to retry query immediately if a `GetContent` request fails; experiment with different policy variations

- Decoupe the drop target and drag source functionality of `ShareList` into two classes, and do the data transfer between the two classes properly via data exchange; this will significantly expand the GUI code base footprint

Readers gung-ho for writing JXTA code should not have any problem finding opportunities to enhance this skeletal `WroxShare` application.

Summary

In this chapter, we have examined a P2P application development case study: the `WroxShare` content sharing utility. This JXTA application follows the "content sharing network application pattern" and illustrates how to go about designing and coding such applications.

We have leveraged the versatile CMS service available with the JXTA platform to share content, and written our application code directly to the platform API. We have discovered how to partition a GUI-based JXTA application by using a foreground GUI thread/background JXTA thread paradigm, loosely coupling the two threads with a shared data structure that reflects changes through the model of the MVC design pattern provided by Swing.

Testing the application, we have reflected upon the impact an apparently trivial design decision has on a P2P system, noticing that the set of issues and concerns, when designing application over a network with non-deterministic topology, is quite different from conventional design issues that we face.

By now, you should be fully comfortable with designing and coding JXTA applications. We have the high-level EZEL, enabling us to quickly create or prototype JXTA applications ideas. We are also familiar with the JXTA platform API, and can program directly to the component view offered by this API.

The foundation we have covered in this book will enable us to move forward with our own endeavors in the interoperable P2P world enabled by JXTA. With the emerging P2P world's endless but yet unleashed possibilities, the world is your giant clam!

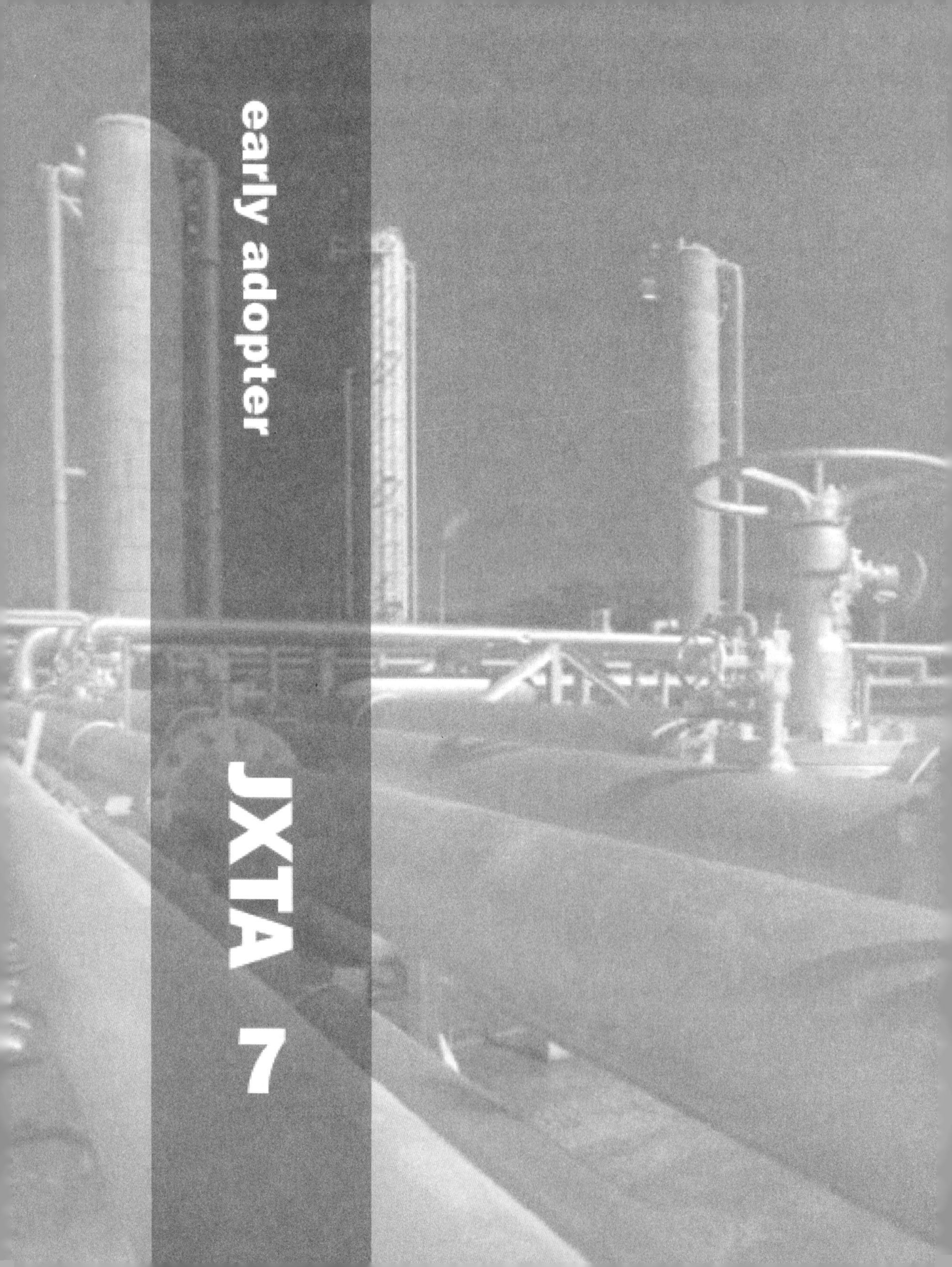
early adopter
JXTA
7

The Future of JXTA

JXTA is an important evolutionary technology development arriving at a very significant time. It provides the research community with a functional substrate upon which to experiment with ideas in modern distributed computing. In this post dot-com decade, where interest in academic research is at a historical high, JXTA has the ability to become the de facto test-bed for some of the most promising ideas in this exciting arena. Meanwhile, libraries such as EZEL offer current day client-server system gurus – looking for some long-lacking intellectual stimulus – an opportunity to sample a taste of the network-centric P2P anarchy that JXTA embraces. Bring these two polarized groups into one global gathering place, jxta.org, could result in the germination of juxtaposed systems where P2P technology works in harmonious competition with existing server-centric systems. From this primeval soup of ideas we can expect to see a new foundation emerge, that will challenge and drive the minds of software and systems engineers for years to come.

In this final chapter of the book, we will give a whirlwind survey of some of the most exciting upcoming technologies that the JXTA community is currently experimenting with. Hopefully, at least one of them will intrigue you enough to bring you into the folds of the community. Better yet, these projects will provide you with a base of open source code for you to create the next P2P "killer application".

7

Security for Distributed Systems

JXTA was built with security in mind from day one. Provision for security is built-in right down at the protocol and message format level (for example, every advertisement in JXTA has a `credential` field built in). This enables all interoperating implementations of JXTA to share a common security model and/or service. This model, however, is left open to the implementers of individual JXTA systems to define.

What JXTA Implements Today – Secured Pipes via End-to-End TLS

Right out of the box, JXTA supports a form of security for communicating peers (mainly through the secured pipe abstraction). The actual implementation is end-to-end TLS (Transport Level Security) providing a level of guaranteed data integrity, confidentiality, and guaranteed peer-authenticity when communicating through a "secured pipe" virtual channel. The supporting API library also provides application access to lower-level RSA, RC5, MD5, and SHA-1 encryption and hashing algorithm implementations.

Under this "secured pipe" scheme, the peer at each end of the pipe can be authenticated (against digital certificates that are exchanged), the messages that pass between the peers will be encrypted on-the-fly using a shared secret encryption cipher – a cipher whose shared secret key will only be known to the two peers involved.

A Spectrum of Trust

Workable production deployment of TLS requires the issue and distribution of X.509 digital certificates from a "trusted source". The traditional web-based model (specifically the HTTPS, or HTTP over SSL implementation – where SSL is synonymous with TLS, since they are different versions of the same technology) requires a centralized Certification Authority (CA) to issue these "certs". This model proves to be overkill, and relatively expensive, for many applications of JXTA, and indeed goes broadly against the concept of pure peer-to-peer networking in the absence of centralized control. The JXTA community, through a white paper proposal detailing a project entitled Poblano, provides a workable alternative solution. This proposal recommends that the JXTA infrastructure should be designed to accommodate a spectrum of trust, encompassing less-robust (but nevertheless highly functional) self-signed certs, PGP-like co-signed certificates (PGP stands for Pretty good Privacy, and is widely used in e-mail encryption), all the way to the full-fledged CA generated certs. This will enable the JXTA application designer to deliver the "best fit" trust solution (within the spectrum) for their specific problem at hand.

The Poblano white paper's full title is *Poblano, A Distributed Trust Model for Peer-to-Peer Networks*, and was developed by Rita Chen and William Yeager at Sun Microsystems. You can download it in PDF format from the JXTA web site documents page, http://www.jxta.org/project/www/white_papers.html.

Decentralized Network Trust

Furthermore, the Poblano proposal takes a stab at the design of a set of fully distributed trust and confidence network metrics that can be used to implement trust systems in the P2P environment. More specifically, there are algorithms for establishing the trust level between:

❑ One peer and another

❑ One peer and a particular piece of content being propagated through the network

The Poblano recommendations are fully distributed and do not require any centralized entity to operate, enabling a Poblano system, theoretically, to be massively scalable. It relies on rating of confidence, based on a keyword (or specific metric), by individual peers of other peers (or content) that they may come across. An implementation of the proposal will be incorporated into the JXTA core, as well as several upcoming complementary services for JXTA (like the CMS, which we've met in our WroxShare design – see http://security.jxta.org/ for more details).

Content Addressable Networks

Content Addressable Networking (or CAN for short) is a hot new research area that is destined to make an impact in many fields. The idea is to treat an entire network as a huge hash-table containing key-value pairs. The implementation requires the maintenance of a distributed, non-centralized index of information supporting the "hash". This distributed index is typically kept among the participating peer nodes in the network, or an elected subset. The non-centralized index implementation will ensure that the network hash-table is always accessible as long as one node remains active or alive in the network. Another significant property of a CAN is the existence of a deterministic upper bound for search – the maximum hops required to find the content of interest. This can be very desirable for applications that depend on distributed searches (such as content sharing networks). Academic implementations have been described in OceanStore and Publius (see the resources section at the end of the chapter for details).

Of course, the JXTA community cannot possibly let such a brilliant idea slip by without attempting a physical implementation. In fact, the developing J2ME (Java 2 Micro Edition) implementation of the JXTA core uses CAN as a highly efficient and performance-enhancing means of discovery (or query resolution). In the longer term, it is foreseeable that this implementation may migrate to the mainstream J2SE implementation (most of the CAN action at jxta.org is centered around the JXTA Distributed Index project – see http://di.jxta.org/).

JXTA Discovery Mechanisms

The JXTA specification does not specify the means by which Peer Discovery Protocol messages are to be sent over a particular network transport. The current implementation uses four different way of doing this. The following is a short discussion of each.

Rendezvous-Based Discovery

This is the bootstrap discovery mechanism supported inherently by the JXTA platform. It uses the network of rendezvous (a discovery broker network) to propagate queries throughout the group. While workable, this is not necessarily the most efficient discovery method (depending on the algorithm used by the rendezvous network to achieve discovery), and really should be used only when bootstrapping a peer or when there is no higher-level application-specific alternative (the three possible alternatives covered next or others based on specific knowledge of a network's topology or configuration can also expedite discovery). However, because rendezvous-based discovery rides on top of JXTA's network virtualization layer, it enjoys the transparent cross-transport support that is often difficult to achieve otherwise.

IP Multicasting

In corporate and intranet scenarios, this is frequently a useful means of discovery. IP multicast messages are used to broadcast messages within a pre-configured multicast group to perform the discovery. The maturity of IP multicast support in operating system software and network hardware makes this a highly workable means of discovery on a P2P system that supports it.

Content Addressable Network

Used currently only for the J2ME (Java 2 Micro Edition) implementation of JXTA, this discovery scheme uses the hash-table like quality of a CAN implementation to quickly resolve peer endpoints.

Discovery via Out of Band Means

This is essentially a wide-open "escape" means of discovery because it does not use any JXTA mechanism. In other words, it takes advantage of application-specific functionality to send an "advertisement" between the peers that need to communicate within the P2P network. Since only the application designer will know how the peers in an application should work together, this can frequently provide the most efficient means of discovery possible for a specific application scenario.

Others?

Some experimentation is currently being performed in the field of discovery-by-proxy. Peers without direct access to a rendezvous node can have their discovery queries routed to a rendezvous node through a locally accessible node that has a connection to a rendezvous – acting as a proxy. This form of discovery is not formalized yet, but holds great potential in the near future for the incorporation of limited-resource devices into JXTA networks.

It is likely, as the decentralized, distributed networking industry matures, that JXTA will increase the number of discovery mechanisms available.

Content Sharing and Distributed Storage

Combining JXTA Search with CMS will give a highly workable solution to distributed content management and sharing. However, the possibilities of distributed storage and content management go far beyond this single implementation.

JXTA enables a networked community of users to keep a set of content available within that community in a non-centralized and fault-resilient manner. Furthermore, by implementing the appropriate propagation and expiry policies, it is possible to:

❑ Ensure only the most timely and demanded content survives in the long term, automatically removing (or archiving into long term storage) content that is no longer desired

❑ Move and replicate frequently content that is most in demand, increasing the probability that peers in the community will be able to access this content

❑ Automatically migrate copies of content towards the population that most likely (probabilistically) will want to access that content

The above statements are pipedreams for developers on conventional centralized networks, but distinct near-future possibilities for P2P system designers.

"Disk in the Sky" Implementation

Instead of storing and propagating complete pieces of content throughout a P2P network, there is a school of thought that attempts to leverage the high-availability and fault-tolerant P2P network itself to store content. The idea is to chunk the content being stored into small pieces (encrypt these pieces if storing on a public network) and propagate it out to the P2P network for redundant storage. When it comes time to retrieve the content, the individual pieces (or perhaps replicated redundant copies of the pieces) are fetched from the network, and reassembled. This enables one to utilize the storage capacity and capabilities of a network of peers to implement a fault-tolerant storage subsystem. Faster overall throughput than from a single server can be achieved, since multiple requests for pieces are answered in parallel by multiple storage peers. It also has application in sending content across a harsh (volatile or insecure) communications environment – by making the content retrieval request from a different peer than that which performed the storage operation.

Global Distributed Search: Dream Search Engines

Implementing an efficient yet high-performance search mechanism for a networked world where nodes may suddenly come and go, and one where no centralized repository of gathered information exists, sounds like a daunting exercise. The best "workable solution" to this fascinating problem is still the topic of academic discourse. Much research still needs to be performed in quantifying and qualifying the alternative schemes that are proposed. JXTA, not wanting to be left behind, has a complete implementation of a "workable solution" that you can use and deploy today. It is JXTA Search a distributed search system.

Reference JXTA Search Service: InfraSearch

The JXTA search service is based on the work of a company called InfraSearch. InfraSearch was acquired by Sun Microsystems in early 2001 and several of its engineers joined the team that works on JXTA. When you survey the current thinking on distributed searching, you inevitably find that all the effort centres around the question, "How do you perform a search that is better than an exhaustive one by incorporating some additional knowledge about the content being searched?" Most solutions revolve around the building and maintenance of a distributed index of this "additional knowledge".

In some current implementations, such as web search engines like Google, this "additional knowledge" is the understanding of how the query engines of leading web sites work, combined with a distilled knowledge of actual crawled pages. In many cases, data is "scraped" from a web-page by knowing the layout of such a page. While workable for web search engines, these sorts of schemes will not work too well for the arbitrary content (images, sounds, code, data in any format) that may be shared by JXTA nodes.

The JXTA search service relies on the decentralized registration of "search information providers" to obtain this "additional knowledge". Who better to know the nature and optimal access method of the content than those who own the content themselves?

Operational Model of JXTA Search Service

As a "true" JXTA service, the JXTA Search Service is defined in terms of a set of interoperable on-the-wire protocols based on the exchange of XML-based messages. The reference implementation is done in Java, but other alternative implementations are definitely possible.

The protocol requires a generic convention for describing how to formulate a query for a specific "search information provider" and how to interpret the resulting response. The protocol is named the Query Routing Protocol (QRP). The QRP also includes a means for supplying metadata search criteria used in locating the set of most appropriate "search information providers".

The JXTA search service operating model involves a network of search hubs (akin to the rendezvous network used to propagate queries). Any peer with sufficient resources to support the JXTA search service can become a search hub. These search hubs take registrations from "search information providers". "Search information providers" can be JXTA nodes or web sites, bridging the Internet into the JXTA world. The registration includes metadata of the content being provided, as well as a description of how to query the content. The network of hubs collaboratively index and maintain this distributed database of metadata, and field requests from "search information consumers" for such information.

During operation, a consumer will query its nearest hub using QRP. The hub will determine the most appropriate provider in collaboration with other hubs in the network, and send a response back to the consumer. This enables search based on metadata on the content, as well as the query method desired for the content.

Wide and Deep Search

The JXTA Search service is said to support "wide and deep searches". In lay terms, it enables the largest cross section of search consumers to conduct the most exhaustive search of the widest possible selection of data sources.

JXTA itself supports a diversity of endpoints, allowing devices from PDA to supercomputers to work together in a decentralized network. This provides a wide coverage of potential search consumers.

To enable "wide" searches, JXTA Search has the ability to combine both the Internet and contents kept on JXTA nodes (databases, gateways into conventional search services, etc.) into a single search space. This is enabled by abstracting the access method into the QRP, enabling the "search information providers" to tell the consumer how to perform the actual query against the source.

The Truly Universal URL

Imagine the day in the future when the URL as we know it today gets revised to include the entire JXTA Search supported space, and you will see the potential impact of JXTA. Remember, since the JXTA Search service can index content from *any* searchable source, JXTA peers can be established to incorporate all sources of searchable data globally. Browsers supporting this unified URL would then have the capability of searching (and accessing) all the searchable content in both the Web of today, and the JXTA "web to the power of n" of the near future. This is the vision of JXTA's creators.

Other Cross-Discipline P2P Explorations

There are many other fascinating explorations of how P2P networks can be utilized in various other application domains, including but not limited to business, mobile agents, education, financial transactions, web services integration, etc. The following is a partial snapshot list of the on-going open source projects that are being managed at **www.jxta.org**. This list is sure to grow, and interested readers should consult the community web site for the latest authoritative list.

Classic Applications

`myjxta`	Formerly known as Instant P2P, a showcase application for what JXTA can do – currently a chat and file-sharer combination
`dfwbase`	A knowledge base that consists of a database at each peer
`gnougat`	An attempt to put decentralized file caching over JXTA
`jnushare`	A file-sharing application, part of the GISP (Global Information Sharing Protocol) exploration
`jxtaprose`	A discussion group application that works over JXTA, doubles as a graphical peer browser
`project2p`	Applying JXTA to P2P sharing of project information
`p2p-email`	E-mail-based group discussion over JXTA
`rosettachat`	A chat application featuring translation capability based on locale

Development Tools

`parlor`	Application framework
`jxtabeans`	JavaBean-like component for creating JXTA applications
`brando`	P2P Java source sharing
`jxme`	JXTA core implemented on J2ME, functional on PDAs
`jxta-c,` `jxtaperl,` `jxtaruby,` `objc-jxta,` `pocketjxta`	Other, non-Java, interoperable implementations of the JXTA core
`di`	Exploration with distributed indexing
`tini`	JXTA-enabling this embedded system wonder – the Java VM on-a-stick
`jxta-rmi`	Implementing the Java RMI semantics over JXTA
`networkservices`	Integrating web services into JXTA
`jxta-wire`	Many-to-many communications, base of propagation pipes

Business Applications

`compute-power-market`	Experimentation in a econcomics-driven marketplace based on JXTA
`payment`	Secure and anonymous payment system over JXTA

Education Applications

`edutella`	Actually exploration for implementing RDF-based metadata for JXTA networks, but initially used to exchange education resources between universities around the globe

Outer Limits

`ipeers`	Exploration of agent-based AI technology in the context of P2P JXTA networks
`search`	Distributed search component of JXTA
`jxtaspaces`	Implementing distributed shared memory semantics over JXTA
`jxtavfs`	Virtual file system implementation over JXTA
`jxta-grid`	Parallel processing over a cluster of JXTA peers

Pasture to Unleash Your Imagination

In the coming months and years, innovative software engineers from all over the world will congregate at www.jxta.org – to debate and design, to test alternative implementations, and to explore the applications of JXTA. This closely knitted open source community will likely influence the destiny of contemporary distributed software as we know it. You, too, can become part of this pioneering event that may change the landscape of distributed software design forever.

7

Incubating a Bleeding Edge Global Meritocracy

To get JXTA off to a good start, Sun has taken a no holds barred attitude towards the initial commitment of resources towards the project. The startup cast of characters in the JXTA community represents one of the most eclectic collections of current thinkers and "doers" in the distributed software technology scene: from folks who have worked in the trenches in Sun's own concurrent distributed computing endeavor, Jini, to architects of the Chorus distributed real-time operating system; from engineers experienced in the implementation of Java on small devices, to those intimate with the Cray genre of massively parallel computing, to core engineers from InfraSearch. Combine this with Sun's experience with decades of high performance operating system development, plus distributed hardware design experience, and you'll see that the JXTA "seed crowd" has the ability to attract and challenge some of their brightest peers (no pun intended) working both in academia and the upper echelons of professional system design. Hanging around the active JXTA community will give you the feeling that you're working in the world's bleeding edge think-tank, in a relaxed yet globally competitive environment. There doesn't seem to be a single day that passes by where the latest distributed research paper isn't discussed; nor any contemporary new exciting algorithm/idea that can escape without someone building a working prototype. The JXTA community is a world where learning never stops; where not only the best ideas survives, but the most radical challenge and occasionally flourish; an extended campus where the ivory tower daydreamers collide on a daily basis with the pragmatic front-line "get the job done" infantry. It truly is Ginkgo Biloba for an engineer's soul.

Resources

OceanStore: An Architecture for Global-Scale Persistent Storage, John Kubiatowicz, David Bindel, Yan Chen, Steven Czerwinski, Patrick Eaton, Dennis Geels, Ramakrishna Gummadi, Sean Rhea, Hakim Weatherspoon, Westley Weimer, Chris Wells, and Ben Zhao. University of California, Berkeley, http://oceanstore.cs.berkeley.edu/ . Appears in *Proceedings of the Ninth international Conference on Architectural Support for Programming Languages and Operating Systems (ASPLOS 2000),* November 2000.

Publius: A Robust, Tamper-evident, Censorship-resistant Web Publishing System Marc Waldman, New York University; Aviel D. Rubin, AT&T Labs-Research; Lorrie Faith Cranor, AT&T Labs-Research. Presented at the 9th USENIX Security Symposium (August 2000).

7